Last Curtsey

THE END OF THE DEBUTANTES

~

Fiona MacCarthy

faber and faber

by the same author

ERIC GILL
WILLIAM MORRIS
BYRON: LIFE AND LEGEND

First published in 2006
by Faber and Faber Limited
Bloomsbury House, 74–77 Great Russell Street
London WC1B 3DA
This paperback edition first published in 2007

Typeset by Faber and Faber
Printed and bound by CPI Group (UK) Ltd, Croydon, CR0 4YY

A CIP record for this book
is available from the British Library

ISBN 978-0-571-22860-7

4 6 8 10 9 7 5 3

With her widely acclaimed book *Eric Gill*, published in 1989, Fiona MacCarthy established herself as one of the leading writers of biography in Britain. This was followed by *William Morris* (1994), which won several literary awards, including the Wolfson History Prize and was described by A. S. Byatt as 'one of the finest biographies ever published in this country.' *Byron: Life and Legend* (2002) was praised as 'one of the great literary biographies of our time' by Mark Bostridge in the *Independent on Sunday*. Fiona MacCarthy writes regularly for the *Guardian* and lives in Derbyshire.

Further praise for *Last Curtsey*

'MacCarthy remembers these parties in toe-curling detail, but she also remembers the houses in which they took place, and one of the many fascinating aspects of this thoroughly absorbing book is the way in which she positions each party, in all its social inanity, within a broader, grander, history of the house and its previous inhabitants.' Frances Wilson, *Daily Telegraph*

'In an acute analysis of the decline of British aristocratic society, [MacCarthy] combines personal memoir and insider history with deft skill and dazzling style.' Iain Finlayson, *The Times*

'Fiona MacCarthy's fascinating, often very funny memoir . . . [An] illuminating and subtle book.' Juliet Nicolson, *Sunday Telegraph*

'MacCarthy is well placed to write an elegy, albeit not a terribly mournful one, for this particular moment because she knows, and understands, both the old world (of the debs and their mothers, engaged in an exhausting battle for eldest sons) and the new (the one embodied by John Osborne, and that ironing board he stuck up there on stage).' Rachel Cooke, *Observer*

'What makes this book a delight is its intellectual panache. It begins with personal experience and moves effortlessly into an analysis of society that has richness and depth.' Frances Spalding, *Sunday Times*

'Stylishly written, intelligent and witty, this book is a revealing portrait of that social world written by one, who driven and empowered by greater ambitions, escaped and took the future into her own hands.' Deirdre McQuillan, *Irish Times*

'[An] intelligent and fascinating account.' Anne de Courcy, *Daily Mail*

'MacCarthy is good at evoking the texture of life at a point of social transition. Her book is a welcome corrective to the 'iconic moments' school of documentary history . . . *Last Curtsey* deals in the historical reality of mixed feelings and cultural collisions.' Rosemary Hill, *London Review of Books*

Contents

❧

Illustrations

EPILOGUE

Preface

This book has been a kind of double coming out for me. For many years I could not bring myself to talk about the Season, hardly even think about it. Especially in the 1960s, when I was working for the *Guardian*, the debutante Season was my taboo subject, an unmentionably embarrassing secret history. How could I expect anyone to take me seriously once they knew I had been amongst the final group of debutantes to curtsey to the Queen?

What has happened to make me change my mind, after so many decades? It is a natural condition of ageing to lose some inhibitions and to see things that once seemed worryingly shaming in a different perspective. By the time you reach your sixties you achieve a glorious imperviousness to what other people think. Viewed from this distance, the final year in which debutantes performed the curtsey to the monarch, breaking a tradition of two hundred years, has historic and sociological importance. In 1958, the year of the last curtseys, the so-called upper classes, to which the debutantes and their families belonged, were already showing signs of a loss of confidence. We were there right on the edge of the socially challenging, sexually revolutionary and, from the point of view of the establishment, destructively satiric 1960s. The end of the curtsey was part of the whole story of England in a particular, and often very anguished, condition of evolution and flux.

This book is partly a defence of debutantes against the cartoon image of the vacuous and flighty socialite. An 'ex-deb' is a phrase that still has a dismissive connotation. This is a facile and patronising view. Yes of course there are still debs of the unreconstructed kind, easily identified by their clothes and vowel sounds as they bray to one another across Sloane Square. But the girls who curtseyed with me in 1958 have been as much affected as women in any other section of society by the profound changes to the expectations of women over the past half century. When people talk of 'the hard way up' they automatically think of women overcoming the disadvantages of being born into poverty. But there is a Poor Little Rich Girl syndrome too. There could be a considerable struggle in surmounting hidebound parental attitudes, the spoken or (equally lethal) unspoken pressures to conform, the minimal education given to a daughter whose future was viewed solely in terms of a good marriage and the paucity of career opportunities available to most of my contemporaries. A bonus of this book has been the scope it gave me to renew old contacts with my fellow-curtseyers and to examine the often very enterprising and surprising ways in which their lives developed from then on.

Perhaps what has motivated me most of all has been the feeling that I was witness to a scene so far removed from present-day experience, so strange and so arcane, that it is worth recording. That last Season of last curtseys was part of a period which is now almost forgotten, the details of which are disappearing fast. Some of the background information is now beyond retrieval. When I approached the palace while researching this book a spokesman for the Royal Archives refused my request for the full list of girls who made their curtseys in that final year on grounds that this would constitute a breach of privacy under the Data Protection Act.

The debutantes themselves are inexorably ageing. It came as a shock to me to realise that some of the girls who went with me to the palace – and some of the debs' escorts I remember dancing energetically to Tommy Kinsman and his band – are already dead. But I have been lucky in finding many people with still vivid memories to draw on and the photograph albums and diaries of girls who did the Season in 1958 have been a valuable resource. 'It was such a peculiar thing to have done', as one ex-debutante recently remarked to me. Peculiar indeed: both in terms of the elaborate social rituals that lingered through the post-war years and in the underlying concepts of elegance, good manners, belief in protocol, love and respect for the monarchy, deference towards your betters, courage, kindness and idealism, qualities which before long appeared impossibly old fashioned. 1958 was the watershed between the lost worlds of our parents or our grandparents and the world which we know now.

Last Curtsey

CHAPTER ONE

Presentation at the Palace

In 1958 – the year in which Khrushchev came to power in Russia, the year after Eden's resignation over Suez, two years after John Osborne's *Look Back in Anger* – the last of the debutantes, myself among them, went to the palace to curtsey to the Queen.

Aristocratic teenage girls had been making their deep curtseys to the monarch for the past two centuries. This most eccentric of tribal initiation ceremonies had been evolved by Queen Charlotte, wife of George III. The Lord Chamberlain's announcement that it would be ceasing after 1958 prompted a record number of applications for the final presentations held at Buckingham Palace in mid-March, like a wave of panic-buying once famine had been forecast. One mother was said to be presenting all her four daughters. In total 1,400 girls were to curtsey in three batches of four to five hundred, in ceremonies spread over three days. Following the rules that a debutante had to be presented by a relation who had herself been presented, a formal application had been sent to the Lord Chamberlain by my mother who herself had made her curtsey in 1925, wearing the then obligatory ostrich feather headdress and white dress with a long train.

I still have the stiff buff card with its raised gold insignia EIIR. It bears the message 'The Lord Chamberlain is commanded by Her Majesty to summon Mrs Gerald MacCarthy and Miss Fiona MacCarthy to an Afternoon Presentation Party at Buckingham Palace on Tuesday the 18th March, from 3:30 to 5:30 o'clock pm.' The dress code was now less formal than in my mother's presentation year. Ladies were instructed to wear day dress with hat. Gentlemen had a choice of morning dress or non-ceremonial day dress, esoteric instructions presumably immediately intelligible to our parents' still mili-

Invitation to the palace (left); and Fiona MacCarthy dressed for her presentation in blue wild silk and black kid gloves

taristic post-war generation. The Lord Chamberlain directed that 'If in possession swords should be worn.'

So it happened that on a cold and blustery spring afternoon I joined the troupe of well-bred gels, their parents and their sponsors assembling along the iron railings outside Buckingham Palace for what turned out to be an ordeal of a wait. There was to be a lot of waiting on presentation day and indeed throughout the London Season that succeeded it: endless hanging around, filling up the spaces, exchanging sometimes desperately sprightly small talk, sipping at a drink. What made that wait outside the palace so peculiarly memorable was not just the savage weather assailing the poor debs lined up in what *The Times* reporter called their 'flimsy finery', exposed to 'rough winds shaking their chiffon and light silks'. It was the deeper certainty that this whole old world of privilege and upper-class frivolity was doomed. As shown in faded press cuttings the scene seems to encapsulate a strangely melancholy period quality. Moustached fathers in their toppers, proud mothers swathed in mink. A certain bitter sweetness, an end of empire feel. *The Times* noted the 'valedictory spice about the familiar pageant of the debutantes on their way to a brief moment of glory in the State ballroom'. There were crowds outside the palace, kept at a discreet distance, staring at the toffs as in an Ealing comedy. On the final day of presentations two young blades in bowler hats drove up The Mall in a vintage Rolls Royce tourer, holding up a placard crudely lettered GOODBYE DEAR DEBS.

Debs and their parents queue outside the palace, March 1958 (top); and
Sonia York, her parents and friends arrive for the presentation ceremony

Debs' escorts mourn the end of presentations

At last we were inside and ascending the Grand Staircase, an ostentatious sweep of Carrara marble with bronze balustrade. Up the red carpet the debutantes were entering an *Alice in Wonderland* world of stagey pomp and comic fancy dress. Beefeaters in their ruffs were stalwartly in attendance. Placed at strategic points throughout the palace were distinguished ancient soldiers, members of Her Majesty's Body Guard of the Honourable Corps of Gentlemen at Arms, recalled to duty for the afternoon presentations, and giving the scene an air of spectacular unreality with their plumed helmets, their heavy gold epaulettes and quasi-medieval halberds, held ready to root out the traitors in the crowd. The debs were now denuded of their tweed or camel overcoats, thronging through the palace, eyeing one another as if entering heat one of an old-time beauty contest, which in a sense it was. The presentation ceremony marked our entry into a complicated, sometimes cut-throat competition that could shape a girl's whole future. We were on the starting line for the thing called 'coming out' which, in its old and precise sense, meant a young girl's rite of passage out of the schoolroom and into society, once she became of marriageable age. The ritual was once connected with menstruation's onset. Society doctors in the Victorian age advised the delay of a young girl's menstruation as long as possible, ideally until her formal 'coming out'

1958 debs coming to make their curtseys in full-skirted dresses and little petal hats: from left, Sally O'Rorke, Julia Chatterton, Victoria Bathurst Norman, Jane Dalzell

at seventeen, prescribing a strict regime of cold baths and exercise in the open air to allow her to make full use of the valuable formative years of puberty. The debutante would then emerge, butterfly from the chrysalis, to parade before the eyes of her prospective suitors in 'the full perfection of womanhood'.

By 1958 such brutal delaying tactics were abandoned. Girls' bodies matured earlier: I had started menstruating at the age of ten. But in a sense our development too had been retarded in the stultifying of female ambition and the deadening of our critical sense. In the contest for a suitable husband, ideally titled, landed and with money, originality had never been high on the agenda. Sameness and acceptability were of more value. In 1958 we looked alike in full-skirted calf-length dresses, long kid gloves and tiny hats constructed of myriad petals or soft feathers perched on our carefully waved hair. Whether the dresses had been made by a couturier, Victor Stiebel and Norman Hartnell being the prestige names, or run up by the deb's mother's village dressmaker, the final effect was curiously similar. I was wearing blue wild silk, the favoured fabric of that Season, and everywhere I looked were other girls in rustling skirts in the uniform light blue, turning Buckingham Palace to a shimmering silk sea. The atmosphere, although excited, was peculiarly docile. You could hardly call us teenagers: we were altogether too formal and submissive, imitations of our mothers, clones of the Queen herself, here at court in our court shoes.

The curtseyers had now been separated from their sponsors who were seated in the heavily ornate Edwardian Ballroom, all pilasters, giant doorways and appallingly bad sculptures, where they were entertained with a selection of light music played by the String Band of the Irish Guards. The debutantes were corralled into an ante-chamber known as the Ball Supper Room where we sat in rows on stiff gilt chairs for what seemed hours. Looking round I recognised quite a number of the others, old connections from the intricate networks of the past: the assemblages of nannies pushing glossy baby carriages in Kensington Gardens and Hyde Park; children's parties where we played interminable pass the parcel and suffered the often tearful disappointment of being left chairless in musical chairs; dancing classes where the little girls were taught the sailor's hornpipe; skiing classes in Mürren, in the Bernese Oberland. Sharing such distant memories were girls linked through our age, our education, our family connections, the tribal relationships of London and the counties. Most of all we were shaped and motivated by the friendships and expectations of our mothers. By the standards of today we were appallingly naive. Sitting waiting, chatting nervously, the debutantes held tight to two small cards issued to 'all unmarried ladies'. Evidently these cards had magic powers. The first, the white card with beige borders, bearing the mystic message TO BE PRESENTED, had to be yielded to the Lord

Chamberlain on entering the ballroom where Queen Elizabeth II and the Duke of Edinburgh sat enthroned under a crimson canopy adapted from the Imperial *shamiana*, redolent of the then relatively recent British rule in India. The Queen's aunt, the Princess Royal, was also on the dais on the day I curtseyed, while the Mistress of the Robes and the Ladies in Waiting were seated behind the royal party. Having passed what was described reverently as 'the Presence', the second green card gave the debutante her entry to the reception in the State Rooms once her obeisance was done.

The long procession of virgins – for the vast majority of upper-class girls of seventeen were virgins in 1958 – passed in front of a young queen who not so long before had been a virgin herself. She had married Prince Philip in 1947 when she was twenty-one. From her height on the dais the Queen surveyed these serried ranks of girlish innocence, earls' daughters, generals' daughters, a Lord Mayor of London's daughter, English roses from the shires, fresh-faced girls with the slight blankness of their class and inexperience. There was a softness and sweetness and also an inherited silliness of manner, a gasp in the voice, a giggle and a flutter, in these participants in what Jessica Mitford, in her book *Hons and Rebels*, described as 'the specific, upper-class version of the puberty rite'.

Penny Graham and her great-grandmother the Dowager Lady North on their way to the palace

The first of the very last debutantes to curtsey, a tall, elegant, amusing girl called Penny Graham, daughter of the racing correspondent of the *Daily Express*, owed her prime position to her aged sponsor, her great-grandmother the Dowager Lady North who had not been to court since she herself had been presented to Queen Victoria. Lady North, by now in her late eighties, was decreed too frail for queuing and was spirited in early through the Entrée Entrance, a discreet side entrance of the palace. It helped that Penny's cousin was on duty as a member of the Royal Body Guard. Penny was wearing oyster-coloured silk with a petticoat in which her heel caught in mid-curtsey, a small debacle which the Queen pretended not to notice. Four hundred girls, four hundred curtseys, each a thing of minor drama. A deep curtsey to the Queen, then three side steps to curtsey to Prince Philip, seated on the throne beside her. Did the Queen address the debutante? As I remember, she did not. The ceremony had an air of semi-sanctity, a little like a Church of England confirmation. Extract a smile out of

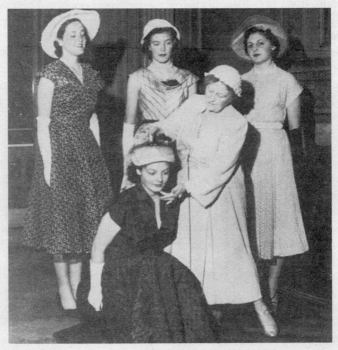

Madame Vacani training debutantes to curtsey

Prince Philip and it counted as a triumph. He was seen to give a wink at the very daring deb with the Nefertiti hairstyle who was wearing a tight-fitting sheath of mauve, ruched chiffon designed by Victor Stiebel: not for Dominie Riley-Smith the standard blue wild silk. The procession of the nubile formed, dissolved, reassembled as name after name was shouted out by the Court Usher. Later, when I read Marina Warner's *Monuments and Maidens*, her brilliant study of the allegory of the female form, it was easy to relate her historical account of the idolatry of virgins to my own all too personal memories of maidens processing past their monarch in 1958.

The curtsey itself was part of the mystique. It was a question of leg-lock: left knee locked behind the right knee, allowing a graceful slow descent with head erect, hands by your side. Avoidance of the wobble, definitely frowned upon, relied on exact placing of the knees and feet. The technique had been passed down through the generations of debutantes who learned it at Vacani's School of Dancing, at 159 Brompton Road in Knightsbridge, a few blocks down from Harrods. The school was founded by Marguerite Vacani, a widow, and her sister, both professional dancers, early in the First World War. My mother learned her curtsey there. It was assumed that I too would book my session at Vacani's. Other dancing schools might purport to teach the curtsey. But as far as the deb world went there was no substitute. Madame Vacani, as she styled herself, a squeaky voiced, effusive, highly powdered tiny lady, had made herself the high priestess of the cult. She had something of the manner of a genteel sergeant major as she trained prospective debutantes: 'Now darlings, throw out your little chests and burst your little dresses.' Once learned never forgotten, like bicycling or skiing. I believe I could achieve a Vacani curtsey still.

The knowledge that these were the final presentations made the occasion peculiarly poignant. Impossible to be there and not be conscious of the long line of our predecessors, going back to those late eighteenth-century ingénues led in by their powder-haired aristocratic mothers to curtsey to Queen Charlotte on her birthday feast. The scene was then relatively private and domestic. But gradually the system had been formalised. By 1837, when Queen Victoria ascended the throne, the term 'debutante' was in general use and young girls would be summoned to Queen Victoria's drawing rooms, then held in St James's Palace, to mark their entrée to society. The dress code was at this point the elaborate long white court dress with ten-foot train, mystical white veil, the ostrich feather headdress, elbow-length white gloves. The protocol surrounding presentations was strictly hierarchical. If the debutante before her was the daughter of a peer, Queen Victoria would kiss her; if the daughter of a commoner, the debutante would kiss the Queen's proffered hand. Once successfully married, the young bride would be presented again by her mother-in-law; symbolically, when the bride returned to court to curtsey she would come in triumph, wearing her wedding dress.

Cynthia Charteris, later Lady Asquith, in the white crêpe de Chine dress, long white train and headdress of white feathers in which she was presented to King Edward VII and Queen Alexandra at the age of seventeen

Here we were then, the descendants of Lady Clodagh Anson who made her curtsey in 1898 to a by then aged Queen Victoria, a diminutive but still imposing regal figure seated on a low throne-chair that made access to her perilous: '. . . you had to make a deep curtsey to get down low enough'. To her near contemporary Lady Sybil Lubbock, mother of the writer Iris Origo, who curtseyed the next year in low-cut white chiffon on a freezing winter day:

. . . there was something almost Chinese about it. We were dressed like this in order to pay homage to our venerable Sovereign, who, in her youth, had looked her best with her plump white shoulders well exposed. These were our ceremonial garments, to be worn out of respect to her, no matter at what time of day or in what weather she chose to receive us.

Lady Sybil made her curtsey unsteadily, balancing her unwieldy train over one arm while the opposite hand clutched her fan, her gloves and handkerchief. It was as clear to debutantes of that early generation as it was to the girls of 1958 that palace presentation hovered on the borderline between dignity and farce.

But it had a mad, sad beauty this long chorus line of privilege. Lady Diana Manners, the future Lady Diana Cooper, presented in 1911, at the second court of the new King George V, wearing an ivory brocaded crêpe de Chine dress with a cream net train sprinkled with pink rose petals and real diamond dewdrops, a *tour de force* of a costume she had designed herself. Vita Sackville-West, presented at court by her mother Lady Sackville, in a white satin gown with a Buckingham lace and chiffon bodice, the satin train a cloudy mass of tulle and silver bows. Betty Vacani, niece of Madame Vacani, queen-empress of the curtsey, who curtseyed herself in 1939, rose to poetic heights in her description of the scene at Buckingham Palace: 'After the presentations, the King and Queen walked down the line of debutantes and dowagers and as they passed everyone curtsied. It looked like the wind blowing through the flowers.'

The decorative elements of the presentation ceremony masked its serious, even ruthless, *raison d'être* in the stratification of society. By the mid-nineteenth century the annual presentation had gradually become the key event in a formalised connection of the monarch and the court with the Season and society. Presentation acquired an important role in the regulation of society in Britain. It became a kind of bulwark, defending an elite inner circle and securing the channels to power, influence and wealth. To put it at its crudest, the curtseyers were in, the non-curtseyers excluded from the myriad royal enclosures, members' tents and other well-defended spaces in which the well bred were separated from the riff-raff. The making of the curtsey raised the expectations of, at worst, a socially suitable marriage, since girls had few opportunities to form liaisons away from their restricted social sphere. Through the centuries, the details of presentation altered. Queen Victoria's more sober Afternoon Drawing Rooms gave way to the ostentatious splendour of Edward VII's late-night gatherings at Buckingham Palace, in which the debutantes were beautifully illuminated in the newly installed electric light. In the early 1920s, following a fashionable raising of the hemlines, presentation dresses were permitted to be shorter and trains reduced to eighteen inches from the heel. Debutantes of that period contended with the problem of anchoring their ostrich feather headdress on a shingle haircut. By the 1920s, too, the several miles of carriages queuing for the palace had been replaced by a long line of large black chauffeured motor cars. But such changes were minor. The systems, aims and attitudes surrounding presentations remained almost totally entrenched.

Inevitably presentations were affected by external events and political commotion. No courts were held in Britain in the First World War, the war which brought an end to several European monarchies. Evening courts and garden parties were cancelled by the Coal Strike of 1921. On 16 March 1939 news of the German invasion of Czechoslovakia ousted the Court Circular, with its report of the previous evening's presentations, from the pages of *The Times*. During the Second World War presentations were once again suspended and parents were faced with great practical problems in bringing out their daughters, as Ted Jeavons comments gloomily in Anthony Powell's novel of wartime England *The Kindly Ones*. By 1947, when the palace announced the revival of presentation parties, 20,000 debutantes were waiting to apply. Because of the large numbers, garden parties were organised so that debutantes could be received *en masse* and then, once it was realised that English summer weather could not be relied on, the ceremony moved indoors, to the Palace State Apartments. In 1951, individual presentations to King George VI, a monarch who believed in court ceremonial, revived: the ceremony had an extraordinary staying power. There were laments that the afternoon presentations lacked the glamour of the old evening courts: 'The splendour of the 1930s had vanished for ever', wrote a regretful Duchess of Argyll.

There was less possibility of anarchy or drama: 'Now, there were no evening courts and no ostrich feathers, no chamberpots either, or knickers falling down', complained Philippa Pullar, a debutante presented in a calf-length pink dress in 1953. Certainly the post-war courts had lost a little of their glitter. But the eventual cessation of court curtseys is less remarkable than the fact that young girls' presentations to the monarch continued, essentially unaltered, for so long.

Why did presentations end in 1958? For many years there had been rising criticism from within that the system was failing in its mission of upholding social exclusivity. External forces, social pressures, were seen to be eroding the sanctified relationship between God's anointed monarchy and God's anointed subjects. Or, in more agricultural terminology, the wheat was no longer distinguished from the chaff. In the early period of presentations when the immediate court circle was limited to just a few hundred aristocratic and landowning families, all of whom knew one another, the debutante intake was easily controlled by the Lord Chamberlain himself. His role was to root out undesirables, especially women with a less than blameless past. But from the mid-nineteenth century the system had been gradually forced to open out to include the daughters of families whose fortunes had been made in industry and commerce. For those with no inherited grasp of protocol, etiquette manuals were circulated, giving hints on the correct behaviour at court, and from 1854 Certificates of Presentation were issued. Laments that the floodgates of society had opened to *arrivistes* and imposters, negating the pure principles of presentation, had begun at least as early as 1861 when *Queen* magazine commented:

The crowning mischief, as we take it, is the way in which presentation at court is now so vulgarised, that it has lost all value and meaning as a title to social distinction. Formerly, presentations were confined to the true aristocracy of the country, the peerage, the superior landed gentry, persons of distinction in art, science and letters and the holders of offices of dignity under the Crown. . . . It is no longer so. Presentations are now so vulgarised that literally ANYBODY who has sufficient amount of perseverance or self-confidence may be presented. The wives of all Members of Parliament are presented and they in turn present the wives and daughters of local squires or other small magnates. There is no knowing where this is to stop.

According to David Cannadines's study *The Decline and Fall of the British Aristocracy* the number of presentations more than doubled during the last twenty years of Queen Victoria's reign, many of the additional debutantes being the daughters of self-made plutocrats from Britain, the Empire and the United States. In 1841, 90 per cent of women presented at court had been from the aristocratic and landowning families. By the end of the nineteenth century the proportion of debutantes from aristocratic families of ancient lineage was less than half.

Was there any point in continuing a practice so devalued? In 1957, the doyenne of society columnists, Mrs Betty Kenward, the *Tatler*'s 'Jennifer', was voicing her own doubts about whether presentations should continue, recalling in her memoirs: 'In my humble opinion the Season was becoming rather a racket! More and more people were trying to buy their way in.' Princess Margaret's conclusion was similar, if more crudely expressed: 'We had to put a stop to it. Every tart in London was getting in.' Jennifer was especially incensed by the commercialisation of the presentation ceremony by ladies who had an entrée at court, having been themselves presented as debutantes, who took fees for presenting motherless girls or girls whose mothers were disqualified from presenting their own daughters because they were divorcées or because they had not been through the ceremony themselves. 'I knew of two peeresses and a commoner who did this very successfully for several years, and there were probably masses of others.' They made money not only from presenting girls at court but shepherding them through the Season, introducing them to other debutantes and organising dances for them. Nor were they necessarily effective in these launchings, which were often money wasted. Jennifer remembered one poor widowed father 'spending a fortune on a spectacular dance for his daughter, who had very few invitations in return'. The palace, sensitive to accusations of links between presentations and commercial profit, was by this time taking soundings from Jennifer and others. A friend of the Queen's arranged to have a quiet drink with Jennifer who claims to have been open on the racketeering aspects of the Season: 'I told her very frankly all I knew.'

The mood towards the monarchy itself had altered subtly since the reverent euphoria of Coronation Day, 2 June 1953, when Queen Elizabeth II was crowned in Westminster Abbey attended by Lady Anne Coke, Lady Jane Willoughby, Lady Mary Baillie-Hamilton, Lady Rosemary Spencer Churchill, Lady Moyra Hamilton and Lady Jane Vane-Tempest-Stewart, ex-debutantes and all of impeccable lineage, only or eldest daughters of the nation's senior peers. A maid of honour had, by definition, to be maidenly: Lady Rosemary Spencer Churchill, engaged to be married, postponed her wedding to preserve her maid's credentials. The main function of the maids of honour was to carry the Queen's twenty-yard-long train of heavy purple velvet as she processed up and then down the long aisle of the abbey. The Coronation was in fact the last fling of old-time pageantry. The monarchy, and its long close links with an exclusively upper-class section of society, would soon be coming under unprecedented fire.

The end of presentations was a symptom and a symbol of wide changes in Britain in the middle 1950s. The debacle of Suez, followed by the resignation of Anthony Eden, the Prime Minister, destabilised the country with a force that is quite difficult to describe to those who were not there. When Nasser nationalised the Suez Canal on 26 July 1956, the action signified the end of Empire for the British. It was a traumatic episode, shaming not only in the underlying political arrogance of the British government but in the bumbling hopelessness with which the crisis had been handled. Suez forced us to revalue our sense of our importance in the world: almost overnight Britain's potency had dwindled. This crisis of confidence was also retrospective, casting doubts on the hallowed traditions and courtly prerogative of Britain's past. It was a time when the whole standing of the monarchy was being called into question. There was public criticism of the Queen's role in the appointment of Harold Macmillan as Eden's successor as prime minister in preference to the expected candidate, Rab Butler. This compounded widespread doubts about the palace's handling of the love affair between Princess Margaret and her recently divorced equerry, Group Captain Peter Townsend, in 1953. In this conflict between errant love and royal duty there were obvious echoes of the pre-war scandal of the love of Edward VII and Mrs Wallis Simpson which resulted in the King's abdication in 1936. Since then public opinion had grown more sophisticated. Townsend's virtual banishment to Brussels showed the palace clinging to what, in a more sexually realistic post-war Britain, appeared an outdated moral code.

Up to 1957, the traditional Buckingham Palace summer rituals of debutante presentations, garden parties and Royal Ascot continued according to the reassuring pattern. In personal terms the royal family had had an easy ride. But the days of automatic deference were ending. Behind the scenes there was anxiety, rising to horrified indignation as press criticism of the Queen and her courtiers, up to then off limits, became uninhibited veering towards rude. One of the earliest snipers at the royals was Malcolm Muggeridge, left-wing journalist and professional iconoclast. In an article in the *New Statesman* in September 1955 he launched into a diatribe of disloyalty, maintaining that the British people were secretly sick of the sight of the royal family and the ingratiating publicity surrounding them. Muggeridge suggested that another sycophantic photograph '. . . will be more than they can bear . . . The Queen Mother, Nanny Lightbody, Group Captain Townsend, the whole show is utterly out of hand'.

More considered, more incisive and dramatically effective, in the strangely neurotic aftermath of Suez, was an article by Lord Altrincham, soon to renounce his title and resurface as respected historian John Grigg. His inflammatory article appeared in August 1957 in an issue of the *National and English Review*, a small-circulation journal which Altrincham then edited, devoted to discussion of the 'future of the monarchy'. With a candour that some readers saw as tantamount to treachery his article belaboured the complacency and frowsiness of the British monarchy, insulated as it was from social challenges of the modern world. Altrincham in full flood was a formidable opponent:

'Crawfie', Sir Henry Marten, the London Season, the racecourse, the grousemoor, canasta and the occasional royal tour – all this would not have been good enough for Elizabeth I! It says much for the Queen that she has not been incapacitated for her job by this woefully inadequate training. She has dignity, a sense of duty, and (so far as we can judge) goodness of heart – all serious assets. But will she have the wisdom and give her children an education very different from her own? Will she, above all, see to it that Prince Charles is equipped with all the knowledge he can absorb without injury to his health, and that he mixes during his formative years with children who will one day be bus drivers, doctors, engineers, etc. – not merely with future land-owners or stockbrokers? These are crucial questions.

So they proved.

Altrincham reserved particular venom for the debutántes, accusing the Queen herself and Princess Margaret of bearing the 'debutante stamp' imposed by their narrow education by 'Crawfie', the royal family's pet name for Marion Crawford, the princesses' Scottish governess who remained their chief companion and confidante into their adulthood. He ridiculed the Queen's style of ingénue prissiness, describing her stilted public speeches as '. . . "a pain in the neck". Like her mother, she appears to be unable to string even a few sentences together without a written text.' He poured scorn on the Queen's entourage which he identified as 'almost without exception the "tweedy" sort': plus-foured aristocratic landowners and their ladies. The royal household had remained 'a tight little enclave of British ladies and gentlemen', embarrassingly white-skinned at a time when it was essential for the monarchy to be cementing good relations with the multi-racial countries of the Commonwealth. What he saw as the court's 'social lopsidedness' was emphasised by the blatant social selectiveness of palace presentations, outdated rituals which Altrincham suggested should have been 'quietly discontinued in 1945'. In Altrincham's vision of a 'truly classless and Commonwealth Court', the only people who deserved to be presented to the monarch were those who had positively earned the right.

It is probable that, even without Lord Altrincham, debutante presentations would have been discontinued. Stung by criticism, the royal family could be seen to be making valiant efforts to get out and meet the people. On the very day that I and my fellow debs assembled at the palace to curtsey to the Queen the Court Circular records that Princess Margaret, attended by her lady-in-waiting, Lady Elizabeth Cavendish, was opening a pensioners' club in Camberwell. It was generally believed in the deb world that Prince Philip had been the prime mover in the ending of the curtseys as part of his sometimes desperate mission to modernise the court and make it more accessible by, for instance, introducing a regular series of luncheon parties to which a social mix of guests would be invited. According to a court source quoted in Sarah Bradford's biography *Elizabeth*, the Queen had planned to do away with debutante presentations in 1957 but 'she carried on with them for one more year just to show that she wasn't going to bow to Altrincham'. At a time when controversy about the British monarchy flared up with unexpected intensity the largely unwitting English debutantes provided a convenient public sacrifice.

The announcement came from the Lord Chamberlain's office on 14 November 1957. The following year was the last in which presentation parties would be held. The Lord Chamberlain provided discreet words of explanation:

. . . for some time – in fact since 1954 – the Queen has had in mind the general pattern of official entertaining at Buckingham Palace, including the problem of Presentation Parties and certain anomalies to which they give rise. Her

Majesty felt reluctant to bring these to an end because of the pleasure they appear to give to a number of young people and the increasing applications for them. These applications have now risen until it has become necessary either to add to the number of these parties or to seek some other solution.

Because of her many other engagements the Queen was said to be unable to increase the number of presentation parties. She therefore planned to substitute additional garden parties, 'which will have the effect of increasing the number of persons invited to Buckingham Palace, both from the United Kingdom and all other parts of the Commonwealth'.

Reactions to the Lord Chamberlain's announcement were mixed. The social diarist Jennifer records in her memoirs the 'great consternation' caused among future debutante mothers and sponsors at the news they were about to be cast out of the palace. She was telephoned constantly by press reporters for her reaction and comments, which she claims she steadfastly refused to give. In my own milieu of debs' mothers and their progeny, a social strata not given to stringent analysis, the response to the announcement was puzzled and a little bit aggrieved. We felt a close personal connection with the royal family, perhaps all the more so because we had been together through the war. Those old enough had listened to, and been uplifted by, the young Princess Elizabeth's wartime broadcasts to the children of England. We identified closely with the day-to-day lives of the royal children as related by 'Crawfie' in *The Little Princesses*, the first (and very controversial) instance of a royal employee telling her own story. Girls of my generation almost knew that book by heart. My sister and I had been dressed in those identical check tweed winter coats with little velvet collars, like the ones worn by Princess Elizabeth and Princess Margaret Rose. When King George VI died, I, then a child of twelve, wore a black armband through the period of court mourning. It was a strong emotional association. When news reached us of the end of presentations there was a feeling that the Queen, on whom we had thought we could count, had now abandoned us. For many fathers it was simply further proof that the country they had fought for was going to the dogs.

However, a *Times* leader gave cautious approval, seeing the end of presentations as the inevitable result of post-war social changes:

. . . the present age is one of transition in the sense that the traditional barriers of class have broken down. It has long ceased to be true that the court is

Fiona and Karin MacCarthy with a schoolfriend Starr Ankersimmons in Kensington Gardens all wearing Little Princess coats

the centre of an aristocracy, the members of which form a clearly recognizable section of the community.

Formal advantages deriving from the presentation no longer exist. The selection of the privileged few has become increasingly difficult and even invidious. The abandonment of a custom that has largely lost its contemporary value is sensible. However, it should not be taken as an encouragement by those who press for a more and more democratic court.

The Times leader writer argued that the idea of the Queen bringing herself 'down to the level of her ordinary citizens is absurd and illogical'.

The popular press, whose gossip columns then depended to an extent that now seems almost unbelievable on the doings of the debutante world, were vociferous in their laments for the passing of presentations. Both Paul Tanfield in the *Daily Mail* and William Hickey in the *Daily Express* gave the news extensive coverage, Hickey wallowing in sentiment as he described the pre-war glory days for debutantes waiting out-side the palace in their cars sustained by champagne, brandy or pâté sandwiches: 'One girl had drunk so much champagne that when she went to curtsey to the King and Queen she fell down flat on her face.' For Hickey this was the end of a certain sort of Englishness: 'Now some-thing of the exclusiveness and glamour will have disappeared for ever.' There was general acceptance that the end of presentations threatened the viability of the London social Season. It had been the set piece of the curtsey to the monarch, the ratification of the young girls' entrée to soci-ety, that provided the Season with its central *raison d'être*.

In 1958, as the final presentations approached, foreign commenta-tors took up the theme. INNOCENT DAZZLE ON HUMDRUM LIFE – US REGRET AT DECISION ran a headline in the *New York Herald Tribune* whose reporter argued that presentations 'made up part of the ordered, stately, and majestic cavalcade of royal life which the British people look on with so much personal pride, no matter what they think about it'. There was regret for the loss of 'gorgeous pomp'.

In the last week the *Daily Express* launched a competition for an 'Epitaph for a Deb' to be sent in on a postcard with a 2$^{1}/_{2}$ d stamp. The winning entry, by Miss Stout of York, was sadly undistinguished:

A sparkling debutante lies here.
Daddy found her very dear.

The runner up was more succinct: 'Oh Deb where is thy fling?'

On 13 March 1958 the William Hickey gossip column was report-ing that 'Deb decorum – acquired at considerable cost in the most exclusive finishing schools – is already beginning to crack at the seams. I hear that there is a gentle-voiced but oh so grim tug of war at most debutante tea parties.' In the press and in private, speculation had been mounting as to who would be the last of the last debs, the final debutante to curtsey. Harriet Nares, described in the *Express* as 'a dainty honey blonde', said her friends had been told of quiet dim cor-ners in the palace in which they could hide in order to arrive strategi-cally late for the line-up for the curtsey. There were stories of money being offered by one deb to another for an exchange of seats in the antechamber in which they waited to be summoned to the Presence. Presentation was still being regarded by traditionalists as 'a symbol of loyalty and humble duty' but among the ranks of the girls to be pre-sented less ladylike instincts were breaking through.

In accounts of the end of presentations pride of place as last curtseyer has often been accorded to the blonde and buxom Lovice Ullein-Reviczky, eighteen-year-old daughter of a former Hungarian diplomat. It is Lovice's image, walking through the palace courtyard flanked by her sponsors, Frederic Bennett, Tory MP for Torquay, and his wife, in her fur tippet, that has acted as a kind of summing up for many people of the true significance of that strange day. It is a lonely image, with an edge of fallen glory. But in fact Lovice Ullein-Reviczky was not the last of the debs, but rather the last deb to arrive at the palace, her sponsor having been unavoidably detained at the House of Commons.

The genuine last deb to curtsey was a girl called Judy Grinling and, in the best traditions of the *Girls' Crystal* school stories we all devoured in childhood, she did not achieve this glory by jostling for position. Her triumph was a matter of her niceness and her luck in simply finding herself on the last gilt chair of the last row. And even then her position was not entirely certain: the debs could have been summoned from the other end. Judy Grinling, who later confessed to a reporter that her eventual curtsey had been 'a little wobbly', was not from a traditional aristocratic family but the daughter of a sculptor, Anthony Gibbons Grinling, who was also a director of W.A. Gilbey, the wine and spirit firm owned by his family. Judy herself was living in France, learning the language and intending to return there soon after she had curtsied. She was casual about the Season, although planning a dance in London later in the summer, nor was she very interested in her sudden accidental prominence as final debutante. Her mother told a reporter: 'I don't think she has any idea of what a Very Important Person she is.' She resisted invitations to give press interviews or to be photographed in her presentation clothes, making a single exception for the American *Life* magazine which was covering this turning point in English history. Judy Grinling had the streak of self-determination which in a period of dawning feminism would affect all social classes, the deb classes among them. For what *The Times* defined as an age of transition Judy Grinling was a very good example of the emergent transitional deb.

There was a dawning feeling by 1958 that the conventional cycle of coming out, courtship and marriage was not the be-all-and-end-all it had by and large appeared to our mothers' generation. A certain superiority about the Season was becoming *de rigueur* in the circles which I knew. In the week working up to the final presentations the *Evening*

Standard ran a series entitled 'Goodbye to the Debs' by Jocasta Innes, herself an upper-class girl who had become a successful journalist. The first of these deb interviewees, Philippa Drummond, posed in her Chelsea house with her black poodle, maintained that her main interest was art and that she would probably work in an art gallery after the Season ('of which' commented Innes 'she takes a more detached view than most debs'). The next girl to be featured, Priscilla Hunter, a stockbroker's daughter, had spent six months living in a French family and taking a course at the Sorbonne instead of the traditional finishing school. Her ambition was now to work her way to America as a nurse.

How had this change of attitude arisen? One clear external influence was William Douglas-Home's popular West End comedy *The Reluctant Debutante*. In his autobiography William Douglas-Home gives an account of a conversation held on Ashridge Golf Course with his friend George Bishop of the *Daily Telegraph* about the new play he was writing, as then unnamed:

'What's the new play about?' he asked me, studying the line of his putt.

'It's about a country girl who doesn't like the London Season,' I said.

'The Reluctant Debutante,' he said, half to himself, as he stooped over his ball.

The play opened at the Cambridge Theatre on 24 May 1955, the action taking place in a flat off Eaton Square, a flat rented for the Season by Jimmy and Sheila Broadbent, superficially silly but ferociously ambitious mother of Jane, the reluctant debutante. Jane's suitor David Hoylake-Johnston, a charmer of dubious reputation, is steadily discouraged by her mother until it emerges, in the final scene, that the sudden death of his great uncle has transformed him into the Duke of Positano. All dukes are desirable in Mrs Broadbent's view of things and in the volte-face of the final curtain she is pursuing him with gushing invitations to dinner with her daughter. The deb was played by Anna Massey, daughter of actor and producer Raymond Massey and actress Adrienne Allen. Her uncle Vincent Massey was then Governor General of Canada. This, her first professional engagement, coincided with her own debutante Season, a peculiar example of drama mirroring reality. To the many debs-to-be who giggled through a plot in which true romantic love triumphs over snobbery the fact that the star actress herself had made her curtsey gave the play an extra twist: Anna was one of us. I had my own brief moment of Anna

Lovice Ullein-Reviczky, the last of the debs to arrive at the palace (left); and Judy Grinling, the last deb to curtsey to the Queen in the final year of presentations

Massey glory, having partnered the future reluctant debutante in a performance of 'In Your Easter Bonnet' from *Easter Parade*. This was in the charity matinée put on by Miss Violet Ballantine, whose dancing school we both attended. I, aged nine, was the gauche clumsy imitation Judy Garland to Anna's much more polished Fred Astaire.

William Douglas-Home's play, an efficient if unsubtle comedy of manners, raked over all the clichés of debutante life: the rival chitter-chatter mothers; the weary father groaning about the expense and the late nights; the caddish debs' delights; the double-barrelled names. It was not that the Season's silliness or even its venality had never been admitted, but it rated

The Reluctant Debutante with its original cast including Anna Massey as the debutante and Celia Johnson as her mother

as a private, relatively inbred joke. William Douglas-Home's play, later turned into a movie by Vincente Minnelli with Kay Kendall and Rex Harrison, made the family secret embarrassingly public. What could a deb do now except plead reluctance? Even the most inwardly ambitious girls were claiming to be doing the Season on sufferance by 1958.

In the history of debutantes one often finds an element of disbelief, an urge towards self-parody. Lady Diana Manners, arriving at the palace in 1911 to make her double curtsey to King Edward VII and Queen Alexandra, recollected that the courtiers had been 'very alarming and martinettish – they shoo you and pull you back and speak to you as a wet dog'. Photographs of the artist Leonora Carrington in her train and ostrich feathers awaiting presentation to King George V in 1934 were a source of fascination when circulated around her surrealist friends. Closer to our own last curtseys, Emma Tennent describes her 1955 debut as a scene from a pantomime: you stood for 'a split second in front of the Royal Family on the dais, before dropping down to perform what looked, from the rear, very like the laying of an egg'.

Its solemnity betrayed even by its own insiders, what hope of remaining respect towards a ceremony already pronounced by the Lord Chamberlain as obsolete? The age of full-blown satire and irreverence would not arrive till the early 1960s, but the satiric possibilities of the end of palace curtseys were already irresistible. Any tone of respect towards the toffs was banished in such knockabout features as that in the *Evening Standard* headed 'SQUASHY' BELCHER OF ROEDEAN MEETS THE QUEEN. Sarah Belcher's father was said to be a heart surgeon. Unusually young to curtsey, at sixteen, she had been fast-forwarded in that final year of applications and was on an exeat from school. The *Standard* showed one picture of 'Squashy', her Roedean nickname, in school uniform and one in the 'fabulously expensive' floral presentation dress made for her in Paris. With the case of 'Squashy' Belcher all vestiges of dignity surrounding presentation vanished in a puff of smoke.

After the ceremony I was ushered into the Green Dining Room with a group of other girls, swirling in in our silk dresses and our little feather hats to be reunited with our parents and our sponsors and mull over, in relentless detail, the afternoon's events. We stood and we sipped tea and munched the traditional post-curtsey chocolate cake provided by the palace, not just debs but greedy teenagers in a country in which food rationing had only ended in 1954. For the more mischievous of the debs there was now the ceremony of the Pinching of the Teaspoons, a project made only slightly less daring by the fact the teaspoons were the property of the palace caterers and not the Queen herself. The chat was inevitably of cocktail parties, dances. There was also the conversation-stopping news that the Norfolk debutante Lois Denny's mother had been killed on the hunting field on the very eve of presentations. She had just taken a house in London for the Season. Debutantes had their particular tragedies.

I do not think I am falsely recalling a sense of the momentous alongside all the frippery. We may not have taken it to a logical conclusion: we were of course by definition four hundred silly girls. But at some instinctive level I feel we understood that the end of presentations signified a formal end to high society and that as English debutantes we were a dying breed.

CHAPTER TWO

Preparations for the Season

Only a small proportion of the 1,441 debutantes presented at Buckingham Palace in 1958 stayed on in London to do the Season proper. Many debs 'up from the country' (as my Chelsea-based mother would have put it, in slightly pejorative tone) returned whence they had come after delivering their curtsey. One of these, Angela Carler, told the *Evening Standard*, 'Riding's my hobby. Mummy is Master of the North Warwickshire Hounds.' The bevy of foreign debutantes presented to the Queen by the wives of their respective ambassadors – for instance the US, Belgium, Italy, with the largest contingent from France – almost all dispersed after the ceremony. The hard core of mainly English debutantes who spent the next four months giving and attending parties and the random succession of events that made up the London Season amounted to little more than two hundred: in her 1958 preview 'Brilliant Vista of the Last Royal Season' Jennifer lists 231 debutante participants and even within this total there were girls who came and went. For the remaining stalwarts based in London, whose non-stop social activities and would-be witticisms provided a whole summer's gossip column fodder, the Season amounted to a full-time job.

Who were these girls? We were a very motley collection compared with the closed society of debutantes in the eighteenth and early nineteenth centuries, when the aristocratic and landowning families converged on London for the Season, balls were held and marriage contracts between the children of wealthy and powerful dynasties were hammered out. Of 168 girls listed by Jennifer as giving dances in 1958 only 17 are daughters of the peerage and therefore irrefutably (this time to quote my nanny) 'out of the top drawer'. Seven daughters of earls and marquesses are listed: Lady Caroline Acheson, Lady

Katherine Courtenay, Lady Fiona Crichton-Stuart, Lady Anne Maitland, Lady Teresa Onslow, Lady Davina Pepys and Lady Carolyn Townshend. It was a sign of the times that Anne Maitland, daughter of Viscount Maitland who was killed in action in 1943, had been upgraded to the rank of earl's daughter after his death. It was also symptomatic of that period of growing casualness towards the London Season in the higher echelons of the aristocracy that the coming out ball at Arundel Castle for Lady Mary Fitzalan-Howard, the Duke of Norfolk's second daughter, had been held over to the following year, when she would share it with her younger sister, Sarah, and her older sister, Lady Anne, whose twenty-first birthday it would by then be. In 1958 Lady Mary would make do with a small dinner dance. Lady Rosemary FitzGerald, granddaughter of the Duke of

Lady Rosemary FitzGerald (right) with a fellow debutante outside the palace on presentation day

Leinster, Ireland's premier duke, unwillingly attended a few debutante tea parties and struggled through her own cocktail party at the Cavalry Club, before defecting from the Season altogether, setting off for travels in the USA.

Jennifer lists ten debutantes with the title of the Hon., which marked them out as daughters of viscounts or of barons: Penelope Allsopp, Mary Bridgeman, Diana Connolly-Carew, Eliza Guinness, Annabel Hawke, Camilla Jessel, Marilyn Kearley, Gail Mitchell-Thomson, Teresa Pearson, Elizabeth Sidney. By no means all these girls were of ancient lineage. Several were descended from the new commercial aristocracy that began to be created in the nineteenth century, gradually intermarrying with the old landowning elite. The Hon. Eliza Guinness came from the famous brewing family originally ennobled by Disraeli: Eliza's dance was to be given by her grandmother, the Countess of Iveagh. The Hon. Penelope Allsopp was descended from Henry Allsopp, another brewer, a relatively modest self-made man created Baron Hindlip by Lord Salisbury in 1886. The Hon. Teresa Pearson's great-grandfather Weetman Pearson was an entrepreneur of energy and vision, an engineering contractor on a global scale

The Hon. Penelope Allsopp

whose elevation to the peerage as Lord Cowdray in 1910 was by no means universally approved. The title inherited by the 2nd Baron Jessel of Westminster, father of the debutante the Hon. Camilla Jessel, dated back only as far as 1924. Lord Jessel had married into the Londonderry family and Camilla's grandmother, the Dowager Marchioness of Londonderry, was to be the hostess at Camilla's ball at Londonderry House. The father of the Hon. Gail Mitchell-Thomson was technically speaking even more of an *arriviste* since his title of Baron Selsdon of Croydon, a place itself a little suspect in smart circles, was bestowed as recently as 1934. Decades of political appointments to the peerage, as well as frequent intermarriage with commoners, had turned the British aristocracy into a hybrid. By 1958, contrary to many outsiders' expectations, little of the blood of my contemporary debutantes could be described as truly blue. This is not to say the Season was a free for all. There were still operable grounds for social exclusion. But these were a matter of language, style and manner rather than the dynastic claims of aristocracy and land.

In that post-war decade of rapid social transition, as the debutante connection with monarchy and aristocracy loosened, my own family background was typically mixed. My mother's grandfather Robert McAlpine was a prodigious example of the self-made man. Born into a mining family in Lanarkshire, he worked as a bricklayer before founding the building and contracting firm that became Sir Robert McAlpine & Sons. He was made a baronet in recognition of his 'continuous and patriotic service' soon after the armistice of 1918. McAlpines had been farsighted in developing new techniques of concrete construction and my great-grandfather became a well-known public figure, popularly known as 'Concrete Bob'. Sir Robert's daughter Agnes, my mother's mother, had married a French diplomat, the Baron de Belabre, a tall, distinguished, rather dilettante figure who had been French Consul at Dover and at Newcastle, was an amateur painter and had written a history of Rhodes. The marriage only lasted for ten years. The baron was unfaithful. My mother was apt to be impatient with my grandmother's intolerance of his vicissitudes, maintaining that she ought to have accepted he was French.

Socially speaking my mother had married a little bit beneath her. In 1937 Yolande Yorke Fradin de Belabre, the girl whose name reminded gossip columnists of the heroine of a medieval French romance, married Gerald MacCarthy, eldest son of a Sherborne

Fiona MacCarthy with her grandfather, the Baron de Belabre, at Bridport (left); and The marriage of Captain Gerald MacCarthy and Yolande de Belabre at St George's Hanover Square on 6 April 1937

country doctor of Irish extraction and his wife, Florence, a diminutive Irishwoman known as Flo. My father was a regular soldier in the Royal Artillery, a regiment of marginal social acceptability. But what my father may have lacked in fashionable credentials was compensated for by good looks, affability and charm. He was a dashing, gregarious figure known as 'Bang Bang', the name by which he first appears in my mother's voluminous photograph albums. He was a wonderful ballroom dancer, a proficient rider and polo player: in almost all the pictures my father is either on or near a horse. His ebullience balanced my mother's much more reticent nature; as they say, he brought her out of herself. My father, by then a lieutenant colonel, was killed in 1943, only weeks after sailing from Glasgow to join his regiment in the offensive against Rommel's army in Tunisia. He perished in the desert, in a random scenario of ambushes and sandstorms. His death was recorded as 'date unknown'. My widowed mother had suitors but she did not remarry. No one ever measured up to my father she would say.

My credentials for the Season were in one sense unimpressive.

Gerald MacCarthy in India in 1937 with his chestnut Arab horse Mistral, winner of many cups (top); Fiona MacCarthy with her mother in her Schiaparelli parrot dress; and Fiona MacCarthy with her father at home on his last leave in 1942

Neither by birth or fortune (for in spite of the McAlpines my mother was hard up) was I up there with the grandest of the debs. But my right to do the Season was never, I think, questioned by my mother, by myself or anyone I ever met. As a family we were positioned in the fluid territory between the upper middle classes and the aristocracy: one of my mother's half sisters was married to Sir Edward Naylor-Leyland, Edward VII's godson. Of my mother's own god-daughters, one married David Stuart, Viscount Stuart of Findhorn, another is the present Duchess of Devonshire. My mother was not snobbish or particularly socially ambitious for her daughters, her great enthusiasm was for ballet and the theatre. My younger sister was already training as a dancer and our household was more like that of the stage-mad children in Noel Streatfeild's *Ballet Shoes* than a social forcing house. But the Season was somehow built into the equation, a matter of conventions and connections so deep-rooted that no one really bothered to discuss it. It was the assumption that in the interval between leaving school and taking up my place at Oxford I'd be dancing, having fun, making friends, acquiring 'beaux' (as my mother's generation optimistically described them). In my mother's circles the debutante Season was simply something that one did.

Historically, the London Season began and ended with large-scale arrivals and departures: the movements of whole households from the country to the town house in late spring and back to the country in late July or August as the shooting season started and, in the heat of summer, London itself became less salubrious. In her memoir *Hons and Rebels* Jessica Mitford describes the removal in the 1920s of the large family, servants and household effects (including wax-wrapped packages of home-baked bread) from their house in the Cotswolds to their seven-storey town house in Rutland Gate as 'resembling the evacuation of a small army'. By 1958, by which time the majority of these enormous aristocratic town houses had been given up, the Season was not so logistically complex but its formal vestiges remained in the announcements in *The Times* Court Circular appearing from early March onwards. For example, on 3 March:

Lord and Lady Rollo and the Hon. Helen Rollo will be at 24 Hilton Street SW (telephone Sloane 4111*) from April 23 for the Season.

The family of the 13th Baron Rollo had arrived from Perthshire.

Major R.A. and Lady Rosemary Rubens and Miss Davina Nutting will be at 11 Cadogan Court, Draycott Avenue, sw3 (telephone Kensington 2821) from today until August 31.

The grave tone of these *Times* announcements suggests an event of national importance. On 1 April the Court Circular informed its readers:

Lady St. John of Bletso has left 1 Herbert Crescent and her future permanent address is 8 Lennox Gardens, sw1 (telephone Kensington 6537).

Lady St. John was the most notorious of the Season's paid chaperones, launching her own little group of debutantes each Season, so the notice of her changed location was essential to trade.

---

*These were the days when London telephone exchanges were still local, defined by names not numbers.

From the point of view of social cachet it mattered greatly where you lived. Over the centuries the different areas of London had acquired their own identity and status. By the interwar period, according to Jessica Mitford, their social character seemed 'as fixed as if it had been determined by some inimitable law of the Universe'. Mayfair was the chosen place of the very rich and fashionable; more artistic, literary and bohemian people gravitated towards Chelsea 'or even Bloomsbury'. Hampstead, Hammersmith or St John's Wood were 'predominantly middle class'. Meanwhile the 'run-of-the-mill squires, knights, baronets and barons' were colonising Kensington, Paddington, Marylebone and Pimlico.

By 1958 Mitford's analysis was still in broad terms valid, though, crippled as they were by high levels of taxation in the post-war period, few upper-class families could afford to live in Mayfair and the boundaries of social acceptability were necessarily spreading out and out. The further reaches of Chelsea and Fulham were no longer considered socially beyond the pale. In this my mother's situation was typical again. The address printed on our deep-blue printed writing paper was 66 Limerston Street, Chelsea sw10. The postcode sw10 was only just becoming viable in upper-class circles, where every nuance counted and the self-appointed arbiters could be ferocious in sorting the genuinely upper class from the socially spurious: a few years earlier the only acceptable sw postcodes were sw1, sw3 or (at a pinch) sw7. The term Chelsea was barely accurate for a street beyond the bend of King's Road in what was technically World's End, a working-class area then in the early stages of being gentrified. My mother had bought the white stucco terraced house, a handsome house with possibilities though still a little shabby, for £5,000 from the maverick politician and horse racing fanatic Woodrow Wyatt just the year before my Season. For my younger sister Karin and myself it was an extra thrilling purchase in that Woodrow Wyatt shared the house with his then mistress Lady Moorea Hastings, daughter of the Earl of Huntingdon, whom he was soon to marry. This, to us, breathtakingly glamorous slim blonde was referred to in the family as 'Lady-Moorea-in-the-basement'. The whole idea of mistresses in basements was a new one, opening out vistas of possibility.

For a debutante Season Limerston Street was adequate. The house had a good-sized first-floor drawing room, with tall windows opening out onto a balcony. Downstairs there was a library that ran through to the dining room overlooking a small garden at the back. My mother slept on the top floor. My sister and I had our bedrooms on the second floor. Isa, our Scottish nanny, had replaced Lady Moorea in the basement. If the house was not grand scale it was not dramatically different in feel or in facilities from the London living places of many other debs. Apart from the few ostentatiously rich and, in my mother's view, therefore somewhat suspect families ('My dear, you should just see the Renoir in the dining room!') many debutantes emerged in their presentation finery from just this sort of relatively modest Chelsea terrace house or South Kensington mansion block apartment. Tiny, cramped mews houses converted from the dwellings of the former grooms and coachmen had also become popular. Few debutante families had live-in servants. The daily would arrive for a few hours each weekday morning. Quite often these houses or flats would be rented for the Season, hence *The Times*'s announcements of the debutante's arrival. Sometimes just a room would be begged from a relation or a friend of the deb's mother and a weekly rate for board would be negotiated: in the make-do-and-mend upper-class life in that post-war period there was nothing shaming in taking in paying guests (or, as they were termed, 'PGs'). A few days after the 1958 presentations *The Times* ran a quasi-humorous article by one of these all-welcoming hostesses who could have been Anthony Powell's Lady Molly. The piece was titled FAMILY CHARING CROSS.

London Season means a convergence of *débutantes* on the town houses of relatives. With us, the only London branch of a widely extended family, our house is permanently a cross between metropolitan hotel, clearing station, and left-luggage office for our kinsfolk.

Her guests were strewn around on twin beds, studio couch, spare bunks, a rather uncomfortable bed chair, four inflatable mattresses originally bought for camping. The article suggests well the rather ramshackle quality of upper-class living arrangements at the time. I remember wandering into the main bedroom of a flat in Brompton Road taken for the Season and spotting, in a chaotic heap of ball dresses and underclothes, the family tiara on the floor.

Preparations for the Season had gone on for several months before the presentations. The crucial decision was the date for the deb's dance, where it would be held and who indeed was paying for it, a tense question in what were felt to be financially stringent times. Did all debs have to have a dance? A few girls did in fact achieve a perfectly successful Season, being asked to all the parties, without giving their own dances, notably Penny Graham, first of the debs to curtsey. But this was a route only for the brave, for girls with great reserves of personality and contacts. For the vast majority of debs the dance acted as the underpinning of their Season, a focus of activity and an essential bargaining point since it was the tacit understanding that girls you invited to your dance would ask you back.

In the old days of the Season the girl making her debut was the sole star of the evening, the centre of the ritual, an upper-class equivalent of Queen of the May. This was becoming less usual with the advent of two-hostess or even three-hostess debutante dances in which families combined, sharing the expenses. There could be as many as four debutantes coming out together. Of 118 coming out dances pre-announced by Jennifer in her *Tatler* preview of the 1958 Season, 43 were shared. The sharers might be sisters or sisters-in-law combining to launch two debutante cousins. Some of these joint hostesses were, if not relations, old friends. But, with the curious randomness of Seasons in the fifties, some pairings were more like a marriage of convenience between mothers who were not necessarily compatible, introduced to one another by helpful mutual acquaintances. My mother's partner in this enterprise had been produced for her by Helen Vincent. Lady Vincent, daughter of the First World War commander Field Marshal Sir William Robert Robertson, was an old but not, I think, a very understanding friend. The friend of this friend, Petie Burness, was a tiny, dark, vivacious woman whose sister, Patricia Medina, was a minor film star who had started her career as a teenage actress in British pre-war movies before going to Hollywood with her then husband the actor Richard Greene, Robin Hood in the TV series in the fifties. Petie was a little film starry herself. My mother, who could be uncharacteristically catty about Petie, complained that she was never parted from her mink, and indeed there was a day of reckoning in Harrods when animal rights campaigners moved in on her with spray guns. The Burnesses were richer and more showy than my mother who, though hardly Bohemian, considered herself arty. Petie's husband, Kenneth, was a shipping magnate and a member of Lloyd's. Their lavish house on the corner of Cadogan Square had a balcony-terrace overlooking the square gardens on which drinks were served in summer. It was a mismatch in that the Burness's style of life and level of expenditure was not really compatible with ours.

Whatever her misgivings my mother was not one to renege on her commitments. The MacCarthy–Burness (or Burness–MacCarthy) dance was to take place at the Dorchester in June. The fixing of the date for so important an investment in a daughter's future could not be left to chance. London and country dances within reach of London were held in the three months from May to July. This space could get congested with dances overlapping, sometimes two or three a night. Dances in more distant areas of England – for instance Shropshire, Yorkshire and Northumberland – were scheduled for late July and August. Irish dances were centred around the early August Dublin Horse Show; Scottish balls coincided with the shooting in August and September. More London dances were held in the so-called 'Little Season' which began in early October and straggled through the autumn. If humanly possible a clash must be avoided with another daughter's debut, and especially an event of obvious glamour and extravagance which might siphon off your own most hoped for guests. This planning could be nerve-wracking and there were many pitfalls, some resulting in embarrassing apologies in *The Times* explaining that because of unforeseen circumstances the date of an already-announced dance had now been changed.

The cannier mothers consulted Betty Kenward, 'Jennifer', who had been the *Tatler*'s social diarist since 1944 and who, fourteen years later, was an astonishing repository of knowledge of the working networks of the upper class. An upright, beautifully coiffed and elegantly austere figure, dedicated to upholding proper standards of behaviour in a world in which they seemed in imminent decline, Jennifer took it upon herself to regulate the Season, keeping a careful ledger of dance dates already booked and bestowing the free dates on grateful mothers, resembling the goddess with the cornucopia. Like Vacani's curtsey lessons a solemn consultation between prospective dance-givers and Jennifer was a staple of the Season, part of the mystique. I think my mother was secretly a bit in awe of Jennifer, although joking about her trademark strings of pearls and velvet Alice bands. She and Petie returned from their afternoon audience in the *Tatler* offices, having been allotted 10 June for the dance at the Dorchester, with evident relief.

The next thing to organise was the coming-out photograph. Every debutante I ever knew had had one done and indeed you can find these nubile young girls' portraits still standing on the sofa tables and grand pianos of 1958 debs now of pensionable age. As well as being private

Betty Kenward, the social diarist Jennifer, with her son at a London wedding in the 1950s

celebrations of a daughter's entrée to society these formal studio portraits had a public function. Portraits of the best-looking and/or best-connected girls would be selected by the social editors of the magazines *Tatler* and *Queen* to illustrate their February previews of the coming Season, establishing a kind of pecking order amongst the debutantes-to-be. In tone the enterprise was strangely close to that of *Spotlight*, the illustrated casting directory for the theatrical profession, an upper-class version of 'pick your starlet'. Vital statistics were not given but implied as, for example, in the caption to the portrait of Penelope Riches given a full page in the *Sketch*, the third of the London social magazines, competitor of *Queen* and *Tatler*, which was soon to be defunct:

Penelope Riches is the lovely daughter of Mr and Mrs Edward Riches, of Cadogan Gardens, who also have a place near Canterbury in Kent. Miss Riches has the perfect model-girl figure, and great grace and poise. It is her ambition to become a model and rise to the dizzy heights of stardom in this profession, in which the top girls rival the stars of stage and screen. Her curtsey should be perfect.

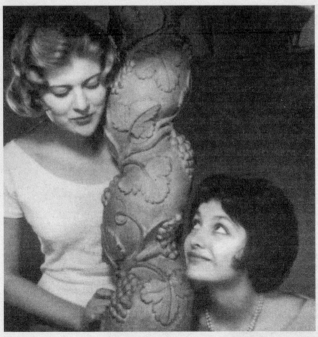

Alexandra Bridgewater and her cousin Georgina Milner photographed by Tom Hustler

It is interesting to see in this write-up the incipient signs of celebrity culture which would in the end engulf the debs.

The portraits themselves mark a turning point. The old names of the established society photographers – Madame Yevonde, A.V. Swaebe, Bassano and Lenare, who had photographed many of our mothers – were still in evidence in 1958. The majority of portraits were still the conventional head and shoulders shots of girls in pearls, girls in off-the-shoulder satin dresses, girls perched on brocade sofas with a glimpse of a family heirloom or a heavy gilt-framed painting in the background. But there was a growing tendency towards the more romantic flamboyant stagey image showing the influence of the widely circulated velvet-mantled portrait of the Queen painted by Pietro Annigoni in 1954. F.G. Goodman's photographic portrait of Georgina Montagu-Douglas-Scott, debutante niece of the Duchess of Gloucester, a sacrificial virgin in a grandiosely melancholic landscape, certainly has the Annigoni touch.

Lola Wigan, whose portrait by Tony Armstrong-Jones was used on the cover of *Queen* magazine. It challenged the conventional twinset-and-pearls image of the debutante, setting a new style of society portraiture in 1958

Younger photographers were gradually taking over from the famous interwar portraitists of society and royalty. Dorothy Wilding's Bond Street studio employed a staff of around forty in the late 1930s and extended over several floors. The portrait Wilding took of Henrietta Tiarks, 1957 Deb of the Year, was in effect a swansong. In 1958 she sold her studio to her twenty-four-year-old assistant, Tom Hustler, for a mere £3,000. Hustler introduced a quirkier, almost surrealist approach to debutante photography as in his double portraits of the two cousins Georgina Milner and Alexandra Bridgewater, relations and rivals in their year of coming out. These are beautiful, witty, slightly unnerving studies in ambivalence.

The other rising star of society photography was Tony Armstrong-Jones. He too was in his twenties. His portrait of Lola Wigan, the cover picture for *Queen* magazine's February issue 'FIRST NEWS OF THE 1958 SEASON', was a breakthrough in two senses, bringing a new informality to society photography and redefining the image of the debutante. Armstrong-Jones photographed Lola not in a twinset, not even in a choker, but with a suggestive stretch of naked shoulder. Quite possibly the deb was naked to the waist. He invested her with a sweetness and a nonchalance, a Reluctant Debutante in beautiful reality. Here in 1958 is a face of the sixties, the vulnerable but self-determined waif, a girl of the style soon to be popularised by Jean Shrimpton, the most famous model of the time. Within weeks of the *Queen* cover, Lola Wigan was a debutante cult figure. The *Evening Standard* reported: 'Miss Lola Wigan, a rare, exquisite deb with Pre-Raphaelite face and cascading hair, was told that Polish students had posted her photograph (by Tony Armstrong-Jones) on the walls of an art school in Warsaw.'

There were mutterings among the debs' mothers that Lola, although she came from nowhere, had a good chance of becoming the next Deb of the Year.

The February publication of the list of dances and girls' portraits made it possible for mothers to check through and assess the competition, pinpointing the main dances and most glamorous of debs. The followers of form now came into their element. If the illustrated previews of the Season resembled a casting directory they also had overtones familiar to the horse-racing fraternity to which so many families of the debutantes belonged. In that sense we were all promising young fillies, to be pondered over, prodded, trained up and made the most of.

Margaret Whigham, later Duchess of Argyll, Deb of the Year in 1930

The Season was put over as 'having fun', sheer pleasure. But right from the beginning we felt a sense of duty to, so to speak, our trainers, as if England expected us to do our best.

Predictions began early over who would be 'Top Deb', seen at all the smartest parties clasped in the arms of the most eligible men. Though coming-out had originally been an internal affair, with little personal publicity directed at the debutante, the scene had altered greatly in the brasher 1930s. Much to the horror of the old-guard aristocracy debs became newsworthy. The first of these was Margaret Whigham, later Duchess of Argyll, acclaimed Deb of the Year in 1930 amidst rumours that her wealthy Scots-American father had financed a considerable publicity campaign. Other highly publicised debs of that same year were Lady Bridget Poulett, sister of Earl Poulett, and Rose Bingham who was to become the Countess of Warwick. As Margaret Whigham saw it, 'We seemed to fill the gap between the picture postcard beauties of World War I and the star models, such as Barbara Goalen and Fiona Campbell-Walter, after World War II.' On this rise to semi-stardom she admitted she had had assistance from friends who were newspaper gossip columnists: 'Don', the Marquis of Donegal, Viscount Castlerosse, Tom Driberg, originator of the William Hickey column. For the first time the debutante became a household name with a physical persona recognisable enough for the angular and slender Margaret Whigham to appear in numerous newspaper cartoons:

. . . they usually made me baleful looking, with large sunken eyes and a square jaw jutting out from an elongated neck. I was regarded as a trend-setter, and was apparently the first girl to wear pearl-coloured nail varnish that was luminous at night.

Through the decades Debs of the Year had come and gone, with no one quite approaching Margaret Whigham's brittle notoriety. In 1957 the consensus of opinion had settled fairly early on Henrietta Tiarks, daughter of an international banker Henry Tiarks, a director of Henry Schroder and a member of the Dollar Exports Council. Henrietta's grandfather F.C. Tiarks, Governor of the Bank of England, was embroiled in the Anglo-German Fellowship set up in 1934 to foster contacts with Germany. This fellowship was in effect a channel for Nazi propaganda. But such family embarrassments were never mentioned, perhaps barely even thought of, as Henrietta's Season went from strength to strength. The sleek-haired, slightly slit-eyed and

Henrietta Tiarks, Deb of the Year in 1957, at a ball at Claridge's with Prince Alexander Romanoff and (far left) Charles MacArthur Hardy

Oriental-looking beauty pictured sitting with her mother at Queen Charlotte's Ball; Henrietta at a dance at Claridge's, half smiling, with Prince Alexander Romanoff sitting at her feet. As Deb of the Year, Henrietta had been classic: her Season in London had been followed the next year by a second triumph in New York. Henrietta was destined to be Marchioness of Tavistock, then Duchess of Bedford. Who had the stamina to succeed her in 1958?

In our year the winner of the Top Deb contest was less obvious. Though Lola Wigan looked the part she was naturally reticent and had no pushing mother in the background. The names of a number of alternative contenders began to be bandied about with a slight air of desperation. The *Sketch* alighted on Miranda Smiley whose dance was to be held at her grandmother's house, Parham Park in Sussex: 'Miss Miranda Smiley might well prove to be "deb of the year". She is endowed with great good looks, is studying the piano and is really talented.' The fact that she also played the piano accordion was noted as a further bonus point. Elfrida Eden, niece of the former Prime Minister Sir Anthony Eden, was another possibility put forward by the *Sketch*: 'She is well in the running for the title of "debutante of the year".' But it was pointed out that Elfrida had her own, rather different ambitions. She had her mind set on becoming a professional ballet dancer. Elfrida, who had trained with George Goncharov and also studied with Vera Volkova, is pictured *en pointe* in her tutu, performing a solo from *Swan Lake* at a charity matinee. The photograph is captioned A DEBUTANTE ON HER TOES.

Four other debutantes were picked out as strong contenders by the *Evening Standard*. Mary ('Minnie') d'Erlanger, daughter of the newly knighted Sir Gerard d'Erlanger, Chairman of BOAC, was said to start with the advantage of knowing the Duke of Kent through her sister; in addition her face photographed well. Georgina Ward, daughter of George Ward MP, the Secretary of State for Air, was described as an attractive girl who aimed to be an actress, having won medals for monologues and lyrics. The Duke of Windsor, a close friend of her uncle the Earl of Dudley, was likely to be at her Dorchester dance. Zia Foxwell, whose mother Lady Edith was married to the film director Ivan Foxwell, was also in the running. She was sharing her dance with Georgina Montagu-Douglas-Scott, the Duchess of Gloucester's niece. Melanie Lowson, described as 'a strawberry blonde with a passion for stamp collecting', had the advantage of a mother, Lady Lowson, who was the most successful Lady Mayoress that London had had for a decade. But in spite of famous fathers, lavish dances, royal connections, none of these girls succeeded to the title. They were all passed at the post, as we shall see, by a country girl called Sally, a relative outsider with an intrepidly ambitious mother, Mrs Arthur Croker-Poole.

In any case by 1958 the title itself had become a bit *déclassé*. Like other aspects of the Season it was being diminished by ridicule and satire. Later in the summer an amateur play, *The Deb of the Year*, a comedy whodunnit written by Lady Aylwen was performed to a fashionable audience at the Scala theatre in aid of the NSPCC. Lady Aylwen, not content with appearing in the prime part of the debutante named Lola, cast herself in a lesser role as well. The novelist Denise Robins, in a cap and frilly apron, played Germaine, the French maid.

The role of the ingénue Lady Davina Delville was acted, tongue in cheek, by a previous year's debutante Marika Hopkinson. The part of the murderer was taken by Charles MacArthur Hardy, described in the *Evening Standard* as 'that large, handsome and superannuated deb's escort now laughingly known to his friends as "the Clive Brook

of Green Street" '. Clive Brook had appeared in such popular successes as *Gioconda Smile* and *The Count of Clérambord*. In this star part
of the murderer, Charles MacArthur Hardy, the epitome of smoothness, parodied himself and effectively sent up the London Season. The
villain was unmasked in the Ritz in Paris. The critic in *Queen* magazine may have complained of cruelty to audience in the theatrical disaster of the upper classes playing the upper classes. But according to
the *Standard* 'the audience howled' in its appreciation.

In the early weeks of 1958 our mothers were working hard at circulating. In mid-February, Gladys Boyd, the *Sketch*'s social editor,
reported:

There is little more than a month to go till the Presentation Parties in mid-
March and the mothers of all the debutantes (of whom there is a record number this year) are now having the time of their lives making all the detailed
preparations to give the girls the time of *their* lives! It's a most exacting and
tiring job; some mothers love it, some loathe it; but I think the majority of
them enjoy the gay lunches and small dinner parties which they give to meet
each other and generally plan for the Season as carefully as if it were a season
of International Opera or a Festival of Britain.

The organisation of the Festival of Britain, held in 1951, was still a
prize example of a triumph of logistics. The mums' lunch was another
ritual of the Season that had recently become the target for mild satire:
How to be a Deb's Mum by Petronella Portobello ('who has been
one'), a comic epistolary novel of debs' mums strategies in launching
darling daughters, had been published successfully the year before.

What were these gatherings of mothers really like? They were relatively small and intimate: twenty or thirty mothers meeting in a private house or flat, rarely in a club or a hotel which would have been
considered rather nouveau, redolent of rootlessness. My mother held
two lunches, rather crowded affairs, in our Limerston Street house.
Coronation Chicken was inevitably on the menu: this collation of cold
chicken in a creamy sweet-sour sauce was originally evolved by
Rosemary Hume of the Cordon Bleu Cookery School and first served
by the Constance Spry finishing school students at the celebration
lunch in Westminster Hall for foreign delegates attending the
Coronation. The recipe remained a staple of upper-class entertaining
for many years to come. The debs' mums' lunches at Limerston Street
would have been prepared jointly by my mother and our nanny, Isa.

There were no upmarket takeaways in those days, and we did not employ a cook. The food was not, by today's standards, at all sophisticated. The most popular pudding served at the lunches given by the mother of Thalia Gough, a deb of the next Season, was made by their daily woman from packages of Raspberry Frood Mousse whipped up with cream and decorated with fresh raspberries: 'We used buckets and buckets as the Season wore on.'

Most debutante mothers were still young, although to us they did not seem it. The majority were in their early forties or even their late thirties, having married and borne children relatively early. Quite a high proportion were single mothers in the sense of being widows like my mother or divorcées. Many had suffered the emotional casualties of war, and were now remarried. It is striking how few of the 1958 debs' mothers still had the same surname as their daughters. From the family point of view this was a confused scene. Our mothers were women of a certain social background, bound together by what Peregrine Worsthorne has described so well as 'the invisible bonds of memory': shared nurseries, shared day schools, their own now distant comings out and wedding days and christenings, divorces and bereavements, inextricably linked in the detail of their lives. They were linked by their appearance, nicely dressed in the printed silk suits with the hats, gloves and little clutch bags recommended by that season's fashion editors 'for lunching in town'. The most glamorous debs' mothers were elegant and rangy, with the look of Osbert Lancaster's Maudie Littlehampton, the charm of her silliness mingled with hauteur. These women sounded alike; helter-skelter in delivery with lavish use of 'dahling!' They were united in recognition of proper social values, of what constituted morally acceptable behaviour. Although many would admit that they themselves fell short of it, and some of the debs' mothers' lives were fairly rackety, these were the standards they upheld for their daughters. For all their vicissitudes they showed a crazy courage in rising above personal disaster, sexual betrayal, financial decline and what they foresaw (when they chose to think about it) as the end of England as they knew it. Like the Hoffnung cartoon of the orchestra still playing as the *Titanic* gradually, inexorably, sank into the ocean, our mothers dressed up, chattered on and planned another London Season. In their way they did their best.

After lunch, as the over-percolated coffee was distributed in tiny Wedgwood bone china cups, the business of the day began and the debs' mothers rummaged in their bags for their little leather books. This was exchange of address time. Notes were made on dates and places of cocktail parties and balls planned for spring and summer. Names of nice reliable young men who could be brought in to balance up the numbers were discussed. Though such strategies would hardly have been needed in the days when the Season was small and self-sufficient, by the 1950s 'the List' as it was called, a kind of register of eligible debs' escorts, circulated round the mothers. One version was headed 'Jeunes Hommes' although the mothers detected that some of the escorts (like Charles MacArthur Hardy) were already getting grizzled. Debs' delights would be deleted once they got engaged. If there was, as has been claimed, the List's corollary, a black list of young men to be avoided on the ground of their being NSIT (the code name for Not Safe In Taxis) or MTF (Must Touch Flesh) my mother did not divulge it. A futher categorisation of the young men was apparently VVSITPQ: Very Very Safe In Taxis Probably Queer.

Could an outsider break into this close circle of debs' mothers? Yes, but only if she had a lot to offer. To some extent in the deb world of 1958 the cutlet for cutlet principle prevailed and a mother who was planning a really lavish ball could be forgiven for being Jewish – at a level of society in which a certain anti-Semitism was almost automatic – or in trade or 'not quite right' in other ways. She would certainly have needed extreme determination, and the hide of a rhinoceros, to enter this hyper-critical milieu in which social ineptitude was a running joke. Those who did not understand the unwritten rules were ridiculed. There were right clothes and wrong clothes for every occasion: I remember the horror when I proposed arriving in red shoes at a house party in the country. There were right words and wrong words, and the wrong ones would arouse a barely concealed shudder.

The question of language, intonation and accent was the hardest for a would-be ascender through the class structure to master. My mother and her friends were fascinated followers of the debate raging in the 1950s over 'U and non-U' language. This originated in a learned article by Professor Alan Ross entitled 'Linguistic Class-Indicators in Present-Day English', which first appeared in an obscure Finnish philological periodical *Neuphilologische mitteilungen* in 1954. Ross's argument was that in the middle 1950s, as the old class demarcations of education and wealth had been eroded, distinctions of language were the sole remaining factors in distinguishing the upper classes from the middle and the lower classes. What had started as a relatively academic exercise in defining upper-class ('U') usage in relation to non-upper class ('non-U') became a much more widespread subject of controversy when the writer Nancy Mitford took up Ross's thesis, expanded upon it and made it more amusing, in an essay 'The English Aristocracy' published in 1956, with cartoons by Osbert Lancaster, and a joke non-U poem by John Betjeman, the future Poet Laureate, under the title *Noblesse Oblige*. What follows is Mitford rewriting the professor on U versus non-U vocabulary:

cycle is non-U against U *bike*.

dinner: U-speakers eat *luncheon* in the middle of the day and *dinner* in the evening. Non-U speakers (also U-children and U-dogs) have their *dinner* in the middle of the day.

greens is non-U for *vegetables*.

home: non-U – 'they have a lovely *home*'; U – 'they've a very nice *house*'.

ill: 'I was *ill* on the boat' is non-U against U *sick*.

mental: non-U for U *mad*.

toilet paper: non-U for U *lavatory paper*.

wealthy: non-U for U *rich*.

She adds her own favourite examples of *sweet* – non-U for *pudding* – and *dentures* for *false teeth*, while reminding her readers that when, in her novel *The Pursuit of Love*, Uncle Matthew speaks of his 'dentures' he does it as a joke.

Can a non-U speaker become a U-speaker? In this linguistic minefield Ross concluded that an adult could never achieve complete success 'because one word or phrase will suffice to brand an apparent U-speaker as originally non-U (for U-speakers themselves never make mistakes)'. Nancy Mitford, from her impeccably U viewpoint as Lord Redesdale's daughter and with a trace of superiority towards Birmingham-based Professor Ross, was not entirely convinced about this, maintaining that usage changes very quickly and that she, in 1956, knew undisputed U-speakers who pronounced girl '*gurl*' – 'which twenty years ago would have been unthinkable'. However, she concluded, 'it is true that one U-speaker recognises another U-speaker almost as soon as he opens his mouth'. So it was with the debs' mothers and their close-knit coterie. Since then a proportion of upper-class children have adopted quasi-classless voices and deadpan intonation in a not always convincing attempt to counteract the cut-glass accents and exclamatory poshness of their parents. But in 1958 upper-class speech and vocabulary was still uniform, a bastion of U-ness, the last-ditch defence of social exclusivity.

While all this frenzied activity was taking place amongst the mothers, the debutantes themselves were staying hidden. We were still in training, most of us at so-called finishing schools in England or abroad. The *Sketch* editor wrote sanctimoniously 'no girl would willingly give up this period during which she changes gracefully from a schoolgirl into a charming debutante'. There was the subtext by which a finishing school was considered a safe haven for a girl at a time of awakening sexuality. These were the days before the pill. The fear of impregnation was a real one for both mothers and their daughters. An early unplanned pregnancy would jeopardise the Season, not to mention marriage prospects. Pregnant debutantes were contradictions in terms.

One of the largest London finishing schools was the Monkey Club in Pont Street. The Monkey Club girls had a formidable principal, the Hon. Griselda Joynson-Hicks, daughter of the 1st Viscount Brentford. A rival establishment, ten-minutes' walk away in Queen's Gate, South Kensington, was named, in the same spirit, Cygnets House. Here cygnets were transformed into swans under the guidance of Mrs Rennie-O'Mahony, a war widow who had founded her school in 1945. The academic content of the course was very lightweight but girls were trained in social skills and public speaking. They were lectured on dressing to look elegant. Cygnets were expected to be expert at opening bazaars. At the annual Cygnets Ball, held at Claridge's, attended by proud parents and their friends, the emergent swans would enter to the band playing Tchaikovsky ballet music from *Swan Lake*.

Other parents preferred to send their daughters to the continent. Finishing schools in Paris had more cachet, and for parents who remembered the city's pre-war glamour, Paris was a sentimental link with their own past. The choice was between Mademoiselle Anita's, where the girls attended classes by day and lodged out as paying guests with approved French families, or residential study-homes. The Comtesse de la Calle kept the biggest and socially the smartest of the live-in finishing schools in a villa near the Bois de Boulogne. Madame Paul Verlet at Les Ambassadrices in the Boulevard Berthier took in eighteen pupils. Madame Harel-Dare ran a smaller and, in theory,

more artistic establishment at Neuilly. My mother, having had it recommended by the friend of a friend who already had a daughter there,
settled on Madame Boué's Study-Home, a finishing school for a dozen
or so English girls in a large apartment in Rue Erlanger, Auteuil.

I was the late arrival, in early January 1958, having stayed at boarding school to take my Oxford entrance. The other girls had been at
Madame Boué's since October. It might well be wondered why, after
five years at Wycombe Abbey, having taken 'A' and 'S' levels, including one in French, I needed any further finishing. The need was never
questioned. The finishing school was part of the pre-Season ritual as
far as my mother was concerned. I think she secretly hoped I would
acquire a bit more polish. Wycombe Abbey, though rock solid educa-
tionally, was not a *soigné* school. So I joined the little group of
Madame Boué's pupils travelling by boat train from Victoria and then
by Channel ferry, a gaggle of English girls in headscarves and cashmere coats. When we arrived, exhausted, at the Auteuil apartment
Madame Boué bustled to the door to greet her *petite famille* as she had
done every term since 1920, only interrupted by the German
Occupation. We were never told what had been the fate of Monsieur
Boué but for many decades Madame Boué had been a woman on her
own, like the principals of all the other finishing establishments, like
Madame Vacani and her dance school, making a living from the per-
ceived needs of the English upper classes. Her *enfants* were packed
into Madame Boué's flat, two or three per bedroom. The classroom
was also the dining room. The salon was crowded with ornate stiff-
backed chairs on which, in the evenings, we practised sitting gracefully
and made far from fluent conversation in obligatory French.

During our time at the Study-Home the girls were marched along to
watch Madame Boué receive a decoration at the local town hall. This
was the insignia of a Chevalier dans l'Ordre des Palmes Academiques,
conferred for her services to education. She was overjoyed and her
pupils were pleased for her. But I cannot really say the decoration was
deserved. Education at the Study-Home was very rudimentary. Besides
French conversation there were lessons in commercial French, given
by Brigitte Bardot's aunt, a faded, pinch-faced woman who referred to
her niece with a fond anxiety. There was musical appreciation: after
lunch on Tuesdays, a middle-aged Frenchman came in and played
Charles Trenet on a wind-up gramophone. From time to time,
Isabelle, the cook, would be prevailed upon to receive us for what

passed for cooking lessons, adding to her already considerable burden in providing meals from a small ill-equipped kitchen for a dozen hungry girls. We were taken to the Louvre and planted in the crowd to listen to official lectures of interminable dullness. No escape, since Madame Boué sent a chaperone to guard us, a small, harassed and presumably very ill-paid woman whose bare legs would turn raw and purple in the cold. In the evenings we wrote up our journals, anodyne recordings of the day's events, and stuck in picture postcards of buildings visited: the Sacré Coeur, the Saint Chapelle, Les Invalides. When Madame Boué settled down each night to her self-imposed task of checking through these journals did she ever wonder whether we were learning anything at all? I really do not think so. Give or take fencing lessons, dressmaking classes or a ballroom dancing course, this was the curriculum on offer at every other finishing school for English girls and its content and value was not scrutinised by parents for whom, on the whole, the education of daughters seemed of little relevance. Making a good and happy marriage was the thing.

Of the dozen girls in Madam Boué's *petite famille*, six of us were going on to do the Season. The *famille* subdivided, as if by some unwritten law, into the smart girls and the rest. The ringleader of the smart set was Lady Sarah Jane Hope, a fair-haired snub-nosed young beauty whose father, the Marquess of Linlithgow, had been held at Colditz in the special wing reserved for potentially influential prisoners. Sarah Jane had the upper-class bolshiness one finds in the heroines of Nancy Mitford's novels, banging out 'Frankie and Johnnie were lovers' on the upright piano in Madame Boué's salon. Her bosom friend was Jane Holden, a strapping blonde from Norfolk who put herself over as the epitome of experience and sophistication. Jane told enviable tales of her rapturous evenings with 'dreamy men'. The dreamiest of all was named as Henry Blofeld. When I met this legendary lover some years later both he and I were writing for the *Guardian*. He had metamorphosed into the cricket correspondent, familiarly known as 'Blowers', a convivial but hardly a Byronic figure in that hearty sports department where the men called out 'Well caught!'

Life at the Study-Home had its frustrations and its longueurs. As teenagers we had all read the nihilistic novel *Bonjour Tristesse* written by the young Françoise Sagan. She was said to have composed it in the cafés round the Sorbonne where she was a student. *Bonjour Tristesse* caught the feeling of the times exactly when it was published in 1954.

For girls growing up in England Sagan's atmospheric story of Cécile, the doomy seventeen-year-old, living with her irresistibly attractive widowed father and observing his numerous brief love affairs, had been our education in Frenchness. We loved the novel's mordant sexiness and the more rebellious could see themselves as Cécile, the symbol of disaffected youth. But Françoise Sagan's Paris and the world of Madame Boué's Study-Home had few connections. Apart from approved outings to the Sunday morning service at the British Embassy Church and stilted exchange tea parties with the pupils of the Comtesse de la Calle, our movements were restricted. Madame Boué was paranoid about preserving our virginity, even demurring about allowing us to visit the Musée Rodin in case the more erotic of his sculptures played havoc with our latent sexuality. She was obsessed with the dangers of the white slave trade, demonstrating the ease with which a chloroform handkerchief could be pressed over the face by villainous abductors lying in wait for English victims. We were virtually imprisoned in Auteuil. With colossal ingenuity, inventing a respectable evening party to which all had been invited, one of the *petite famille* provided an escape route and one evening we found ourselves in a poky flat on the Left Bank, drinking crude red wine with three amorous Moroccans. The Moroccans were so far outnumbered by the rather anxious and self-conscious English girls the evening turned out to be less than Saganesque.

Madame Boué would occasionally override her fears of abduction and rape and accede to girls' requests for exeats with relations or with parents' friends. A title would work wonders. She beamed with delight when Gabriel Waddington, a deb-to-be from Ireland, daughter of the racing trainer Nesbit Waddington, was fetched from the flat one night by Prince Aly Khan, though she would perhaps have been less approving had she known that her charge was being taken to the floor show at the Folies-Bergère. My mother's cousin, the current Baron de Belabre, was also welcomed warmly. He and his wife invited me to weekend lunches at their immaculate town house in St Cloud. It was here I learned the lesson, inexperienced as I was, that it took very little for the elegant and elderly relation to turn into the seducer. So much for Madame Boué's warnings of the white slave trade. This was sexual peril very close to home as Serge led me to the library, proffered a succession of leather-bound books with beautifully engraved pornographic illustrations, began to stroke and cradle me with what even I could recognise as enormous skill. What was I to do, half frightened, half enjoying? The decision was made for me by the sudden entrée of Genevieve, the Baroness, announcing tea, diffusing the drama with precision timing, as in a Feydeau farce.

Our sheltered environment kept us unaware of the disturbances in Paris through that winter: the riots at St Nazaire shipyard; the worsening crisis in Tunisia; the warfare between rival Algerian terrorist groups in France, with many killed and wounded, strangled corpses left lying in suburban Paris streets. What we registered more keenly in Madame's Study Home was the death a few weeks earlier of Christian Dior. The great couturier had died at the end of October 1957 at the age of fifty-two. His introduction of the 'New Look' in his first postwar collection in 1947 had helped regenerate the depressed French textile industry by demanding yards of fabric for its full-skirted designs. The New Look, with its nipped-in waist and blatant femininity, had become a symbol of the resurgence of Paris as the capital of elegance and style. Madame Boué mourned him deeply and, sensing the enormous post-war impact of Dior's creative genius, so I think did we.

Madame Boué's Study-Home constituted a bizarre prelude to the Season, a Paris winter in which our girlishness was frozen. There was no development: we remained as we had come. Yet those months at the Study-Home had made a bond between us. Later in the Season, coming across Sarah Jane or Sally or Gabriel or Coral at a party, we would greet one another like old soldiers with peculiar shared memories, veterans of an arduous posting in far lands.

When we returned in March the mothers' lunch parties were ending. Reflecting successful contact making and campaigning, the invitations were beginning to come in. 'Caroline has 300 invitation cards on her mantelpiece,' Caroline Butler's mother, Mrs Derek Hague, told an enquiring journalist. 'I've answered half of them – being a deb's mum is hectic.' Invitation cards, to be up to standard, were of very stiff white cardboard with slightly embossed lettering following the formulaic

Mrs Arthur Nicoll

at Home

for her daughter

Miss Rachel Nicoll

at the Savoy – River Room

Even though Mrs Nicoll was clearly not at home, or not in her own home, the lack of logic was not noticed. These invitations had a gravity, a lingering sense of serious purpose in a young girl's debut. No light-hearted little sketches of party balloons and – horror! – flat-bottomed champagne glasses emanating bubbles. There was 'U' and 'non-U' even in invitation cards.

Some of Annabel Greene's many invitations to debs' luncheons, tea parties and cocktail parties in the spring of 1958

Back from Paris we were thrown straight into the debs' own luncheon and tea parties. The time had now come for the girls to meet each other. These gatherings followed the same pattern as the lunches for the mothers, being all female affairs, but they tended to be larger and would often be held in a club or a hotel. There were two hundred debs at the first luncheon I went to, a party given in the Park Suite at the Dorchester by Lady Lowson, the ex-lord mayor's wife, an energetic and eternally youthful-looking woman who, when asked by a reporter whether she found planning her daughter's Season arduous, gave the withering reply: 'I had enough practice organising receptions at the Mansion House.' Lady Lowson had already launched her elder daughter, Gay, whose satisfactory engagement to the Earl of Kinnoull would be announced in 1961. Her attention was now focused on her younger daughter, Melanie, for whom she had already held a London cocktail party. A ball at the Savoy had been announced for May. No effort had been spared. In terms of the 1958 Season this was the ultimate in coming out.

I knew every nook and cranny of the Dorchester since my great-grandfather's firm, McAlpines, had built it and the family owned it. I had been in and out of the hotel since early childhood. All the same I found this first debs' luncheon party very daunting. My hostess, slim and gracious in her pale-grey sack dress, following the latest style; Melanie standing beside her in coral pink greeting the long line of her contemporaries who, though only seventeen, behaved like thirty-five. Most wore hats and carried gloves, balancing their black leather or suede handbags on the elbow. Since this was a fork luncheon you needed expertise in juggling your plate and fork and glass. Whatever the demands, these girls exuded confidence, though some have since admitted to feeling very nervous at the start of the Season. My own reservations centred on my lack of social graces: I was a solemn girl, a reader, a Shakespeare fanatic, and I could not do the chatter. The idea of a whole summer of frivolity alarmed me. Also it dawned upon me there were far too many Fionas: Fiona Crichton-Stuart, Fiona Freeman, Fiona Pilkington, Fiona Sheffield. Even Melanie Lowson, my young hostess, had been christened Melanie Fiona. All right, there were even more Penelopes or Pennys. But Fiona, chosen by my mother after the poet Fiona Macleod, a name I had always regarded as original, was appearing overused by 1958.

There were two or three weeks of this forced fraternisation among the debutantes. Not all lunches had the discreet formality of Melanie Lowson's at the Dorchester. More were a matter of twenty girls assembling with friendly hoots and giggles in a little house in Chelsea and sitting on the floor. Sitting on the floor was a feature of the Season: it was lucky we were agile. I had two debs' lunches of my own at our home in Limerston Street where I have a feeling my mother's staple Coronation Chicken made a reappearance. I went to a debs' tea party given by the girl whose dance I would be sharing, Jennifer Burness. Up to then, strange as it must seem, I had not even met her. All arrangements had been made by our two mothers while I was away in Paris. The tea party was an elegant affair for five or six girls sitting round the mahogany table in the downstairs dining room in the Burness house in Cadogan Square. The manservant poured our tea from a Georgian silver teapot. It was hardly believable that we were still teenagers. The scene was positively middle aged. Jenny was tall, dark, beautiful, languidly friendly. We would always be kind to one another but were certainly not soulmates. Her cronies were worldly girls whom I immediately identified as by far my superiors in social expertise.

This was especially true of a friend of Jenny's, Countess Carolyn Czernin. Carolyn was the daughter of Count Manfred and Countess Maude Czernin. The Count, from an aristocratic Polish family, had been an ace war pilot, fighting with the RAF. Carolyn, although only sixteen when she made her debut, was already suggesting the world weariness of having endured a hundred complicated love affairs. Carolyn was cool before the word had acquired its current adulatory connotation. She gave the impression then, and later, of knowing exactly how to handle men. Even now Countess Carolyn remains a potent figure in my personal mythology. I was and am still haunted by her as the paradigm of the woman of experience, the sort of woman with whom I could not conceivably compete.

In between this multiplicity of social engagements it was shopping, shopping, shopping. I had only very recently discarded my school uniform of navy serge gymslip and Wycombe Abbey blazer with the words 'In Fide Vade' (Go Forth in Faith) emblazoned on my bosom. I had other clothes for holidays, but little that was suitable for this highly competitive would-be grown-up life. My mother and I scoured the shops for cocktail and dance dresses. The dress for my own dance was to be made at Worth but, like most of the clothes of my contemporary debutantes, the remainder of my wardrobe came not from couturiers but 'off the peg' from the eveningwear departments of the Knightsbridge department stores: Harrods, Woollands, Harvey Nichols. For deb's mothers and their daughters Harrods, in particular, became a way of life, almost a home from home with its familiar routines. We would rendezvous in the Banking Hall, with its capacious green leather chairs, then eat a light lunch in the Silver Grill before descending the escalators to the fashion floors. My mother's generation had a touching faith that Harrods, in those days – unlike now – a very dignified department store, could meet all possible customer requirements, from christening robe to shroud. Besides the department stores, mothers and daughters went on searches in the local 'Madam' shops. Our mothers' favourites were Nora Bradley in Knightsbridge or (slightly more downmarket) Wakefords in King's Road with its buxom, blonde and heavily mascaraed sales ladies, alternately flattering and bullying, telling you that you looked lovely when you obviously didn't. Left to myself I much preferred Bazaar, the more modern and informal fashion shop which Mary Quant had opened in King's Road in 1955. But the style of the Season was still conservative, fixed in the gracious-lady idiom. Our full-petticoated cocktail dresses and our ballgowns mostly bore the more conventional labels of Frank Usher, Jean Allen, Susan Small.

The shopping list was long. A minimum of six dance dresses, of which one must be white for Queen Charlotte's Ball in May. Two or three of the dresses needed to be long and relatively formal, for the grander balls in London; the others could be short, for dances in the country. Debs also needed several day dresses in silk or chiffon, suitable for Ascot, Henley, the Fourth of June at Eton. Further necessities were shoes and gloves and handbags and especially hats in what was not only the year of the last curtsey but also the year in which the wearing of hats for social occasions was done with a conviction that would not be seen again. Some girls had hats specially made by, for example, Aage Thaarup, the Queen's milliner, or by Simone Mirman. But once again the department stores were the main source for our straw cartwheels, those fashionable hats shaped like upended flower pots and little toques with tulle on top.

There were also the underclothes. Enduring long blush-making fittings by large sales ladies in small box-like cubicles in the lingerie department, the debs of 1958 were equipped with corsetry. Even so-called Youthcraft Girdles were garments of horrible complexity, more like a suit of armour than mere underclothes, encasing our young bodies in what was advertised as a 'firm but flexible elastic net'. These panty girdles had detachable gussets and suspenders. Were they specially designed to discourage intercourse? As would-be seducers from the fifties still remember they were hideously difficult to negotiate.

Elizabeth Arden's 'Blue Grass' perfume; Yardley 'Feather Finish' cream powder for restoring perfection to the face; Goya's 'Kiss Again' lipstick. The brand names of that period bring back with sudden clarity those few busy, worried weeks at the beginning of the Season, weeks of unprecedented acquisition and, for my mother, alarming expenditure. The more ingenious debs' mothers managed to cut corners, for example having ball dresses run up out of old curtains. Tessa Prain, a deb of our year, had an ally in a society dressmaker whose clients brought in their couture clothes for alteration. The dressmaker surreptitiously made a toile. So Tessa wore Balenciaga copies through the Season and we all remember how fabulous she looked. But there were many mothers who showed signs of mounting anxiety, faced with an outlay they could not easily afford.

In a *Tatler* article in April 1958 Judith, Lady Listowel gave a detailed analysis of what a Season actually cost, comparing the minimum possible outlay with the cost of a money-no-object Season.

	Shoestring Deb	De Luxe Deb
mums' luncheons	£25	£100
dinners	£60	£600
debs' teas etc.	£10	£50
mum's dresses	£80	£500
Ascot tickets	£14	£14
hairdressing, taxi, etc.	£50	£250
deb's 4 cocktail frocks	£50	£250
" 7 evening frocks	£90	£450
" 2 Ascot frocks	£30	£120
" 6 pairs of shoes	£22	£60
" 4 handbags	£10	£25
" 24 pairs of nylons	£10	£12
" suit	£12	£48
" coat	£15	£50
" evening wrap	£6	£30
" 5 pairs of gloves	£4	£16
cocktail party	-----	£600
dance	£225	£5,000
Total	**£713**	**£8,125**

Today's equivalent totals would be about £11,000 for the shoestring budget, more than £120,000 for the deb de luxe. Lady Listowel ends her article by saying that the level of expenditure was really not the issue. The decisive fact is what any given girl will make of her own Season:

I know girls who have been brought out on a shoestring, and had the time of their lives. I have seen poor little rich debs weep in the cloakroom because they were 'lost' – they had no young men to dance with . . .

It was indeed a world in which only the fit survived.

CHAPTER THREE

Cocktail Parties

The early weeks of preparation in the choosing of the wardrobe, issuing of invitations, the visits to the hairdresser, the primping and the preening, had been a purely female tribal ritual. It was only once the curtsey had been made and the debutantes were formally certified as nubile, or to put it more crudely, let loose upon the market that we were to catch our first sight of the ostensible object of the exercise. From mid-March, at cocktail parties, we began to meet young men.

These parties began in presentation week and continued into April. Some were held in private houses but more often they took place in a hired room in a hotel or London club, the Cavalry Club being a favourite venue with families who almost all had equestrian connections through their regiments, their hunts, horse-racing, polo playing. It could be embarrassing to admit you had no horse. Some hostesses sought out more original locales. One early cocktail party, given for Penelope Agnew, daughter of the managing director of *Punch*, was held in the *Punch* offices. The phrase 'enjoying a joke', overused by desperate caption writers in the social magazines, now took on a new meaning as the debutantes were pictured 'laughing over an old volume of *Punch*'.

Usually cocktail parties were from 6.00 to 8.00, though a few were cocktail dances, going on into the night. The cocktail dance was a recent innovation which met with disapproval from the old guard who felt that boundaries were getting dangerously blurred. Cocktail parties would sometimes feel a little bit half-hearted, the staking of a claim in the Season by a hard-up or lazy mother who felt an obligation to the launching of her daughter but who hoped to get away with cocktails instead of a full-blown dance. Only the hostess with the mostest

Allegra Kent Taylor and Pamela Walford at their joint cocktail party
at 6 Hamilton Place

would invest in a cocktail party in addition to a dance. A cocktail
party held early in the Season would advertise a girl's credentials and
ensure she was invited to the most important dances. Girls given cocktail parties in addition to dances had an immediate entrée to the ranks
of the top debs. My mother, having fixed the date for my joint dance
with the Burnesses to be given at the Dorchester in June did not, so far
as I remember, contemplate a cocktail party. There was a sense of
betrayal in our household when the covertly ambitious Petie Burness
sent out her invitations for a cocktail party for her daughter Jenny to
be held in presentation week.

What formula did these London cocktail parties follow? They were
not for the faint-hearted. Hot and crowded, semi-formal in their dress
code with girls in scoop-neck satin, men in uniform dark suits with old
school or regimental ties. Apart from the debs' parents, a few middle-
aged friends and some elderly relations, these were essentially parties
for the younger generation to meet and greet each other, everybody trying hard. Although nominally cocktail parties, the drinks served were
not sophisticated, less a matter of a sidecar or a James Bond-style

Martini than a sticky gin and orange. The canapés kept coming round on silver platters: little squares of cheese and pineapple on cocktail sticks; miniature sausages, warmed up and slightly charred; tiny chicken *vol-au-vents*, twirls of smoked salmon in brown bread and a horrible invention of the period, the 'dip', a cream cheese mix the consistency of porridge into which you dunked a strip of raw carrot or a stick of celery. The chatter was continuous and shrill. The sound of the Season once heard was never forgotten. The boom of anecdotes, the ebb and flow of shrieks and murmurs: a brittle, self-confident yet melancholy sound that issued from the drawing rooms of Knightsbridge and Belgravia on London summer nights. Lady Antonia Pakenham, the future Antonia Fraser, remembered the effect these sounds of revelry had had on her when she was still too young to do the Season:

As I listened to the noise of the cocktail parties drifting out of the open French windows, it was like the sound of the hunting horn in the ears of the hound puppy not yet old enough to join in the chase. It excited me; and it filled me with anguish at the same time.

The cocktail parties gave us our first sight of the fathers, presumed to be somewhere in the City while the mothers held their luncheons and the debs their teas. The reluctant deb's father was becoming a stock figure, exemplified by Evelyn Waugh whose daughter Teresa was presented in 1956. The entry in Waugh's diary for 15–16 March shows a typical male irritation at these complex rituals in which the females set the pace:

Irene Ravensdale was giving a cocktail party for debutantes. I thought I could be helpful to Teresa so offered to take her. Since Laura [his wife] had fittings at dressmakers I was obliged to take the early train which was crowded – Thursday being a day when the Duke of Beaufort does not hunt.

Waugh was staying at the Hyde Park Hotel:

I was not dressed when Teresa arrived to use my room between a debutante tea and cocktail party. I fled to Whites, drank a lot of Bollinger '45 and felt better. At Irene's house there was a crowd so dense I did not attempt to enter the drawing room but sat with the butler in the hall.

Fathers kept to the outer reaches of the Season. Their role was mainly that of the financier of an enterprise that was, in its detail, left almost entirely to their wives. Fathers of country debutantes only rarely inhabited the flats and houses which their wives had taken for the Season, coming up to London when summoned for a party at which their presence was considered necessary, retreating the next morning back to their estates. Cocktail parties, being briefer and less onerous, were more acceptable than fully fledged deb dances to fathers who, according to Gladys Boyd, the *Sketch*'s social editor, 'often studiously avoid all "deb" dances except their own'.

The figures of debs' fathers drifted in and out of the parties of that summer, the host whose hand you shook at the end of the reception line, the tall man with the moustache who made sure you had a drink. Fathers appear as afterthoughts in Jennifer's effusive *Tatler* reports of the Season's London gatherings: 'I also met Mr. Stephen Twining, who was helping to make Jean and Annette's party a success' . . . 'Her father Major Shirley was there to help entertain their friends; and of course Colonel A.E. Croker-Poole and Mr Roger Wethered were there too.' But even if of peripheral interest to Jennifer, for whom the Season was a primarily female institution, to me, who had no father, other debutantes' fathers were objects of envy and fascination. One deb, Joanna Priest, indeed had a father who could almost have been mine. Brigadier Robert Priest was also a career soldier in the Royal Artillery. Having survived the war he was now in command at Woolwich, the regimental headquarters, still always referred to by my mother as 'the Shop'. One lunchtime Joanna's friends were bussed out there for a party in the commandant's house, forty debs in their floaty summer dresses converging on that dauntingly masculine military place. The brigadier identified his old comrade Gerald's daughter and we talked about my father, the only time I ever met a friend from his old regiment. There were to be more unexpected loomings up and revelations. The Season by its nature created a bizarre succession of convergences, surprise realignments of old family connections as we, the new generation, were emerging. It subsisted on recurrent replayings of the past.

Most debs' fathers kept the vestiges of military rank, even if no longer serving. In Britain in the fifties the war was still the ever-present topic. The week of presentations coincided with the premiere of Sir Michael Balcon's epic film *Dunkirk* starring John Mills as a heroic British corporal leading his small band of soldiers through the German bombardment to the French beaches to await the rescue fleet of small civilian craft. To children growing up in the war the Dunkirk story remained riveting, however many times we heard it. Some of our fathers had actually been there and some had died there. Dunkirk has been described as an elegy for the last generation of the aristocratic officer class. Almost all survivors had carried the distinctive attitudes and manners of the war years over into peacetime. Still upright in their bearing as if on a parade ground, these now middle-aged men were creatures of convention, showing the emotional reticence of those long attuned to an exclusively male society bound by its own rules and its accepted code of bravery.

Many of the 1958 debs' fathers were still living according to this wartime code of chivalry. Some had suffered horribly in battle and in prison. Stephanie Perry's whole family – her father, mother, her older sister and the infant Stephanie – had spent four years in Stanley prison camp, Hong Kong. Margaret McKay's father, George McKay, was captured in Greece and then transferred to the prison camp for officers at Kassel, Germany, where Douglas Bader was, for a time, a fellow prisoner. He endured a cruelly austere regime for the next four and a half years. When POW No.49 returned to England he was a barely recognisable emaciated figure, his weight having reduced to seven and a half stone. Almost all the fathers who fought in the Second World War had been shocked to lose close friends and near relations. Twenty-three peers and thirty baronets were killed on active service. Sudden deaths could thrust survivors into new responsibilities and alter the expected pattern of their lives. Andrew Cavendish, who had assumed himself to be merely the younger son of the Duke of Devonshire, heard the news while fighting at Montecatini in Italy in 1944 that his brother Billy had been killed by a sniper's bullet, making him his father's heir. He became 12th Duke of Devonshire on his father's death in 1950, faced with the task of raising over £90 million pounds to pay the old duke's death duties. It took twenty-four years. This is an extreme example, but many of the soldiers of my father's generation had their lives reshaped by the chanciness of war.

They emerged from that long period of separation from their country and their families, fighting in Europe, Africa or in the east, to find a world completely different from the one they had expected. *The Times* had predicted, as far back as 1940, that the war would bring about a changed society in Britain: '. . . the new order cannot be based on the preservation of privilege, whether the privilege be that of a country, of a class, or of an individual'. And so it had turned out. War damage to their property, the scarcity of servants, the reduction of affluence as the landowning classes were financially penalised by higher taxes and a huge increase in death duties which stood at 80 per cent in 1950: these were serious setbacks but relatively technical. What was more psychologically wounding was the fact that these war heroes were not acclaimed as such, but subjected to a barrage of opprobrium and ridicule as class resentment intensified in the post-war period. The change of heart was illustrated cruelly and, to those in my mother's milieu, shockingly when Winston Churchill, the saviour of the nation, failed to be re-elected as prime minister in the first election after the war. What they dreaded was that this was the prelude to a regime of Welfare State socialism.

The upper classes received a direct onslaught in a book called *Declaration*, a volume of essays by seven Angry Young Men, as they were christened by the press, and one Angry Young Woman – Doris Lessing. The Angries had been brought together by an enterprising young publisher, Tom Maschler. *Declaration*, published in 1957, was leftist in tone and highly critical of England. One of the contributors, film director Lindsay Anderson, compared coming back to England from abroad to going back to the nursery:

. . . the outside world, the dangerous world, is shut away: its sounds are muf- fled. Cretonne curtains are drawn, with a pretty pattern on them of the Queen and her fairy-tale Prince, riding to Westminster in a golden coach. Nanny lights the fire, and sits herself down with a nice cup of tea and yesterday's *Daily Express*.

The colonel class, my father's class, the Tory fathers of the debu- tantes were jeered at by John Osborne in a fiercely anti-establishment essay 'They Call it Cricket' in which he asks, 'Are we going to contin- ue to be fooled by a class of inept deceivers, are we going to go on being ruled by them?' In his play *Look Back in Anger*, first performed at the Royal Court in 1956, John Osborne created a significantly poignant character in Colonel Redfern, bewildered by the impulse which has taken his well-nurtured daughter Alison to live with the left-wing ranter Jimmy Porter in a one-room flat in a large Midland town. John Osborne describes Redfern as a large handsome man of about sixty:

Forty years of being a soldier sometimes conceals the essentially gentle, kind- ly man underneath. Brought up to command respect, he is often slightly with- drawn and uneasy now that he finds himself in a world where his authority has lately become less and less unquestionable.

Watching the play, my heart bled for Colonel Redfern. In the course of the Season I met many Colonel Redferns, bemused and vaguely disappointed, looking for a role again, pouring another gin.

These were lost heroes, the fathers of the debutantes. This was not to say that they could not enjoy a party. Not all were as curmudgeonly as Evelyn Waugh. Once persuaded that the launching of a daughter was a duty the fathers did their best to make a pleasure of it. Pre-war party-going reflexes sprang back into activity as the fathers exerted their considerable charms, acting the soul of courtesy with dowagers, flirting with the mothers, eyeing up the girls. Well-bred men of that period now had a new role model, a comforting fantasy of sexual expertise. 'Enter James Bond who attracts dangerous women like a highly charged magnet' – the *Daily Express* ran a feature on Bond and his exotic retinue of 'naked sirens' in the same week in 1958 in which we made our curtseys to the Queen. James Bond was the invention of a writer of exactly the debs' fathers' generation and background. Ian Fleming was born in 1908, educated at Eton and Sandhurst and had had a notably good war, working in naval intelligence. The persona of James Bond was created in the vacuum that followed the tension and excitement of the war years. The character was born from that sense of loss and melancholy. In James Bond the officer class was fighting back. The first Bond novel *Casino Royale* was published in 1953. It was followed by *Live and Let Die* in 1954, *Diamonds are Forever* in 1956 and *From Russia with Love* in 1957. In the figure of James Bond, cruel, debonair, ironic, the wartime man of courage was reworked for an age now more cynical and flashy. The redundant Colonel Redferns were transformed and glamorised into Agent 007 with his seductive accoutrements: the 1933 $4^1/2$-litre Bentley, the Morland cigarettes with a triple gold band, the Beretta automatic secreted underneath the dinner jacket. It would be exaggerating to claim that the majority of fathers saw themselves as James Bond, but there was certainly a nuance. I can say that the debs' fathers, in the mood, were more attractive than the gaucher and less worldly-wise young men.

The fragmentation of the family was clear at cocktail parties, the first public events of the Season in which debs were on show with their fathers and their mothers, their stepfathers and stepmothers. At many of these parties the receiving line revealed the full complexity of post-war upper-class family relationships. One of the earliest deb cocktail parties, described in the *Sketch* as 'most delightful' (the recurring adjective for cocktail parties), was held at the House of Lords and 'given jointly by Lady Kilmuir and Mrs. Oliver Poole for Lady Kilmuir's god-daughter, Miss Caroline Tonge, Mr. Oliver Poole's third daughter, Miss Marian Poole, and Mrs. Oliver Poole's daughter by her first marriage, Miss Zara Heber-Percy'. The air of unreality was increased by the fact that Lady Kilmuir's husband, Lord Kilmuir the Lord Chancellor, received the guests in the full dress of his office. For me it was another of the mystical convergences since I knew two of the girls in question, Marian Poole and Zara Heber-Percy, before they knew each other. Meg Poole had been in my class at Miss Ironside's School in Kensington, a serious curly-headed child as Shakespeare-obsessed as me. She had played Helena to my Hermia in an infant production of *A Midsummer Night's Dream* and indeed she later became casting director at the Royal Shakespeare Company. Zara Heber-Percy and I had been at Miss Violet Ballantine's dancing classes and had performed together in her charity dancing matinees at the Adelphi Theatre, singing the little ditty which introduced these valiant but, I fear, painfully amateur performances:

> *We are the pupils of Miss Ballantine,*
> *We hope to amuse you with our song, dance and mime.*
> *We'd rather dance for you all day,*
> *But our mummies and our nannies say*
> *It's not good for us – They make a fuss.*

Oliver Poole MP – Eton, Christ Church and the Life Guards – was then Deputy Chairman of the Conservative Party. By 1958 these two childhood friends of mine were united by Meg's father's remarriage to Zara's mother. Zara was a good deb, eager, beautiful and sparkly. Meg, already training to be a stage manager, was a bad deb, recalcitrant and sulky. Here they were, like the girls in *Cinderella*, thrown into unexpected sisterhood.

Once past the greetings line, you were propelled, like the missile from the launcher, into an already thronging, noisy room. Cocktail parties faced the deb with an additional ordeal in that you arrived on your own, unlike dances where you came in a party with the people you had dined with. The first test was in locating somebody you knew and attaching yourself to the group in which they were, edging inwards and joining the conversation as best you could. The next test, a far more taxing one, lay in the necessity to establish a fairly quick rapport with the man most likely to invite you out to dinner. In 1958 there was no question whatsoever of a female issuing an invitation or paying for any of the evening's expenses. The urgency of attracting a man willing to take you on to a restaurant was, for many of the girls, a serious anxiety. It would be a badge of failure to return home in a taxi when the party came to its inexorable end in the middle of the evening, just when family dinner would have reached the pudding stage. It was not that many mothers would be positively nasty. But an early return generated disappointment. Popularity with men was the whole business of the Season. Since, in general, the escorts' level of intelligence was a good deal lower than the debs', we made ourselves sillier in order to get through.

Cocktail parties were the phase of mutual appraisal before the Season proper. It was estimated by the social diarists that between two hundred and three hundred young men were on the regular circuit of deb parties. Who were the debs' delights and were they in fact delightful? As we wended our way from Allegra Kent Taylor's cocktail dance at 6 Hamilton Terrace to Raymonde Steinberg's cocktail party at home in Portland Place to the 'charming six o'clock' (as Jennifer described it) for Dominie Riley-Smith in the Dorchester's rooftop Penthouse Suite, with debs and their escorts spilling out onto the roof garden, we had plenty of opportunity to find out.

There was a little hard core of super-smooth professionals, perennial debs' escorts now well into their thirties who had been doing the deb rounds for a decade. One was David Ashton-Bostock, a man-about-town so well practised in approach he could have been a suitor in a Noël Coward comedy. Charles MacArthur Hardy, a rich Australian with a house in Cambridgeshire, was by now so well known a fixture of the Season that gossip columns named him 'Charles Champ' and *Woman's Mirror* ran a photographic feature illustrating his ability to extricate himself from tricky situations: 'the Heavo', 'the Brush-off', 'the Cool Clinch', 'the Surprise Chin-Chin', 'How He Kisses a Girl if He's Not in Love'. However, these all too experienced debs' delights were the exception. The men we met during the Season of 1958 were fairly young, not much older than the girls, often still nineteen or twenty. Some indeed were still at school. The vast majority of the regular debs' escorts had been to Eton, with a few Harrovians thrown in. All deb parties had contingents from Oxford or

Archetypal debs' delight Charles MacArthur Hardy conversing with his hostess, Lady Lowson, at the cocktail party for her daughter Melanie

Cambridge: it was as if no other universities existed. It also goes without saying that no debs' delight was black. Some were wonderfully polite, especially to the mothers, the most polished of the lot being David Buchan, Buchan of Auchmacoy, Chief of the Name of Buchan, recently a Captain in the Gordon Highlanders, who had presumably acquired his perfect sense of protocol as ADC to GOC in Singapore. The rowdiest and most obnoxious delights were future landowners and farmers in training at Cirencester Royal Agricultural College who ran amok together, urging one another on like the football hooligans of a future age.

By far the largest source of debs' partners was the army, in particular young officers of the Household Brigade regiments: the five Guards regiments consisting of the Grenadiers, the Coldstream, the Scots, Irish and Welsh; the two cavalry regiments, the Life Guards and the Royal House Guards, the latter being known as 'the Blues' (to those who knew). The debs' escorts were drawn mainly from the smartest of these regiments, the Grenadiers, the Coldstream and the Blues, in which almost 10 per cent of officers were titled or were heirs to titles. Here too there was a strong bias towards Eton: at this period the Colonel of the Coldstream Guards estimated that half his officers were old Etonians. There was also a strong hereditary factor, since so many of the officers were sons of former officers in the regiment. Andrew Sinclair, himself an Old Etonian who did his National Service with the Coldstream, gives a more or less accurate picture of an inbred and indolent masculine society in his satiric novel *The Breaking of Bumbo*, published in 1959. At the time it was regarded as shockingly disloyal, a betrayal of his officer class, depicting as it did the fixed hierarchies and deadening routines of military life at Wellington Barracks (referred to by its inmates in quasi nursery terminology as 'Welly B'). He brought out the childish arrogance of the spoilt young officers, 'little scarlet gods, little bowler-hatted gentlemen', each with their personal soldier servants, reduced by hours of boredom on officers' mess duty to drinking far too much and taking potshots at the ducks in St James's Park.

For many young Guards officers the Season provided the evening's entertainment with, at best, three cocktail parties to choose from, and later in the summer, two or three deb dances preceded by dinner parties. This entertainment was practically free, the only costs being laundered shirts and a bread-and-butter letter to your hostess. For regiments based in London, the routine was convenience itself. Once military duties ended at four, the young officers were free to have tea in barracks, take a bath and, assisted by their soldier servants, change for the evening's events. They had hardly returned from the night's dances when it was time to report for military duties: there were plenty of tales of hung-over brigade officers fainting with exhaustion while lining some London processional route. It is not perhaps surprising, considering the lack of variation in their lives that, as I remember them, these well-connected officers, especially the regulars, were limited in outlook, stunted in conversation. On the other hand, when these strong silent men invited us back to their barracks for lunch or drinks, there was a gorgeousness about them in their military uniform which reminded me of Lydia Bennet in Jane Austen's *Pride and Prejudice* and her susceptibility to men in 'regimentals'. In 1958 we were still susceptible.

The escorts had a kind of pecking order, as the debs did. What debs' delights did the more ambitious mothers have their eyes on as a future son-in-law? The most obviously covetable was HRH Prince Edward George Nicholas Paul Patrick, Duke of Kent, who succeeded to the title as a child of six when his father was killed in a wartime flying accident. The young duke, seventh in succession to the throne, was now twenty-two and a lieutenant in the Royal Scots Greys. Hostesses were eager to invite him to their parties. In manner and appearance – courteous, sporting, rather chinless – he was an almost cartoon version of the perfect debs' delight. But he remained elusive. He seemed to prefer girls rather older than we ingénues. Through the spring and early summer of 1958 he was attached to Janet Bryce, to the chagrin of the mothers. Still worse, from August onwards, there were rumours of a more serious romance with Katharine Worsley, the daughter of a Yorkshire landowner, whom he was to marry in 1961.

Six runners up to the duke as top escorts were featured in the *Sketch* at the beginning of the Season: these were the twenty-six-year-old Duke of Atholl, whose father had been killed in the war in Italy, and who had succeeded to the ancient Scottish title in 1957; twenty-eight-year-old Prince Alexander Romanoff, of the Czarist Russian family, said to be 'a good dancer, and on most hostesses' lists of escorts'; Jeremy Thornton, stepson of Sir John Johnson Bt., 'a keen dancer, but a keener rider to hounds'. The debonair-looking young Jeremy was doing National Service, stationed with the Blues at Windsor. Paul Goudime, 'a gay companion' – the term 'gay' having as yet no homosexual connotation – was soon to go to Cambridge to read Science: his chief hobbies were shooting and motoring. The Hon. Michael Spring Rice was introduced as the twenty-three-year-old younger brother of Lord Monteagle of Brandon: 'A popular escort, he is gay and an excellent dancer.' Educated at Harrow, he was making banking his career. The last of the *Sketch*'s selection was Peter Tapsell, described as 'a brilliant young man of twenty eight – a budding politician of great promise'. He strikes one as already rather different from the rest in that his school was Tonbridge, not Eton or Harrow, and his Oxford college, where he took a first-class degree in modern history, was Merton, not the much more fashionable Christ Church. Peter Tapsell, born in Hove to a father whose regiment was an obscure one – the 39th Central India Horse – was to have a successful career as a Conservative MP. His first marriage was to the Hon. Cecilia Hawke, daughter of the 9th Baron Hawke. Peter Tapsell, who was eventually knighted and remains one of the longest serving of MPs, is a very good example of the easy infiltration of the deb scene by a non-aristocratic but plausible young man of ambition and intelligence.

A cruel joke was perpetrated on a notoriously pushing deb's mother, Mrs Arthur Croker-Poole, who had only recently adopted the double-barrelled surname, presumably hoping it would add extra gravitas to the family and better the prospects of her daughter Sally. She had previously been contented to be known as Mrs Poole. Their neighbours in the country called the family 'the Frogponds'. There was something about Mrs Croker-Poole's all too blatant social climbing that tempted people to send her up. A mischievous acquaintance, Peter Walwyn, telephoned pretending to be an *Evening Standard* journalist. He told her he had just heard the news that her daughter Sally was engaged to the Duke of Kent. Unlikely as this was, Mrs Croker-Poole believed the story and, according to one witness of the hoax, 'went into paroxysms of excitement'. The story is a very good example of the sadistic humour of the upper classes and also a reflection of Mrs Croker-Poole's limitless ambitions for her daughter, ambitions which seemed at first sight unrealistic but in the end achieved their object. Since the Croker-Pooles lived opposite my mother's house in Limerston Street we watched fascinated at the unfolding of what often seemed like a Restoration satire of social manoeuvring and sexual bartering.

The Croker-Pooles were an Indian Army family. Sally's father, a lieutenant colonel, had returned to England in 1947 when Independence came. He now had a rather menial but very hush-hush job, said to be in the fingerprints department at Scotland Yard. Colonel Croker-Poole and Sally's brother Anthony, a plump, amiable but less than sparkling figure, were kept largely in the background, though Anthony had a walk-on role from time to time as Sally's stooge. Even before Sally came out, Mrs Croker-Poole perfected her technique of keeping out the competition. The autumn before the Season, Penny Graham, a strikingly attractive girl, had been invited to the Croker-Pooles' house in Berkshire for the weekend. She had only been there a few hours when her hostess summarily dismissed her, producing the excuse that one of the men had cancelled, making the numbers uneven. This proved to be untrue, but Penny was packed off back to London in the train. Another fellow-debutante and old family friend, Auriol Stevens, was given similar treatment at the cocktail party given for Sally at the Cavalry Club. Auriol, a tall, willowy, auburn-haired girl who, much to Mrs Croker-Poole's alarm, had brains as well as beauty, having passed her Oxford entrance, was whisked away from any eligible men and introduced to the elderly aunts and doting grandparents who sat around the fringes of debs' parties. Almost fifty years later Auriol still remembers Mrs Croker-

Poole with hatred: 'She was my enemy.' At the end of a girl's luncheon party at her London house, Mrs Croker-Poole took the other debs aside for a confidential conversation in the bedroom: 'Please be kind to Sally. The Season will be hard for her. She's just *so* beautiful!' Sally herself is the enigma of these stories. What was she really feeling? She seemed to go along with her mother's machinations. She had put herself over in the Season's early weeks as a simple healthy country girl, describing herself proudly as the owner of three horses. But the Season was to change her. Sally was destined to acquire a lot more horses after her eventual marriage to the Aga Khan.

Beyond the aspirations of their mothers, what were the hopes and expectations of the debs themselves? An obvious answer can be found in the romantic novel *Borrowed Time* written by Zia Foxwell, one of the 'top debs' of 1958. The setting and the characters are recognisable. Her hero is Harry, 4th Baron Wrightson, aged twenty-two and 'at the top of every deb's mum's list for the past four years'. As Zia describes him 'his tall athletic physique, dark saturnine features and heavy lidded eyes lent him an air of dangerousness which most women found irresistible. His title was also an advantage, as was his adequate income – not that he was very rich.' Harry Wrightson was due to take possession of the family estates, inherited from his grandfather, in three years' time. Meanwhile he was living in 'a decent bachelor pad in a good part of London'. He drove a red Austin Healey, wore a Cartier watch and 'impeccably tailored shoes'. He was reputed to be terribly fast and at the top of the list of NSITs. The novel culminated in a, for its time, quite explicit sex scene as the 4th Lord Wrightson makes love to the virgin Deb of the Year: 'He felt the shivers of desire run over her as all the while he stroked her soft skin.' This was the stuff of our most simple fantasies.

But by then there were other elements encroaching. The working-class hero loomed on the horizon in series of films of northern realism made in the late 1950s in gritty black and white. Our metropolitan debuts coincided with *Room at the Top*, the film based on the novel by Bradford-born John Braine and set in a small town in Yorkshire. In this classic of 1950s upward mobility the rampantly opportunistic Joe Lambton seduces and marries the local tycoon's daughter while carrying on a passionate affair with an unhappily married older woman. For me at least the uncouth glamour of Joe Lambton as played by Laurence Harvey undermined the effete charm of the debs' delights.

There was also *Look Back in Anger*'s Jimmy Porter, the scourge of old-time England and seducer of its daughters. I saw the play in its original English Stage Company production at the Royal Court with Kenneth Haigh as Jimmy Porter, Mary Ure as Alison. I was with Susannah York the actress, who was then at RADA. Susie was living with us at Limerston Street, one of the theatrical PGs my theatre-loving mother favoured. It was another of those random friend-of-friend arrangements. Susie's mother was a crony of my Aunt Cynthia's. Two upper-class girls together, we sat huddled in our seats, watching transfixed as the curtain rose not on a drawing room with tall French windows, which we were so used to in West End comedies, but a scruffy and untidy one-room flat in the provinces. Left of stage was not a chintz sofa but an ironing board on which the beleaguered Alison is toiling while Jimmy lays into the appalling bourgeois values that had nurtured her – and us. Kenneth Tynan, reviewing the play in the *Observer*, called it the best young play of the decade, lauding its political courage and emotional power. He said he doubted if he could love anybody who did not wish to see *Look Back in Anger*. People sometimes say that this was Kenneth Tynan at his silliest. But was it so ridiculous? I know I felt the same. At the time, to the late teenagers we were, the play seemed alarming and amazingly exciting in its fierce iconoclasm, its hints of sadomasochistic sexual relationships, its glorification of real life and raw emotion in contrast to pernicious conventionality. Osborne's play stayed in my mind, providing an unsettling perspective on the Season. It was one of those works of art that shaped a generation. In a way *Look Back in Anger* was to alter my whole life.

The narrowness of education available to upper-class girls in those days now seems positively startling. The thinking – such as it was – was that educating a daughter to the level considered necessary for a son was unnecessary, unjustifiably expensive and indeed might prove positively harmful, overtaxing the brain of a girl destined for marriage, bringing up her children, running a household and finding time for a moderate amount of charitable work. The boarding schools most favoured by the mothers of the debs – Heathfield, Southover Manor, St Mary's Ascot, Downe House – operated a relatively languorous routine, producing boy-mad girls with no sense of urgency, in contrast to the tightly packed curriculum and energetic sporting activities of Cheltenham, Roedean or my own school, Wycombe Abbey, geared to the production of good citizens. In the deb world, I soon discovered, motivation was suspect and 'How frightfully brainy!' was a pejorative response. It dawned upon me then that this was a society dictated by an automatic separation of the sexes into merely functional, decorative women and ruminating and decisive men, symbolised by the way the women departed *en masse* at the end of dinner leaving the men to their politics and port. At a dinner party one night in Woking I was taken to task by my host, a stockbroker I think, for commenting on the Torrington by-election, recently won by the Liberal candidate, Mark Bonham-Carter. It was made only too clear that my opinions were not wanted. Debutantes don't have opinions. Only four of the full-time debs of 1958 – Auriol Stevens, Teresa Hayter, Annabella Loudon and myself – had places at university that autumn. We were known in the gossip columns, with a hint of disapproval, as 'the blue-stocking debs'.

In the fifties women's role was almost totally subservient. In my early teens I read avidly if anxiously a manual of instruction compiled by my favourite novelist Noel Streatfeild. It was called *The Years of Grace* and directed specifically to 'growing up girls at that difficult age'. Beside hints on how to behave at parties, how to train as a secretary, how to make yourself attractive to the opposite sex, there are chapters on such sports as tennis, riding, skating, swimming with the overall advice 'Every girl ought to love sport, but if she wants to be nice and adorable and completely feminine, she will let men win ALWAYS.' Debs were in a no-win situation, only more so. We were taught to give in gracefully to a set of circumstances in which men only inherited their family estates and women very rarely had control of their finances. My widowed mother went through regular humiliating rituals of asking for handouts from the McAlpine family office where her inheritance was held for her in trust. In a world in which marriage was still regarded as a girl's sole fulfilment, indeed a social duty, success in effect meant surrendering our separate identities. A married woman took the name of her husband. Even her Christian name would disappear. We were branded, like sheep, as the possessions of our husbands. For example, at the party held to celebrate Frances Sweeny's engagement to the Duke of Rutland, the *Tatler* noted the number of 'young marrieds': Mr and Mrs Billy Abel Smith, Mr and Mrs Robin Stormonth Darling, Mr and Mrs Jocelyn Stevens, '. . . both very bronzed just back from a wonderful holiday in the Bahamas'. Fifty years later we imagine women to be liberated; but there are people who address me as Mrs David Mellor even now.

Group photograph taken after the marriage of Lady Mary Maitland and the Hon. Robert Biddulph in April 1958

At the beginning of the Season how did we see it ending? Put before us as an example of the conventional ideal scenario was Lady Mary Maitland, older sister of our fellow-debutante Anne Maitland, whose marriage to the Hon. Robert Biddulph, elder son of Lord and Lady Biddulph, was pictured in the magazines in early April. The wedding had taken place at St Margaret's, Westminster, an obvious place for a standard grand wedding of this kind featuring the same hymns, same prayers, a similar small body of family retainers past and present mingling with the guests. The bride herself is the archetypal English deb, light brown haired, slim, pretty, with an innocent sweet face, in her white silk faille wedding dress with pearl embroidered bodice of guipure lace. The skirt of the wedding dress fans out into a train. The bridegroom, the Hon. Robin, wears the traditional black tail coat, mole grey waistcoat and striped trousers, white carnation in his buttonhole. Ten bridesmaids attend them, six adult and four children, all in delphinium blue organza. The little bridesmaids clutch their bouquets. It is a formal but a rather homely scene, the expected female ritual that follows presentation. The carefully posed photographs exude a kind of certainty that Lady Anne and Lady Elizabeth, the bride's sisters, will soon themselves be brides. Except for the fact that presentations had now ended the pattern promised to replicate itself perpetually.

But was this really what we wanted? Some debs had started wondering. Such fixed ideals of marriage were being destabilised by 1958. It was not only the long-running Princess Margaret and Peter

Townsend saga, revived in the very week of presentations, when they were reported as having spent three hours together at Clarence House, 876 days after their forced parting. Princess Margaret was now aged twenty-seven. The banished suitor, forty-three, was said to be looking thin and worn: according to the *Daily Express* 'his grey suit hung on him'. The Queen, absent in Holland, was reported to be irked by Captain Townsend's reappearance. Meanwhile the runaway lovers Dominic Elwes and ex-deb Tessa Kennedy, another notorious couple of the period, were discovered in Havana in a state of penury, hoping that their family would forgive and forget. I remember the reverberations in deb circles when Elfrida Eden's older sister Amelia fell in love with Giovanni Borelli, a handsome burly Italian ferryman and married him 'to exchange the endless bustle of life in London for a home on the lovely little island of Ischia', as the *Sketch* had told us. All at once our visions of a white wedding to the son of a lord at St Margaret's, Westminster fell away. Romance with a ferryman in Ischia was somehow seeming a lot more up to date. When asked by a reporter about her marriage plans, one of my contemporaries, the Hon. Penny Allsopp, 'a sparkling girl in a waist-length necklace', said, 'Debs don't expect to find husbands during the Season – gracious no. What they do is make a lot of friends they can go and see when they are married so they don't have to see too much of their husbands.' By 1958, even in the deb world, a conventional marriage was losing its allure.

Apart from what I absorbed from novels my own view of marriage in action was primitive. The absence of a father meant I had no grasp of the day-to-dayness of it. From my observation, from a distance, of the marriages of my mother's many women friends it seemed that they fell disappointingly short of the sense of sexual ecstasy my reading of fiction (so avid that I once set myself on fire reading Charlotte Brontë by the gas fire in the nursery) had led me to expect. As children we were taken on visits round the comfortable country houses of Aunt Tommy, Aunt Dora and the rest, staying a few days, falling into the predictable routines of mornings in the morning room, a wander round the village followed by a restorative late morning Dubonnet for the adults before taking the dogs out for walks around the fields on routes so well-trodden that even the dogs, it seemed to me, showed signs of boredom. Husbands and wives led largely separate lives, the colonels and the majors married to my mothers' friends spending their mornings in ramshackle apartments at the back of the building known as the estate office or otherwise taking refuge in the library. Both these areas in households where the rules were kept to strictly, even if unspoken, were understood to be the male preserves. Uncle Gerry roared with fury when he found me in his library, the little girl fingering the big leather-bound volumes. The men emerged for lunchtime drinks, sometimes already – as was obvious even to a watchful child – a bit the worse for wear. The drinking culture was pervasive in English country houses in the mid-twentieth century and the whisky bottle in the library posed a constant threat to marriages otherwise reasonably loyal and affectionate, as my mother was often to lament.

Was this really the best that one could hope for, after the long drawn out rituals of marriage? The engagement announcement in *The Times*, the flood of congratulatory letters to one's mother, the infinite preparations for the wedding, the fittings for the dress, the arrangement of the bouquets, the car to the church, the long walk down the aisle, the return to the reception, the display of wedding presents, shooting sticks, silver gilt pheasants, cut-glass decanters, Royal Worcester game casseroles, table mats with hunting prints. These conventional wedding presents had symbolic value. These were artefacts selected to sustain a way of life assumed to be the only valid one, the seal of approval and the blessing for the future handed down from one generation to another. To me at eighteen, at the beginning of the Season, it looked like a disappointment – but perhaps it could be worse.

My favourite aunt, Aunt Ursula, was our family example of marital disaster, the awful fate to be avoided at all costs. Lady Ursula Chetwynd-Talbot ('La' as her friends called her), daughter of Viscount Ingestre and granddaughter of the Earl of Shrewsbury, had been one of mother's oldest, closest friends. Tall, angular Aunt Ursula, perilously shy and hysterically witty, was the only really literary person in our orbit. She was my heroine because, in spite of an attempt to reduce her very prominent Shrewsbury nose by plastic surgery, she still closely resembled Virginia Woolf. I had been given a signed copy of the first edition of Woolf's *A Room of One's Own* for my tenth birthday by my one intellectual cousin Tommy Bishop and it had become my Bible, giving me an intimation of another kind of life, new worlds of female fellow feeling and intellectual rigour. I sensed that in words I could find my own way out. My Aunt Ursula was a professional writer who, if not of the calibre of Woolf, had had several novels published in the

1950s, using the pseudonym Laura Talbot. They are novels of class, critical and edgy, set in the fading aristocratic world she knew. The most successful are *The Gentlewoman* and *The Last of the Tenants*. She also wrote short stories and radio plays.

While I was growing up in London in the fifties La would make brief and always agonised appearances, staying a night or two at the flats in Queen's Gate and later Queen's Gate Gardens where we lived before we moved to Chelsea. Her first husband, Hector Stewart, had died suddenly, soon after their marriage, stricken by a strange paralysis, an unkind act of God. She had then married Hector's cousin, Lieutenant Commander Michael Stewart, her name conveniently remaining Lady Ursula Stewart. But that second marriage soon went on the rocks. By the early fifties Ursula was living with and was eventually to marry Patrick Hamilton, a writer already famous for two gripping stage thrillers, *Rope* and *Gaslight*, as well as for his novels *Hangover Square* and *The Slaves of Solitude*, books which conjure up a shifty, shabby low-life urban England. Patrick Hamilton himself was a contorted character, a middle-class Marxist, an alcoholic with a real-life fascination for the prostitutes he depicts so brilliantly in his novels. He was prone to suicidal depression, entering a mental hospital in the 1950s for a course of ECT. Sexually Patrick Hamilton was very problematic, claiming that his relationship with Ursula was the first time he had found real sexual satisfaction. He was certainly sadistic. La was virtually imprisoned in their house in rural Norfolk. He opposed violently any contact with her friends. Permission to travel to London was hard won. I do not think my mother ever met Patrick, but she hated him implacably. La's stories of horror would upset her for days after. 'That terrible man', she would call him with, for her, an extraordinary indignation. 'No wonder he writes such horrid plays.' The sense of La's suffering left a kind of aura over our cosy, regulated, two-child-and-a-nanny ballet-loving household. If I wanted an example of raw and complicated adult passion here it was.

Ursula's novels are low-key, rather muted, not unlike Ivy Compton-Burnett's but less obscure. *The Gentlewoman*, her best book, is a study in snobbery, a subtle re-creation of the claustrophobia of English family connections, the painful dependencies of the aristocratic entourage. The central character, Miss Bowlby, is a governess employed by the Rushfords of Rushford Hall, inhabiting the indistinct hinterland between the classes, not one of the servants, yet not one of the family. The book is set in the war years, close to the time of writing. There is a strong sense of the old order changing and the inevitable disintegration of England's great houses and the aristocratic way of life they once sustained. In that sense *The Gentlewoman* is as much a landmark of its period as Evelyn Waugh's *Brideshead Revisited* with the difference that Ursula herself had her roots in the doomed, beautiful houses she described.

Rushford Hall is a version of Ingestre in Staffordshire, the grandest and most haunting Jacobean house in England, seat of the Earls of Shrewsbury, Premier Earls of England and Ireland. Ursula's brother John lived at Ingestre, having become the 21st Earl at the age of seven in 1921, succeeding his grandfather. His and Ursula's father, Viscount Ingestre, had died of pneumonia just before the First World War. Architecturally the house is by no means of a single period or style but a series of layerings, accretions, remakings. Behind the wondrous Jacobean façade lie rooms restored by the Victorian architect John Birch when a fire had gutted them in 1882. The north side is John Nash replaying Jacobean. The house itself holds a whole history of changing aspirations and tastes. The stone church beside the house, reputedly by Wren, is crowded out with monuments of the Chetwynds and the Talbots. There are old stables and new stables, an orangery bounded by two pedimented temples. Set within the park, landscaped

Ingestre in Staffordshire, Lady Ursula Stewart's family home, photographed in 1958

Lady Ursula Stewart (the writer Laura Talbot), centre, at Wilton with Mollie Maynard and Yolande MacCarthy before their marriages

to perfection by Capability Brown in the mid-eighteenth century, is a classical pavilion, itself large enough to house a whole family. Ingestre had once been a supreme expression of aristocratic confidence. But by the early 1950s the Earl's sister, and the Marxist's mistress, was sensitive to Ingestre's growing melancholy. After the war, it seemed almost like a stage set, a spectacularly anachronistic place.

The great Pembroke house of Wilton also makes its ghostly appearance in La's novels. Her younger sister Lady Audrey was a semi-invalid who stayed at home in England with her uncle, Lord Pembroke, when her mother, by then married to an American diplomat, accompanied him on postings overseas. My own mother sometimes went with La to Wilton to see Audrey. A Wilton picture in her album for 1936 shows three young women wearing printed cotton headscarves. My Aunt Mollie, my Aunt Ursula, my mother with her adored white Sealyham, Loretta Young. It is still a sunny picture, before any of them married, not reckoning what griefs and turmoils lay ahead.

By the end of April the London cocktail parties were coming to an end and the balls were just beginning. The Berkeley Debutante Dress Show was scheduled for 28 and 29 April. 'Big thing recently was the Berkeley Dress Show goodness they've had it now but oh it was such fun', wrote one of the models, Georgie Milner, in her diary in the hectic deb-speak of the period. The Dress Show had become an institution of the Season. It was held at the Berkeley Restaurant in Mayfair in aid of the National Society for Prevention of Cruelty to Children. The debutante models were selected by Pierre Cardin, the Paris couturier, choosing a dozen girls from a pre-selected shortlist of forty-eight. Cardin would be supplying the dresses for the show. For the girls it was another testing time, a nerve-racking professional assessment of our attributes. We were like the princesses in a nursery story: who would be the fairest of us all?

The Berkeley Debutante Dress Show. The Hon. Penelope Allsopp, Georgina Milner and Gillian Gough model Cardin's clothes

Debs not chosen to be models were given the consolation prize of selling posies to the audience at the Berkeley Debutante Dress Show

We paraded before Cardin in the drawing room of the Duke of Bedford's house in Cheyne Row. The Duke of Bedford was becoming the showman among aristocrats, eager for any chance of publicising Woburn Abbey. He had agreed to be the compère of the show. Many of the debs had anxious mothers in attendance. Jennifer was also present and commented sternly in her *Tatler* column on 'the appalling deportment of most of the girls, who walked badly and slouched along with their heads down. Surely good deportment ought to be one of the most important parts of a girl's education, especially at their finishing schools.' Debs' deportment was not the only thing to be declining on the brink of the sixties: there were much worse things in prospect. We all held our breath while Pierre Cardin made his choice. With commensurate tact he selected Lady Carolyn Townshend, daughter of the Marchioness Townshend who was chairman of the committee of management for the show. He did not select Penny Graham, Mary Groves or Sally Croker-Poole, three of the debutantes who were later to become professional models. Nor was I among the chosen, more understandably. While the fortunate debutantes were led off to be given training for the catwalk by the then well-known model Bronwen Pugh, the rest of us smiled as sweetly as we could and braced ourselves for selling programmes and raffle tickets, the consolation prize for failure, a stiff upper lip being expected of a deb.

Most of us had been to dress shows with our mothers. Mine was regularly invited to Lachasse, a London couture house which specialised in very well-cut tweed. I do not remember my mother ever ordering the expensively discreet coats and skirts that were paraded before us, soft music in the background. But she certainly had her personal *vendeuse*, a woman adroitly balanced on the tightrope between servility and friendship, who would welcome Mrs MacCarthy and her daughter, leading us to our pre-labelled small gilt chairs. Compared with the gentility of London couture dress shows the Berkeley Debs' Dress Show was a bit more of a bunfight, with the reject girls and mothers seated round the catwalk at small tables. The pictures suggest that we ate a hearty tea while the amateur models paraded eighty garments designed by Monsieur Cardin, who had sent over his right-hand man, André Oliver, to supervise the fittings for the show. The parade began with Cardin's fuchsia cheviot suit, progressing to a woollen dress in greige, a yellow and white houndstooth organza dress, a cocktail suit in pale beige *broderie anglaise*. Some girls complained that the clothes made them look too elderly and certainly in retrospect they seem more suitable for a well-off Parisian widow than a girl of seventeen.

The final item was the Wedding Dress. This was the formula in most dress shows of the period. But the fact that both models and spectators were young girls presumed to be in search of husbands gave the bridal grand finale an added edge. In Zia Foxwell's novel of the Season *Borrowed Time*, the question of who wears the Berkeley Dress Show wedding dress provides the central drama of fixation and betrayal. In real life Zia herself was amongst the dozen models chosen by Monsieur Cardin but she failed the final hurdle – she was not to be the bride. That honour went to Lola Wigan, students' pin-up and face of the future with her incandescent slattern-into-angel look. In a tulle and white satin harem-skirted wedding gown the exquisite Lola sailed past us down the ramp.

CHAPTER FOUR

The London Dances

'The first spectacular ball of the Season', as the social diarists described it, was held on the 6th May in the Great Room at Grosvenor House. Four hundred debutantes assembled with their parents and their partners, all of us in long white ballgowns and white gloves. We dined and danced. At 10.30 a signal was given for the hundred and fifty chosen maids of honour to gather in the upper gallery. From there they made a slow descent of the curved stairway like the maidens in a Burne-Jones painting and processed down the vast ballroom trundling in a huge white cake to the March from Handel's *Judas Maccabeus*. This Historic Ceremony of the Birthday Cake was a re-enactment – some might say a travesty – of the annual birthday celebration of Queen Charlotte, wife of George III, held at St James's Palace. When the cake, with its flickering candles, was brought to a halt in front of the guest of honour, the Dowager Duchess of Northumberland, a mass curtsey was performed by the serried ranks of debutantes. They curt-sied very low and rose simultaneously, having undergone a rigorous rehearsal in the morning. Though the curtsey was intended for the Duchess of Northumberland, representing the long defunct Queen Charlotte, the effect was a surreal one of hundreds of debutantes wor-shipping a cake. Queen Charlotte's Ball, strangely combining the solemn and the mawkish, appeared to one later commentator as a mixture of the Nuremberg Rallies and the Dance of the Fairies in the Hall of the Mountain King.

The ball had first been held in 1925, with 181 electric candles rep-resenting the years since Queen Charlotte's birth. Its beginnings were relatively modest. There were only thirty-one white-gowned maids of honour in 1930, the year in which Lady Diana Cooper was Dame

QUEEN CHARLOTTE'S *Birthday Ball for the Débutantes*
GROSVENOR HOUSE, W.1
(Please retain this part)

Table No. 41

QUEEN CHARLOTTE'S
Birthday Ball
for the Débutantes
THE GREAT ROOM
GROSVENOR HOUSE, W.1

RESTAURANT ENTRANCE, PARK LANE

Tues., 6th May, 1958, 8 p.m. to 2 a.m.
Dinner 8.30 p.m. sharp

TICKET £4 4s. 0d. *(including dinner)*
(Exclusive of Wines)

Table No. 41
NOT RETURNABLE

Queen Charlotte's Birthday Ball
FOR DEBUTANTES
Tuesday, 6th May, 1958

Menu
•
Le Consommé de Volaille en Gelée
–◇–
Le Filet de Sole Souchet
–◇–
Le Poulet de Grain en Cocotte aux Raçines
Les Petits Pois Fins
Les Pommes Parmentier
–◇–
L'Ananas et les Oranges Rafraîchies
Le Parfait Glacé Praliné
–◇–
Le Café
•
Grosvenor House   Park Lane, W.I.

Queen Charlotte's Birthday Ball entrance ticket (top); and Dinner menu for Queen Charlotte's Birthday Ball d'Honneur and HRH Princess Beatrice cut the first slice of the cake. The atmosphere was then relatively cosy and domestic with dozens of soon-to-be-redundant nannies of the debutantes crowding the balcony of the Grosvenor House ballroom to watch their charges take part in the procession. No doubt some of them emitted a sentimental tear. The ball increased in importance in the Second World War, when the courts were suspended. Queen Charlotte's took over the court's role in providing the debutantes' initiation ceremony, albeit in conditions of wartime stringency. The debs' partners came in uniform and Queen Charlotte's birthday cake was concocted with dried eggs. By 1944 the ball had become a kind of picnic, with guests bringing their own food and drink. Once the Great Ballroom at Grosvenor House was requisitioned as an American army headquarters, Queen Charlotte's was shifted to a smaller ballroom and was held in two instalments. During the war Bill Savill's orchestra began playing at Queen Charlotte's. The bandleader himself was then in the RAF. Things changed slowly in the deb world. Bill Savill and his orchestra were still providing the dance music at Queen Charlotte's in 1958. But there was the new thrill of the television era with Frank and Peggy Spencer and their 'famous Television Formation Dancers' providing the midnight cabaret.

The girls photographed descending the stairs and making their low curtseys appear innocence personified, their *noli-me-tangere* attitudes intensified by the virginal white of their attire. But there was, as so often in the Season, the competitive undercurrent, the barely concealed resentment of the girls left on the sidelines towards the girls elected to the starring roles. Alas, I was listed in Jennifer's diary as one of the debutantes 'looking enchanting, but not lucky in the draw for the maids of honour who accompanied the cake'. It was small consolation to be invited to come forward to receive slices of the royal birthday cake to take back to my table and distribute to the guests. There were eight or ten people at each round table. Essentially these were family parties, mothers smiling and fluttering, fathers proudly claiming first dance with their daughters, young men chosen as suitable partners for a debutante at her first official appearance at a ball. The strong and silent escort style was particularly favoured: Darel Carey, David Davenport, magnificent young brigade officers, tall, dark and erect. With the terrifying heroism of the upper classes the father of the deb Lois Denny, whose mother was killed out riding on the eve of presentations, had brought his daughter to Queen Charlotte's. 'They are

The maids of honour descending the grand staircase in the Grosvenor House ballroom

now at 21 Wellington Square, the house Mrs. Denny had taken for the Season, and with the help of friends Mr. Denny is trying to give his daughter the coming-out that her mother had planned for her', Gladys Boyd informed her readers in the *Sketch*.

Queen Charlotte's Ball was definitely a night for the tiaras, still *de rigueur* for married women at dances at which the royal family was present. The tiara had its origins in the celebratory garlands and wreaths made by primitive peoples, in the days before metallurgy,

The Dowager Duchess of Northumberland cutting the birthday cake at Queen Charlotte's Ball

using plants and flowers which acquired particular emblematic meanings. There were later more elaborate metallic Greek, Etruscan, Egyptian and Scythian versions, the art of the tiara reaching its ultimate perfection in Western Europe in the nineteenth and early twentieth centuries. Most aristocratic women in the fifties, if they did not own one, could at least lay their hands on a tiara if the occasion was grand enough. The Queen Charlotte's Ball president, the long-serving and wonderfully dignified Dowager Lady Howard de Walden, stood goddess-like in her classical circlet of diamonds, formed like a laurel wreath. Beside her, the resplendent guest of honour, the Dowager Duchess of Northumberland, wore a tiara formed of jewelled feathers, like a headdress from some celestial poultry yard, her earrings dangling, bracelets jangling as she cut the birthday cake. Many of the mothers too were in spectacular tiaras, often borrowed from a friend or relation, or extracted just that morning from the bank vaults. The tiara, emblem of the central rite of passage from virginity to marriage, had special significance within the presentation ceremony. At the full dress evening courts in the years before the war, the mothers or female presenters of the debutantes customarily wore tiaras set with gems. A young woman's bridal tiara bore the complex messages of the language of flowers, an example being the wild rose tiara given by her father, the Earl of Strathmore, to Lady Elizabeth Bowes-Lyon on her marriage to the future King George VI. All those glittering tiaras at Queen Charlotte's emphasised the primitive antecedents of the Season, the garlands and wreaths of ancient ceremony, our origins as debutantes in distant initiation ritual and myth.

The private dances had begun even before Queen Charlotte's, in the panic to accommodate that year's record number of girls making their debut. The first dance I attended was on 24 April: Mrs George Frost's 'small dinner dance' for Miss Leonora Frost at the Normandie Hotel. The term 'small dance' originally signified a dance at which royalty would not be present, allowing a relaxation in the dress code. By 1958 the term had been adopted as a curious formula by impecunious hostesses warning their guests not to expect too much. Colonel and Mrs George Frost need not have worried. I remember a successful and easy-going party, Leonora in spotted chiffon with a black bow at the waist. Spots were in that year, inspired by the much-photographed spotted-silk ballgown worn by Princess Margaret on her West Indian tour. The dancing at Leonora's party at the Normandie was to Tommy Kinsman and his band. Tommy Kinsman was a fixture of the Season, having been catapulted to favour with debs' mums after playing at the ball at Apsley House on the night in 1947 on which Princess Elizabeth's engagement to Prince Philip had been announced. He made the most of his position, resisting the temptation to flirt with all the debutantes who milled around him but encouraging them to add their names to his 'Debs' Drum', Kinsman's trophy of his multiple successes in the Season. Unusually for 1958 the pre-war system of dance programmes was in force at Leonora's party. Each dance was in effect pre-booked, forestalling the agony of being partnerless, but at the same time preventing freedom of manoeuvre as the evening progressed. From that evening at the Normandie I could already see that the Season would be a test of stamina and nerves.

In that year at least forty private dances were held in London between April and July, the debutantes circulating night after night: same faces, same dance bands, more or less the same venues. The most popular places for the London dances were the Hyde Park Hotel, the Anglo-Belgian Club at 6 Belgrave Square (which had the reputation of being cheaper than the others), and the Hurlingham Club in Hammersmith, semi-rural in atmosphere, where the floodlit clubhouse

Tommy Kinsman serenading a debutante

with its spreading lawns and shrubberies provided the illusion – with only a small stretch of the imagination – that you were entertaining in your own small stately home.

The elaborate *mis-en-scènes* of the deb dances had long been a feature of the London summer, creating sudden little crowds and bursts of colour. Looking back on her Edwardian debut Cynthia Asquith recreates for the readers of her memoirs a social London of great confidence and plenty, romantic, hierarchical:

striped awnings, linkmen with flaring torches; powdered, liveried footmen; soaring marble staircases; tiaras, smiling hostesses; azaleas in gilt baskets; white waistcoats, violins, elbows sawing the air, names on pasteboard cards, quails in aspic, macédoines, strawberries and cream, tired faces of cloakroom attendants, washed streets in blue dawns.

For her the scene was invested with a retrospective poignancy: the expectant faces of the girls thronging the ballrooms, 'that shining dewy look of youth on all their faces, so soon to be frozen into grief by the slaughter of the First World War'. In the closeness of the city the sounds of the night's parties reverberated from street to street. Virginia Woolf, a reluctant debutante in 1901, describes in an early essay how the noise of a nearby ball roused her from her bed in Hyde Park Gate. The ball was being held:

Not in our street – but in Queens Gate – the tall row of houses that makes a background to the Mews. The music grew so loud, so rhythmic – as the night drew on & so the London roar lessened, that I threw up my window, leant out into the cool air, & saw the illuminations which told surely from what house the music came.

Now I have been listening for an hour. The music stops – I hear the chatter, the light laughter of the women's voices – the deeper notes of festive males. I can almost see the couples wandering out from the ballrooms to the balconies which are starred with small lamps.

The sounds and smells of the Season seemed somehow to have eaten into the very fabric of the city. 'Though I am deeply thankful that by no terrible alchemy can I ever again be debutante, the sense of excitement is still there when I smell the acrid pot-pourri that the month of May brings to London', wrote Violet Powell, remembering her Season in the years between the wars. Even in the 1950s, when London was in general a drab and muted city, with buildings still bomb damaged, shabby streets of peeling stucco, a little of this glamour lingered. Some summer nights you could recapture the pre-war sense of the centre of London – Mayfair, Hyde Park and Kensington – as an aristocratic neighbourhood, an intimate network of familiar faces, known surroundings. Evelyn Waugh's diary for 1956, the year of his daughter Teresa's coming out, describes a night of wandering from party to party: 'Walking at 2 or 3 from Cadogan Square to Knightsbridge London was full of men in white ties strolling about.'

In its early days, when the Season was the background to family marriage treaties, a girl's coming-out dance would, without question, be held in her own home, in one of the aristocratic London palaces. This remained the case up to the First World War. Lady Diana Cooper listed the grandees' houses where she danced in the year of her debut in 1910: Derby, Lansdowne, Londonderry, Bridgewater, Stafford, the great town houses of the country landowners, 'all magnificent, gilded and marbled, and not to be tampered with', by which she meant that the reception rooms were so architecturally splendid they needed no additional decoration for a ball. Such houses were enormously extravagant to run, requiring a battalion of servants for their upkeep. Many of the houses, once closed down in the First World War for the duration, were never to reopen. Some were sold off and demolished. The old formal style of entertaining began to be eroded, overtaken by the more spontaneous and flighty 'bright young things' parties of the twenties. But even if less ostentatiously splendid, coming out balls in the years between the wars kept some of their old intimate atmosphere. They were still feeling like large gatherings of friends. Joyce Phipps, the writer and comedian Joyce Grenfell, came out in 1928: 'All the parties were in private houses which was lovely. The big set balls in Bridgewater House and Crewe House were thrilling.' Margaret Whigham, the future Duchess of Argyll, recalls in her memoirs coming out in 1930, attending a ball or a reception every night, 'probably at Brook House, Londonderry House, Holland House, Sunderland House or Warwick House', all grand family houses. 'Sadly', she adds, writing in the 1970s, 'many of these no longer exist.'

In 1939, the year remembered with a frisson as the last of the old-time Seasons, a Season overshadowed by the onset of another devastating war, a high proportion of the dances were still being held in London private houses. Parents used their own house or they borrowed a town house from relations. The first dance of that Season was given by their mothers for Elizabeth Hely-Hutchinson and Victoria Douglas and guests danced in the first-floor drawing room of a family house, 16 Cadogan Square. Lady Astor gave a ball for her niece Dinah Brand at her own large town house, 4 St James's Square. Lindsey Furneaux's dance was held at 44 Cadogan Place, town house of Lady Pamela Berry, a relation of Lindsey's parents. The Duke and Duchess of Kent attended. The debut of Ghislaine Dresselhuys, Lady Kemsley's daughter by an earlier marriage, was at Chandos House in Queen Anne Street, the large Adam house that was the Kemsley's London residence. The Duke and Duchess of Kent were at this ball as well.

There were two most mysterious and atmospheric dances in what now seems a phantom Season from which the partygoers have departed with the strange finality of the decorative revellers in Alain-Fournier's novel Le Grand Meaulnes. The first was held in June 1939 and was given by Baroness Ravensdale for her niece Vivien Mosley. Vivien was the daughter of the Fascist leader Sir Oswald Mosley by his first wife, Lady Cynthia, who had died of peritonitis in 1933. The ball was in a beautiful dilapidated house in Regent's Park belonging to a friend of Lady Ravensdale, Maud Allen, a dancer in the free-flowing style of Isadora Duncan. The house was known as the West Wing. That ball stayed in the minds of everyone who went to it. Old ladies now describe it as a scene of wonder which encapsulated the romantic intensity of that pre-war summer. The house had a great wild garden adjoining Regent's Park and the dancers were able to roam out to the long grass.

In July 1939 another curiously memorable party was held at Holland House in Kensington, a marvellous Elizabethan building set in seventy acres of gardens and woods like a country manor house in London. The owners, Lord and Lady Ilchester, had lent the house to the mother of the debutante Rosalind Cubitt. It was a huge dance for more than a thousand guests including King George VI and Queen Elizabeth and Noël Coward. The long history of Holland House gave the night a special resonance. This was a house that had been at the centre of the agonising politics of the Civil Wars: the first Lord Holland was executed for his royalist sympathies. In the eighteenth century Joseph Addison had lived there and the house became a gathering place of London intellectuals and wits. By the early nineteenth century, the time of the 3rd Baron and the inveterate intriguer Lady Holland, the house was one of the great Whig palaces of power. This was where Lady Holland's protégé Lord Byron had his first embattled meeting with his future lover, Lady Caroline Lamb, the start of a liaison that became disastrous for them both.

The Cubitt ball drew its glamour from Holland House's historic connotations, its accretions of memory. The pre-ball dinner was held in the long library. The hosts received the guests at the top of the grand staircase. Dancing was in the formal white and gold ballroom and supper in the 'Joshua' room, where Sir Joshua Reynolds's portraits of eighteenth-century grandees gazed down on the current Queen of England, who was wearing a white crinoline, Queen Eva of Spain weighed down with rows of pearls, and the intrepid old hostess Mrs Ronnie Greville who was now so decrepit she had to be borne in by two footmen but was still dressed to kill in diamonds and blue silk. It was a pouring wet night, rather dampening the splendour. No flirting on the terraces or walking in the formal Italian gardens below the house. Is it only with hindsight the event seems melancholy, a swell party that spelled the end of English social continuity and aristocratic confidence? A year later, in September 1940, Holland House was almost totally destroyed by German bombers. 'Holland House, too, has gone, and I am really sorry', the socialite politician Chips Channon recorded in his diary, adding it to the list of now shattered London houses he had once frequented with such zeal. 'I have been thinking of that last great ball there in July 1939, with the crush, the Queen, and "the world" still aglitter.' The remains of Holland House, that once charismatic building, now stand stranded in Kensington municipal parkland, an appropriately Byronic ruin.

By the time I came out the holding of dances in private London houses had practically ceased, as so much of their pre-war way of life had ended for the British upper classes. 'It is sad that the houses of the great will never again open their hospitable doors,' Chips Channon had lamented as he saw his friends close down and finally sell off their large houses, which were then often converted and divided into flats. Coinciding with the week of the final presentations came the news that Nancy Lady Astor had sold the lease of her London mansion, 35 Hill Street in Mayfair, to a property company for offices. 'Aristocracy no longer keep up any state in London, where family houses hardly exist now', commented Nancy Mitford in her essay in *Noblesse Oblige*. By 1958 deb dances in London residential houses were definitely the exception rather than the rule.

The closest that we came to recreation of old glories was the dance given for the Hon. Camilla Jessel. Camilla was the daughter of the 2nd Baron Jessel. Her mother, the former Lady Helen Maglona Vane-Tempest-Stewart, was a daughter of the notorious 7th Marquess of Londonderry, one-time Secretary of State for Air in the National Government whose possibly well-meant but absurdly naive policy of making friends with the Nazis had ruined his reputation. His widow, and Camilla's grandmother, the Dowager Marchioness of Londonderry, was the hostess for the evening. History was repeating itself dramatically. Lady Londonderry had been the leading political hostess of her generation. Camilla's ball took place at Londonderry House, the eighteenth-century house in Park Lane, opposite Hyde Park, which had been in the family since 1922 and had been the scene of Lady Londonderry's greatest social triumphs. On 12 June 1958, this formidable *grande dame* was once again positioned at the top of the grand staircase where she and Ramsey MacDonald, Socialist Prime Minister of a coalition government, generally believed to be Lady Londonderry's lover, had stationed themselves to receive guests by the hundred at her glittering pre-war political receptions.

Camilla Jessel's coming out was a party full of nuances. There was the irony of her mother, daughter of the enthusiast appeaser of the Nazis, having married a rich Jew, the Hon. Teddy Jessel, son of the industrialist 1st Baron, to the family's discomfiture. Camilla's parents were divorced in 1960. There was a further oddness, endemic of the times, in the fact that Londonderry House, closed down for the war and badly damaged in the Blitz, had been leased in 1946 to the Royal Aero Club, the Londonderrys retaining only the top-floor apartment. The reception rooms were let out for entertaining. The long narrow ballroom, hung with the portraits of three successive Czars of Russia, which the Czars had themselves presented to the family, was already a familiar venue for deb dances. In effect the Dowager Duchess of Londonderry was entertaining for Camilla in a former family home, once a place of great prestige and influence, which in changed circumstances she had had to borrow back.

It was quite a party and another sort of swansong. Hosts and guests dressed sumptuously as if in celebration of the house and its history. Lady Londonderry was in pink brocade with diamonds and a diamond tiara, an absurdly heroic figure of the past, already suffering from the cancer that would kill her in April 1959. Camilla's mother, Lady Jessel, was in scarlet and Camilla herself in a sheath dress of white lace. Of the other Londonderry daughters, Lady Margaret Vane-Tempest-Stewart wore black taffeta with diamonds and turquoises; the youngest, Viscountess Bury, was in a cream brocade dress with a wonderful tiara of emeralds and diamonds. It was a madly sophisticated party in comparison with which many subsequent deb dances seemed more like schoolgirl hops. The Spanish Ambassador and the dramatic Marquesa de Santa Cruz made an appearance, as did the Maharajah and Maharanee of Jaipur, she in a sari, rare brown faces at a 1950s London ball. There was the apparition of the Marchioness of Dufferin and Ava, looking more than ever like a pantomime dame in one of her many bravura confections, a voluminous black organza dress with a black spotted net veil swathed around her head and reaching to the floor. The Duke and Duchess of Sutherland took the floor together, she again in magnificent black taffeta and diamonds. There was not to be another such show-off display of grandeur. The following year Londonderry House was in the news as the scene of a rowdy and much less exclusive coming out which ended in a police raid after debs and debs' delights hurled cushions from the ballroom down into Park Lane, pelting the waiters who rushed out to retrieve them with plates of kidney and champagne glasses, hurling bottles of gin and whisky to 'the poor' below and emptying out boxes of cigarettes onto a tramp, finally embarking on a verbal battle royal with the prostitutes who thronged along Park Lane in those years before street clearance and, not surprisingly, threw insults upwards towards the 'filthy rich'. Londonderry House itself lasted very little longer. In 1962 the building was demolished as the Hilton Hotel rose on the adjoining site.

There were other London balls in lovely and eccentric places. Sally O'Rorke's late summer dance was held at Hampton Court where her grandmother Mrs Karri-Davies had a grace-and-favour apartment. The palace was floodlit and it was a balmy evening, encouraging the debs and their partners to lose themselves in the maze across the palace lawns. Dancing took place in two panelled reception rooms decorated with yellow tulle bows and yellow roses and supper was laid out in the long orangery with an American-style milk bar which at the time was an exciting novelty. Sally, in a white net dress with silver embroidery and silver ribbon hem, looked as pretty and as doll-like as she had been when we both learned ballet from Miss Ballantine.

Sally O'Rorke at her dance at Hampton Court

The most original of the London dances of that summer was Elfrida Eden's. Elfrida too had been a fellow pupil at Miss Ballantine's. The dancing class was a significant place of childhood bonding before the dances proper. As little girls we would be invited to each other's parties: I still have a photograph of Elfie at my tenth birthday tea table, eyes shining with excitement, wearing a tall clown's party hat. Elfrida's father, Sir Timothy, was Anthony Eden's elder brother, an intellectual and historian, an opinionated and irascible character, author of an essay on the aristocracy entitled *The Tribulations of a Baronet* and an erudite two volume history of Durham, published in 1952. His wife, a great friend of my mother's, was a chic, artistic and in her way equally imposing figure, with advanced views on child-centred education. She had founded her own school, known as Lady Eden's School, in two large adjacent houses in Victoria Road, South Kensington. Here Lady Eden, with her second-in-command, Lady Bethune, educated 180 children, girls from four to fourteen, boys from four to eight, in an atmosphere of disciplined homeliness and creative self-expression, with a particular emphasis on dancing, Russian ballet, handicraft and painting. The little girls wore frilled check pinafores, like Kate Greenaway children. Lady Eden was very keen on frills.

The family had their own rooms in the school buildings. Elfie's dance was, naturally, held at Lady Eden's School. The desks, chairs and blackboards were stowed away in a pantechnicon. The classrooms were transformed with flowers, fruit and fairy lights. The party had a dreamlike quality, a Lewis Carroll topsy-turviness, as if the grown-ups had illicitly moved into small children's territory. The debs danced around the schoolrooms and sat out under illuminated trees in what was really the school playground now become a magic garden. Complex adult emotions surfaced. Elfrida, whose party after all it was, cast jealous eyes on her longed for debs' delight, Stephen Drysdale, sitting out with Lola Wigan, the bride from the debs' dress show. I had chosen to wear my newest and, I thought, most glamorising dance dress for the evening, a black sheath dress, very slim fitting, with blue sash. I realised with horror soon after arriving that Caroline Butler, a self-confident blonde I had somehow never liked, was wearing the same dress. The fashion clash was reported in the *Evening Standard*'s 'In London Last Night' column in the semi-satiric tone of the late fifties:

It doesn't happen often – but at a debutante party last night I saw two girls wearing the same dress. And they saw each other.

Strip-cartoon situation. Would they go for the eyes or the throat first?

Said debutante CAROLINE BUTLER, blue-sashed in black lace: 'We smiled amiably.'

Said debutante FIONA MacCARTHY, blue-sashed in black lace: 'When I *saw* her, I wanted to go home and change.

No, I do not come out well from this account. It is clear from the tone of the reporting that although debs were still news they were regarded as ridiculous, particularly debs who answered to the name Fiona, the girl in Julian Slade's musical *Salad Days*. The English upper classes remained, in a way, riveting but their arrogance and insularity now seemed absurd. No one who lived through it could forget the double thinking of that period, the debunking beginning but the snobbery remaining. It was an age of peculiar transition. We were almost but not quite at the end of deference.

By 1958 the norm was for deb dances to be held in big London hotels rather than private houses. With ingenuity and vast expenditure some variation and personalisation was possible even in hotels. For the dance for Georgina Ward given by her uncle, the Earl of Dudley, at the Dorchester, the architect Sir Hugh Casson had designed a Regency-style setting, turning the hotel ballroom into an approximation of the Royal Pavilion at Brighton with artificial palm trees and striped awnings and a pair of giant Regency blackamoors guarding the entrance. The first guest to arrive was Tony Armstrong-Jones, then in his role of smart bohemian photographer, habitually travelling to parties on his motor-bike. A ridiculous number of dukes were at this party: Kent, Atholl, Buccleuch, Devonshire and Westminster. *The Evening Standard* judged Gina's debut as 'the most dazzling Debrett conscious party of the year'.

A few days earlier a fantasy garden had been made in the ballroom at Claridge's for the dance Mr and Mrs Jack Steinberg gave for their daughter Raymonde. The room was hung with a blue silk canopy. The walls were lined with pink silk and hung with white trellises. Pink flowers and ivy leaves were festooned around the room, creating an impression of a medieval bower. Towards dawn the lighting changed and day broke above the dancers. The dance was reputed to have cost £5,000. This, then, was entertaining on a very lavish scale. Raymonde's father was Jack Steinberg, textile magnate, Chairman of Horrockses Fashions, though Raymonde was dressed for her debut not by Horrockses but Hardy Amies. Her mother, the sharp and vivacious 'Baby' Steinberg, born Hannah Anne Wolfson, was the daughter of Solomon Wolfson and sister of Isaac Wolfson of the Great Universal Stores. The great store-keeper himself was at the party: the *Standard* reported that: 'He beamed over his cigar at guests Charlestoning to Paul Adams's band.' In spite of what, in deb circles, were the triple no-go areas of Jewishness, trade and an almost embarrassing amount of wealth all debs' mums wanted their daughters to be at Raymonde's ball. There was not a deb in London who refused the invitation. The drivingly ambitious 'Baby' Steinberg had assembled as her dinner party hostesses the mothers of all the year's top debs – the Hon. Lady Lowson, Lady Edith Foxwell, Lady George Scott, Lady Jessel, Lady Rosemary Rubens, Davina Nutting's mother – as well as Lady Lewisham, the socialite the gossip columns loved to hate, who lived up to her wicked fairy reputation by sweeping in in long red velvet with a satin train. It has to be said that on this evening of her debut the debutante herself was outshone by her mother, looking like a Grecian statue in a draped white dress by Balmain. This was one of the hazards of the Season. Raymonde suffered more than most. In contrast to the mother's brittle elegance the daughter was sweet natured, very shy and rather plump. Underneath the social chatter there was kindness and a fellow feeling among debs and I think we all felt the pain of Raymonde's patent failure to live up to her mother's quite colossal expectations. Raymonde was the poor little princess in our midst.

Certainly there were high points. But the Season developed according to a formula that as it wore on became a bit monotonous. We late teenage girls turned into blasé dowagers complaining at the prospect of yet another dance in the Hyde Park Hotel. These balls were almost always preceded by a dinner party held somewhere else in London, in a private house, a restaurant or a hotel. Dinner parties would be given by close friends or relations of the dance hostess. Opinions differed as to whether the giving of these parties was an honour or a burden. They could certainly make quite a big hole in the budget for the Season. Some bargaining went on over the composition of these parties, one of the more vivacious of the year's top debs being offered as a counterweight to a tongue-tied country girl likely to prove a problem around the dinner table. Discreet attention would be paid to the dinner hostess's own choice in debs' delights. A 1958 deb, Sonia York, has kept her meticulous records of that Season. Her diagrams and notes on pre-dance dinner parties suggest that generally they consisted of ten people: middle-aged host and hostess, four debs and four young men. When Sonia dined with the Hyde Parkers at the Hyde Park Hotel – where else could the Hyde Parkers hold a dinner party? – she was in the place of honour on Sir Richard H P's right. Another dinner was evidently not so satisfactory. She makes a note complaining that the party included 'two very common men'.

What did we eat at these dinners? Hotel menus in those days were still unreconstructed. High society expected an anglicised version of elegant French food. A typical pre-dance menu served in 1958 at the Hyde Park was composed as follows:

Prawn Cocktail

❖

Noisettes d'Agneau Zingara

❖

Haricots Verts au Beurre

❖

Pommes Nouvelles Persillées

❖

Fraises Refraîchies

❖

Crème Chantilly

❖

Café Moka

Hotel menus were still being written in French, the legacy of Escoffier, with the notable exception of prawn cocktail, an import from America. The debs' favourite prawn cocktail – a silver coupe of shredded lettuce, peeled prawns in mayonnaise combined with Heinz tomato ketchup and Tabasco, a few prawns in their shells sitting on the top for garnish – has lived on in my conciousness as the inevitable prelude to the ball.

The recommended menus for hostesses at home were just as bland and boring. Helen Burke in the *Tatler* suggested the following easy-to-prepare menu for a pre-dance dinner:

Consommé Olga

❖

Crêpes de Crème de Volaille
(stuffed pancakes made with young boiling chickens which,
she mentions helpfully, were an economic option)

❖

Pilaff de Riz

❖

Salade de Fruits au Kirsch

The drabness and pretentiousness of post-war formal menus reminds one that it was not long since the British felt they were lucky to have any food at all. The offal queue was a by no means distant memory. My mother, already under the influence of Elizabeth David, whose cookery books were beginning to encourage a new exoticism in the kitchens of King's Road, tried to introduce a Mediterranean zing to the menus she and Isa concocted for our own deb dinner parties. But, as I remember, her gazpacho and the rather outré Parmesan ice-cream wafers she invented were less than a success with the debs and especially their escorts whose tastes in food remained stalwartly conventional.

Waiting at table for these pre-dance dinner parties posed a problem for the hostess. Only mothers on the 'Baby' Steinberg level had a residential staff. The desperate solution was for the father and mother of the deb to do their own waiting, whisking in and out of the kitchen like a substandard Fanny and Johnny Craddock, the famous TV cooking duo of the time. Agonised with embarrassment I sat through just such a scene in a deb's parents' flat in Lower Sloane Street. The hiring of outside staff also had its hazards. My mother, through an agency, took on an unknown butler for one of our dinner parties, first to serve the drinks and then to wait at table. For a party of this size, the dining room was small. The mahogany table was at its full extension, leaving little circulation space between the dining chairs and wall. As the main course was being served, the butler started staggering, colliding with the furniture, slurping the wine onto the table as he poured it, misjudging the distance between vegetables and plates. It was as clear to us as it was to a panic-stricken Isa in the kitchen that our butler had been gulping down the gin between exiting and entering the dining room and was now becoming very drunk indeed. He knew that he was failing us, muttering excuses about his broken glasses. My mother was nice to him, sending him home early. In a way I think we felt responsible for the fiasco. Those who employ unknown butlers have only themselves to blame. I cannot now remember how we solved the butler problem. Not all our deb dinner parties were so farcical. But in our household as in others there was a sense of struggle, a reflection of the general struggle of the upper classes to sustain a way of life for which the underlying practical facilities were ceasing to exist.

The dinner party host and hostess took their party of young people on to the dance. This was the old-time system with the hostess in the historic role of chaperone, making sure her girls were not left stranded without partners and responsible for seeing that she got them safely home. By 1958 the system was not working. The hostess could not be bothered or she had her own agenda. The host might have a duty dance and then head off for the bar. A deb was more or less left to work out her own strategy. At least part of every dinner party was expended in weighing up the possibilities for the evening ahead, hoping you could find a debs' delight responsive enough to see you through at least the first part of the evening. There was always the danger that on reaching the hotel the young men you'd met at dinner would simply drift away. Deb dances could be far from pleasurable. They were often occasions of extreme anxiety. One deb of our year used to make herself sick regularly before dances; presumably she suffered from bulimia. All our grooming and our training had prepared us not to be a wallflower. It was wallflowerdom, public sexual rejection, that was seen as the misfortune almost worse than death. No one wanted to join, if they could possibly avoid it, the gaggle of girls in the fortunately spacious ladies' lavatories, partnerless but desperately trying to be brave, forming small female support groups – girls from Dorset, debs from Norfolk – gossiping and chattering before, at the earliest acceptable hour, around 1.30 in the morning, taking their ignominious taxis home.

Almost any man seemed better than no man. This was the Season's ultimate tyranny. The candidly pejorative descriptions of her partners in Sonia York's detailed records of the dances, which range from 'drunk' to 'ghastly', show the practical hazards that a deb was up against. I learned early on to steer clear of an especially obnoxious group of Chelsea smoothies known as the Rawlings Street Gang. Gatecrashing was rife. It was too easy for a man dressed correctly, looking confident, to time his arrival to coincide with that of the dinner party guests and skirt round the receiving line. The mother's vetting processes proved totally inadequate in eradicating the impostors and the creeps. My contemporary debs remember the group of good-looking young Italian waiters who successfully pretended they were princes and 'turned up all over the place'. But there were sweet amenable young men to be found by those with patience. My saviour from many a deb's nightmare situation was Nicky Branch, an amiable young stockbroker, comfortably chubby, a favourite with mothers, who was asked to all the dances. Nicky Branch and I came to a convenient arrangement. We would be each other's No 2, in effect a reserve partner, dancing together and sitting out together until such time as a potential No 1 girl or man came into view.

These were late late nights. London dances, starting at 10.00 or 10.30, went on till 4.00 or 5.00 a.m., energy levels kept going by gargantuan breakfasts of bacon, eggs and mushrooms, chipolatas, grilled tomato, tea or coffee, toast, rolls and marmalade. By no means everybody stayed at the dances until the bitter end. There was a fashion to set off for an alternative breakfast at London Airport. Air travel still had glamour in 1958. We would head off to Heathrow in an excited cavalcade of MG sports cars and old bangers. There was also a craze for going on to the Hammersmith Palais de Danse and mingling with the London couples of all classes who took ballroom dancing seriously. So sheltered were our lives that things like this seemed fun. Quite often we would slip off with a partner to a nightclub: the Blue Angel, where Noël Harrison often gave the cabaret, or the Condor, a black hole in Wardour Street where couples entwined on big leather-covered benches. Some debs were actually forbidden by their mothers to leave the public arena of a dance and go on to a nightclub, the last vestige of a chaperonage system which had still been more or less *de rigueur* in the years between the wars. My own mother, however, was relaxed about nightclubs. She had always loved the dancing. A night out at the 400 with my Uncle Terry, her regular escort in the years of her widowhood, was her idea of the best possible good time.

Going on to a nightclub made a late night even longer. Regularly I would go to bed at six and get up at twelve, exhausted, with only enough vigour to set off to the hairdresser before making the difficult decision of what I should wear for the next evening's events. Over the years I have often asked myself how a girl so hyper-educated as me got through a London Season so uncritically. Why was I not driven mad by its vacuity? One reason was sheer tiredness. I was, we all were, automatons, drifting mindlessly from party to party. The other, obviously, was the sudden discovery of sex.

The dancing itself was easy. It was almost second nature, it had been central to our culture for so long. Every deb, I am sure, had been sent to dancing classes from the age of four or five. At Miss Ballantine's Dancing School in Herbert Crescent we learned ballet, tap and 'limbering', a kind of gymnastics for which we wore our liberty bodices and blue Viyella knickers. We were encouraged to put the stories of our own

Georgina Milner dancing

lives into dancing. The most extreme example of this was when Miss Ballantine asked us all to dance the rather terrifying narrative of the arrival of a burglar in Victoria Heber-Percy's bedroom while the child was in her bed. Victoria herself danced it, then the rest of the class danced it. Was this some eccentric post-war form of therapy? A popular class, and one with the most bearing on the Season, was the mixed sexes class called 'etiquette'. For this we wore our party frocks while the little boys were dressed in satin or velvet trousers and white shirts. The girls were seated on gilt chairs, their ankles crossed. The boys approached us, made a low bow from the waist and invited us to dance. It was an infant training in approach and invitation, a mating game in miniature, eliciting a chorus of fond 'oohs' and 'aahs' from the rows of nannies who were watching their charges, sitting ranged around the room.

Children's parties, pony club dances, the self-conscious interchanges between girls at boarding school and boys from neighbouring public schools imported for the evening to waltz, foxtrot and quickstep while the headmistress looked on. The children from our background had never not been dancing. By the time we reached the Season's pseudo-sophistication the debs had become the living incarnation of the Noël Coward song 'Dance Little Lady':

> *Though you're only seventeen*
> *Far too much of life you've seen,*
> *Syncopated child.*

Already we were experts at the strange stiff swaying mode of dancing to slow tunes, leaning just slightly backwards, shoulders kept immobile, the right arm stretching downwards, male and female fingers amorously linked. We had experienced the pleasures of the dance as a drug, what Noël Coward described as 'insane music in your brain', as soft romantic tunes gave way to jiving and the Charleston. 1958 was the year of the great jive. The end of the evening exploded into anarchy, the drunken tribal gallop of 'D'ye Ken John Peel', the mad exhilaration of the conga snaking through the grand hotel, from the ballroom to the River Room and on towards the terrace, up the stairs and down the lobbies. The conga was a crazy ostentatious chain of privilege, every dancer clinging to the dancer just ahead as if lives depended on it. The hotel waiters would look on, either envious or cynical but never, of course, attempting to join in.

Fiona MacCarthy with a now-forgotten escort at Dominie Riley-Smith's ball at Claridge's

The dancing was fine; it was the sex that was the worry. The dilemma for the debs was that here they were dressed up, at considerable expense, to be desirable but were not permitted to give in to the male passions they aroused. Why did we accept the taboo on intercourse? Why did the great majority of debutantes end the Season as they had begun it, technically virgins? This in spite of the fact that a great deal of what was then termed 'heavy petting' was allowed, the onus being on the girls to set the limit. Protracted French kissing and caressing of a breast, even a bared one, was quite happily permitted as was the purposeful massaging of the upper thigh. But an escort's hand that strayed too far into forbidden areas between the legs was removed decisively by the debs, as if in unison. How had we reached consensus as to where to draw the line?

It was simply an accepted truth that nice girls didn't. The ethics of the question remained totally mysterious since, in any serious sense, sex was not discussed. There was no sex education at Wycombe Abbey School. Indeed in 1958 there was no sex education anywhere. Between mothers and daughters in my milieu, apart from a few token generalised warnings, likely to have done more harm than good, the basic mechanics let alone the morals of sexual relations stayed shrouded in a blanket of embarrassment. All we gathered was that there were good women we should emulate, contented wives and mothers, smiling protectors of the status quo, on the lines of the Queen Mother whom the debs' mums all adored, as opposed to streamlined, cruellipped, overtly sexy women of whom the prime example, in their eyes, was Wallis Simpson, a temptress, an *American* of doubtful sexual habits who had led the King astray.

Aware of her own inadequacy, at the beginning of the Season, in warning me of possible perils ahead, my mother had passed the job on to Uncle Terry, her close companion in those post-war years. Terry Beddard was a tall, pink faced, balding man, a charmer. An Old Etonian, he appears in his contemporary Cyril Connolly's autobiographical *Enemies of Promise*, described admiringly as a 'Byronic youth'. In middle years he had become less Byronic but retained considerable glory as a champion fencer, specialising in the épée, who had represented Britain at the 1948 London Olympic Games. To the small girls we then were, the sight of Uncle Terry, masked and all in white, leaping down the piste and brandishing his giant sword, alien but still familiar, was a wonderfully terrifying sight. His ordinary, unsporting life was not so marvellous. He had long parted from his wife, Ursula, and his two young sons. He ran a small interior decorating business in Sloane Street. Sometimes, on our way to Peter Jones, my mother and I would call in to visit Terry, descending on his rather dark and unconvincing lower ground floor showroom displaying curtain poles and chintz. There were never any clients. Even then I had the sense this was a doubtful enterprise.

We saw a lot of Uncle Terry. He came on summer holidays. He spent Sunday evenings with us, arriving in good time to mix a perfect dry Martini, wielding the cocktail shaker with some of the male expertise he brought to fencing. After dinner my mother and he would sit companionably, listening to Noël Coward on the gramophone. He did not stay the night. Whether he and my mother were actually lovers both I and my sister Karin, Terry's god-daughter, are still unable to decide. There was a story that they had once taken a room at the Savoy intending to make love there but the packet of French letters Uncle Terry had brought with him appeared to have been sabotaged. He tried one, he tried another, but all of them had holes in. This seems to me convincing, tallying with his general practical incompetence, as does the sequel that he and my mother dissolved into laughter so helpless all ideas of congress had had to be abandoned. They shared a wild and physically abandoned sense of humour, sitting shaking with hysteria through Marx Brothers' films. In their close but not overtly passionate relationship the night at the Savoy may well have proved a turning point. Perhaps after this debacle they had not had the heart to try again.

From this it will be clear that my Uncle Terry was not an obvious choice to be lecturing a debutante on how to navigate the Season and keep herself intact. There was an added reason in that, unknown to my mother, he had made a mild attempt to seduce me a year earlier, having taken me out to dance and dine at a Spanish restaurant in Old Brompton Road while my mother was abroad on holiday. He had invited me back to the flat where he lived with his housekeeper, Miss Hunt. The housekeeper, a rather strict and formidable figure, I suppose had gone to bed. Where Cousin Serge had made a pass at me while showing me his etchings Uncle Terry had asked me to come up and see his ivories, a collection of miniature oriental carvings which he brought one by one out of their display case, pointing out each tiny detail as a way of coming close. Inwardly I was horrified. This was my mother's friend, the nearest thing I had to a father. With what seems to me now extraordinary sangfroid, even ruthlessness, I stood up, pushed past him, fetched my coat and left. Typically of the non-confrontational world I was brought up in, the episode was never mentioned afterwards, not by Terry, not by me. Instructed by my mother to tell me about sex the best that he could manage was, 'A pretty girl like you needs to be careful.' Poor Terry. His heart was hardly in this tricky assignation.

Our beliefs, such as they were, were based on the assumption that men preferred a virgin bride, that the virgin state would actually enhance our chances. In my own teenage generation in the fifties holding on to your virginity for your eventual husband was, for most debutantes, an article of faith. It was not just a matter of simple ignorance or the scare of getting pregnant, though both these entered the equation. We were so unprepared in the mechanics of seduction that being alone with a young man brought on wild panic. One ex-deb now tells the story of how she returned home after a dance to her room high up in a house in Redcliffe Gardens bringing her escort with her. When he started to embrace her she flung open the window, yelling, 'Taxi! Taxi!' The taxi arrived instantly and she pushed him down the stairs.

Beyond the fear of the unknown there was something far more mystical, close to religiosity, in our sheer determination to keep ourselves unsullied, whatever the temptations. You knew who the 'fast' debs were – the Fleurs, the Carolyns, the Pennys – who danced closer than the others and disapproved of them instinctively. Rumours of errant debs who 'disappeared' to have abortions struck horror in our hearts. When one of the more persistent debs' delights, an attractively world-weary young man called David Dickinson, tried to persuade me to sleep with him, saying (probably quite rightly) that it would do me good to lose my sexual inhibitions, I bombarded him with letters in defence of my chastity like the stubbornly virtuous Pamela in Samuel Richardson's eighteenth-century epistolary novel of that name. I suppose I was embarrassed to discuss such a delicate question face to face. I have lost sight of the sort of arguments I mustered but I know that they were prim ones and that these were the letters of a self-righteous debutante.

A certain sexual and social overlapping was beginning. It was by no means at the pitch it would reach in the next decade, in which Christine Keeler, the nightclub dancer and call girl, so fatally attracted both the Russian Naval Attaché and the Minister for War under the benevolent aegis of Lord Astor. But what became a lethal combination of snobbery and sleaze was already visible during the Season of 1958. So it was that one night after a dance I found myself in a lavish, rather flouncy flat off Shepherd's Market. I had come with Giles Havergal, one of my favourite dance partners who later became famous as director of the Citizens Theatre in Glasgow. The gathering that evening in the low-lit flat could have provided him with an atmospheric period piece. Giles himself, then a Guards officer at Caterham, had driven up that evening with Nicky Simunek who was also in the Guards but had not been made an officer. The affably roguish Simunek was not just not safe in taxis. Simunek was unsafe anywhere at all. Also at the party, if you can call a party this disparate collection of about a dozen people, some still in ballroom clothes, lolling listlessly on sofas or stretched out on the floors entwined with one another, drinking a lot of vodka, I dimly recognised another deb, Gillian Gough. Gillie Gough was a tall girl of horse-faced splendour who had been one of the models whom Cardin had hand-picked to take part in the Berkeley Debutante Dress Show. Gillie's mother, Mrs Gough, had threatened to upstage her daughter's debut by becoming 'secretly engaged' to a Dutch rubber magnate, Mr Freddie Harttman, as the *Daily Express* divulged under the heading 'Deb's Mother to Remarry'. Gillie too was a little more raffish than the rest. Who brought her here I do not know. It was a night of many mysteries. Nominally in charge of the proceedings, perhaps the owners of the flat, were two Piccadilly tarts. Bedroom doors opened and closed again. Shadowy half-dressed people came and went. If this was an orgy it seemed a little joyless and to my relief no one invited me to join it. I sat apart from the action, the impregnable virgin, like the figure of virtue in a medieval tapestry.

What I find most interesting is that, *pace* David Dickinson, the chivalric ideal of the virgin-unto-marriage was actually upheld by the majority of men. For our escorts, as indeed for us, the routine of arousal then denial was hardly satisfactory. The mating game without the mating was an arid occupation. But young men on the whole accepted the dead end of heavy petting, enduring the inevitable sexual frustration, going off to seek relief by masturbation or a desperate visit to the Bag o' Nails, a brothel conveniently placed near Wellington Barracks and referred to as 'the Bag' by Guards officers. Most of our dance partners were gentlemanly gentlemen. In 1958 there were still traces in our escorts of the old aristocratic code of honour which included protectiveness and gallantry towards the fairer sex and left them unwilling to perpetrate upon a well-bred young girl a fate which they would not wish upon their sisters. They might try it on, but deep in the psyche was their feeling that intercourse with a nice girl, the kind of girl you'd want to marry, was a species of defilement. They respected the refusal more than the assent. It is also worth remembering that, by the laws of averages, some of the debs' escorts were homosexual, even though in that age of spectacular lack of sexual awareness, they were not, as I remember, recognised as such. At bottom, so to speak, not everyone desired us. The surprise of recent years has been the gradual emergence as bona fide gays of reluctant debs' delights who, at the time, simply did not realise their sexual orientation lay elsewhere.

In 1958, the spring and early summer was a time of international political turmoil with states of emergency declared in both Aden and Ceylon, tensions worsening between the Turks and Greeks in Cyprus, rioting by the extremist Europeans in Algiers. Closer to home, British unemployment figures were worsening, with the decline in jobs attributed to innovations in technology; the Campaign for Nuclear Disarmament was gathering support; in May and June a two-month bus strike caused commotion in the capital; growing panic about over-dressed and law-defying Teddy Boys was highlighted by a *Times* article 'Age Succeeds Class as a Barrier'. The debs danced on, oblivious to all this, and when not dancing appeared at a whole sequence of social events that made up the London Season: the Royal Academy Summer Exhibition; the Chelsea Flower Show; the Fourth of June at Eton; Trooping the Colour; Royal Ascot Week. I was at all of these, feeling an increasing terror that this could be a life's work. Standing around for ever in silk dresses, hats and gloves. As the old ladies died off there were the young ones to replace them in this endlessly repetitive and time-consuming cycle of seeing and being seen.

The Royal Academy Private View at Burlington House was the official beginning of the Season. In 1958, for the first time, 'modern' paintings – formerly in a ghetto of their own – were hung side by side with the traditional. John Bratby's *Adam and Eve* and *Nell and Jeremy Sandford* now appeared in juxtaposition with a Winston Churchill landscape of Cap Martin and Anthony Devas's portrait of the Queen. Not that paintings themselves were the focus of attention in what was less an exhibition than a huge midday cocktail party without cocktails, a gathering of the aristocracy and diplomats, the politicians, artists and literary figures who comprised the then establishment in days when the great and good were standing fairly firm and Sir

Mortimer Wheeler and Sir Malcolm Sargent (both at the exhibition) were still counted as the celebrities. My escort Clive Muncaster, a tall, thoughtful and immensely shy young man, was the son of a then well-known painter, Claude Muncaster, a leading light of the Royal Watercolour Society who specialised in landscapes and seascapes. In 1946, the year after war ended, Claude Muncaster had been commissioned by the Queen to paint a series of pictures of Windsor, Sandringham and Balmoral as her personal celebration of victory. In the year when Clive was courting me his father was showing, in an exhibition of the Society of Aviation Artists, a meticulously detailed panoramic landscape of England viewed from an aeroplane, an interesting reminder of how long the wartime imagery of RAF dawn patrols and Spitfires was lingering in those years after the war. I found Claude Muncaster's work distinctly worrying. I distrusted such painstakingly realistic painting, being at the time more of a Ben Nicholson and Barbara Hepworth girl. My favourite of the paintings that we had at home was a semi-surrealist Paul Nash watercolour cryptically entitled *Ballard Phantom*, showing a twisted seashell on a mysterious shore. Unfairly perhaps I projected my doubts about his father's work upon the unsuspecting Clive. It was a repeat of the feelings that had overwhelmed me when an earlier suitor – Paul, the boy who kissed me at the annual Bradfield dance at Wycombe Abbey School – had invited me to Stratford to meet his mother who, as it turned out, ran a picture gallery which specialised in very brightly coloured historic narrative: minstrel boys, carousing monks, Cavaliers surprised by Roundheads, lurid princes in the tower. That early episode suggested that love was less a question of sexual than aesthetic compatibility. I was convinced then that I could never love a boy whose mother dealt in paintings of drinking cardinals.

The centrepiece of the Royal Academy exhibition was John Merton's portrait of the young Countess of Dalkeith. The painting received the academy's rare 'A' award, signifying unanimous acceptance by the selection committee, the first time this award had been given since the war. John Merton was a popular gentleman portraitist, described in the *Sketch* as having 'less the appearance of an artist than of a typical "English soldier" – which, in fact, he was for many years'. Colonel Merton's Queen Anne house and studio was said to be not far from 'the famous military training-ground of Salisbury Plain'. His subject, the Countess of Dalkeith, was formerly Jane McNeill, daugh-

The Countess of Dalkeith (later Jane, Duchess of Buccleuch). Portrait in oils by John Merton

ter of a judge, John McNeill, QC, who had married the Scottish earl, heir to the Duke of Buccleuch, in 1953. The aristocratic married couple now lived at Eldon Hall in Melrose, Roxburghshire. The earl held the historically resonant appointment of Brigadier of the Royal Company of Archers, Her Majesty the Queen's Body Guard for Scotland. The painting is a quasi-Renaissance composition of the countess swathed in satin standing on a columned terrace with a vista of meadows and mountains. The impression is of feminine beauty and decorum in a setting of territorial power. There is a leavening touch of domesticity in the smaller portraits of the countess in the upper niches in which she appears petting a fantail pigeon and a Siamese kitten which is perching on her shoulder. The painting now looks anodyne but in its period it made a statement of considerable emotional force. At a time when they were threatened, this was a defiant celebration of upper-class values. The carefully-coiffed countess is a woman as she should ideally be, representing aristocratic correctness and serenity in an increasingly ungracious modern world. Her rewards are fame, status and the jewels at her neck.

The countess herself was at the Private View, face to face with her own portrait. Her mother-in-law, the Duchess of Buccleuch, was with her. Mrs Rennie-O'Mahony, who attended the academy with thirty of her finishing school cygnets, no doubt extracted a timely lesson from the painting: 'Tread carefully and this could be you, my girls.' To the debutante world the Dalkeith portrait was both comforting and aspirational. It made an impact far beyond, raising debate and stirring argument about styles in portraiture as representative of post-war British culture and society. Along with Annigoni's portrait of Queen Elizabeth, it reminds us of the lingering romantic yearnings of the time.

My Dance at the Dorchester

With that streak of wilfulness with which the upper classes used to like bewildering the lower orders, the Fourth of June at Eton, a kind of open day for parents and old pupils, was not necessarily held on the 4th of June. In 1958, however, name and date had coincided. The 4th of June was a Wednesday and for once the sun was shining on what had originated as a gala in honour of George III's birthday and evolved into an erratic combination of public school speech day and Thames-side *fête champêtre*.

Victoria Bathurst Norman at the Fourth of June at Eton

Falling as it did in the busiest weeks of London dances the Fourth of June at Eton was a welcome change of scene for the debs thronging around in the role of schoolboys' sisters or recent Old Etonians' chosen girlfriends for the day. Events followed a programme evolved over the centuries. There were the speeches in Upper School where sixth-form boys wearing their formal dress of knee breeches declaimed passages from Aeschylus and Milton, Racine and Oscar Wilde. Visitors to the exhibition in the Drawing Schools were invited to admire a hundred selected paintings by Eton boys including two watercolours by Prince Richard of Gloucester, one depicting a desert scene with snake charmer, another an expedition to the Arctic. Lavish hampers were unloaded from the boots of parents' cars and picnic parties involving several generations of Etonians were held in the lush grass along the riverbank. 'Hulking young Old Etonians drank champagne from the bottle and called their mothers Mummy', William Hickey's *Daily Express* column reported the next day. On Agar's Plough – the cricket pitch – the school team was defeated disastrously by the visiting team, the Eton Ramblers, drawn from old boys of the school captained, as always, by an ancient and bewhiskered Old Etonian 'Buns' Cartwright who had played for Eton fifty years before. As we watched, the school team was dismissed in its first innings for a total of 100 with four ducks while the band of the Grenadier Guards played comfortingly on.

The great set piece of the day was the procession of boats, first recorded at Eton in 1793, for which the oarsmen still dressed up in Nelsonian sailors' uniforms of white trousers and blue jackets, their straw boaters winsomely decorated with English country garden flowers. The moment of drama in the procession comes when each boat draws level with the crowds assembled on the banks of the Thames and the oarsmen stand up, with the synchronised movement of a chorus from *The Boy Friend*, lift their oars on high and raise their boaters to the audience. To our horror, one of the boats overturned, depositing its crew in the river. 'Jolly boating weather' as the song goes: yes indeed. Such small debacles were intrinsic to the Fourth of June at Eton, entering the folklore, strengthening the fellow-feeling of this all-day picnic party for the then elite. In entering Eton, as the old Etonian Henry Blofeld put it, 'you were going into a sort of educational freemasonry which had its own language, its own rules, its own dress and its own way of coping with the world'. All the guests at the Fourth of June knew or at least easily recognised each other. It was a completely inbred scene, replete with the elegance of privilege, the sense of belonging to the best club in the world. Eton was the school that nurtured England's rulers. 'The Tory Ministers of 1990 picnic by the Thames', as the *Daily Express* prophesied, none too accurately. Mrs Thatcher's government was not a predominantly Old Etonian one.

Eton families revolved around the Headmaster, Dr Robert Birley, himself an Old Rugbeian who had, through his office, absorbed an altogether Old Etonian gloss. In his tail coat, silk top hat and rolled-up black umbrella, Dr Birley appeared the perfect benign figure of authority, Mrs Birley at his side in summer floral printed silk. The Duchess of Gloucester steered her young sons round the cricket pitch, boys dressed in Eton uniform of black tail coat and stiff white shirt with carnations in their buttonholes. To the dismay of the debs' mothers the Duke of Kent was once again escorting Janet Bryce. Eton 'characters' made their statutory appearances: Lord David Cecil, the Oxford professor, wearing a bowler hat which emphasised his bird-like features; the Duke of Marlborough in a ducal three-piece pin-striped suit worn rumpled with suede shoes; the Irish Catholic intellectual Sir Shane Leslie in his saffron kilt and bonnet. There was a certain splendour, a rather cranky beauty in the scene as the sun went down and the crowds kept milling round, still drinking champagne and waiting for the fireworks. Towards evening I remember an encounter with a rather maudlin Randolph Churchill, shadow figure of his father, the son without a role, swaying his way through a dusky Eton glade. What made the scene so poignant was the sense that it was passing, that this upper-class cohesiveness was already under threat.

Eton itself was in line for a debunking in a novel by an Old Etonian David Benedictus. His book *The Fourth of June*, a black comedy of school life and English mores, was published in 1962. Far from glorifying the old school, Benedictus revealed Eton as an ugly and squalid environment, a secret society of snobbery and cruelty, violence and torture, in which the physically weak and socially unacceptable boys are routinely victimised. The Fourth of June celebrations, in the presence of royalty, necessitate a frantic cover-up by the authorities of near-fatal injuries caused by the sadistic beating of the stunted, ugly Scarfe, a 'guinea pig' pupil from a grammar school. Scarfe recovers but his spirit has been broken. Benedictus's novel was an insider's exposé of an inbred system of education by which these traditions of callous superiority passed on from father to son within Etonian families in perpetuity unless drastic changes were to be made. *The Fourth of June* attacked, by extension, the moral cowardice of the rulers of the nation. The novel ends with the procession of boats and Eton fireworks. The set piece head of the Queen explodes into a showering of rockets before it literally falls apart.

Benedictus's novel now seems a bit jejune. But like *The Breaking of Bumbo* and *My Friend Judas*, bitter-sweet social comedies by Benedictus's Eton contemporary Andrew Sinclair, it was symptomatic of a time in which Eton's esoteric customs and language – by which Absence is a roll-call for the pupils present – began to seem less than enchanting to the outside world. Eton's academic reputation was to be more seriously challenged by another old Etonian, Professor Francis Sherlock, in Simon Raven's compendium *The Old School*. Sherlock, an Eton Colleger or 'tug' (Eton code for a scholar) of the post-war generation, was highly critical of the cult of ignorance prevailing at the school: 'We openly and constantly repudiated the exercise of the mind, skimped and scamped our school work, blackguarded literature and the arts.' The professor derided the system by which scholarships or exhibitions at Cambridge and Oxford were 'tied' or limited to Old Etonians, arguing that this could only drag their value down. Henry Blofeld tells us in his memoirs that, because he had had a cycling accident, King's College, Cambridge, admitted him 'on trust' from Eton in the 1950s. He had not taken an entrance exam at all.

In *The Old School* Simon Raven, himself an Old Carthusian, attacked the superficial, self-protective manner of the public-school boy as it appeared to him when he arrived at Cambridge:

. . . it seemed to me that most public school boys were pretty easy to get on with, no matter how disagreeable they were at bottom, because they were all conversant with a code of manners that forbade awkward questions, was rich in soothing euphemisms and neat formulae for evading crucial issues, and ensured that in no case whatever should public school men break ranks if threatened or attacked by aliens or renegades (for deserters we certainly had) – by socialists, intellectuals or just plain yobs in the street.

The lack of imagination seemed to him in retrospect especially horrific. There was a barrier in understanding: '. . . what we, as public school or ex-public school men, found moving or amusing, was often to others false, irrelevant or cruel'.

I had been brought up to think the best of Eton. Uncle Terry often flaunted his blue striped OE tie. A favourite story in our household was one about the box at the Eton and Harrow cricket match at Lords. There were three public-school boys, a lady, and no chairs. The Etonian called out 'Fetch a chair for the lady', the Wykhamist fetched it, the Harrovian sat down in it, the joke being that Etonians are by nature commanding, Wykhamists biddable and Harrovians uncouth. I was attuned to admire Etonians' glamour. But I became distinctly less pro-Eton after my experiences at the Fourth of June. I had gone in a small party, three recent Old Etonians – Paul and Miles and Peter – with three debs as their companions. Our function was quite clear to me: to spend the day standing around admiring male sporting prowess, three debs like attendant maidens at a medieval joust. Vistas opened out of myself in years to come at cricket matches, polo matches, three day events, smiling, clapping and encouraging in endless, only slightly varied repetitions of this scene, the role in which Camilla Parker Bowles would prove so adept, offering congratulations, holding out the silver cup. The crunch came when my escort, the sandy haired and dapper Old Etonian Miles Eastwood, not a man of great stature, physical or intellectual, referred to three of us as 'the tiny girls'. Tiny girls indeed! The incident was trivial but to me it had the force of revelation. On the Fourth of June at Eton I became a feminist.

My coming out dance was a week later. The choice of place – the Dorchester – was inevitable. All McAlpine family events took place at the Dorchester or 'the Dorch' as we called it. My mother's own wedding reception had been held there in 1937. As a child I had been taken to innumerable family lunches, christenings and weddings in the hotel my grandfather's contracting firm had constructed and which the McAlpine family still owned. All through my childhood my grandmother, the Baroness de Belabre, lived there with her companion and a fast-changing entourage of ladies' maids. My grandmother was notoriously exacting. With its vast luxurious spaces, its bedroom floors and ballrooms, its retinue of deferential doormen, maids and pageboys, florists, waiters who wheeled in your meals and then reappeared to wheel out the empty dishes, the Dorchester was almost a world within a world. Relatively speaking the McAlpines were new money. The wealth of our family had been created in the early twentieth century, too late for the McAlpines to have acquired a town palace like those of the old-time aristocracy. But the Dorchester Hotel was in its way palatial. The hotel was our own peculiar approximation of a London stately home.

The building of the Dorchester on its Park Lane site directly oppo-site Hyde Park involved the demolition of the mid-nineteenth century Dorchester House, a spectacular town mansion purpose-designed by the architect Louis Vulliamy for the wealthy connoisseur Robert Holford to display his considerable collection of paintings. It was in the face of public protest that this lavish and dramatic classical edifice, conceived as a work of art itself, was razed to the ground in 1929 and its great art collection sold off. Just before the demolition there had been a final ball, which was later referred to as Resurrection Morning. Some of the guests were people from the country who had not been to London for so long that people were surprised to see them still alive. On the night of the ball the once grandiose house was semi-derelict, the carpets and most of the furniture had been removed already and great swags of green leaves were festooned around the walls to dis-guise the patches left where the pictures had once hung.

Rattled by criticism of the demolition, unusual in those pre-conser-vation movement days, McAlpines went to great lengths to accentuate the positive. The Dorchester was to be a marvel among modern grand hotels, an eight-storey concrete edifice faced with terrazzo slabs of cement and crushed marble, polished to a pale gold surface that glint-ed in the sun. The eighty salons and three hundred bedrooms all had their en suite bathrooms which, as was pointed out, was a distinct improvement on four bathrooms for the whole of the old Dorchester House. There was a multi-mirrored ballroom, an open-sided Terrace Restaurant with views across the park, a Grill Room and Sherry Bar whose hispanic decor had been personally approved by the Spanish King Alfonso, an acquaintance of the very grand head waiter, Mr Charles. The Dorchester was built for a new age of high-speed travel, drinking, dancing, pleasure in surroundings of ultimate extravagance.

In a way it seems a curiously hedonistic project for a family so work driven as the McAlpines were. As a young bricklayer in Lanarkshire, the future Sir Robert McAlpine would rise at four a.m. to achieve his personal target of 2,000 bricks a day; in later life he still kept a strict eye on progress on the McAlpine building sites, turning up in his dark suit, brandishing his rolled umbrella, laying into any employees he suspected of slacking. This intimidating figure was known amongst his labourers as 'the Umbrella man'. McAlpine policy was to guard the mainly Irish building workers from distraction. 'Never let Paddy come off the mixer' was the motto among the partners of the firm. The

The clan McAlpine (top left). Sir Robert McAlpine in the centre of the group with his daughter Agnes on the right. Alfred, Malcolm and Granville are in the bottom row; Sir Robert McAlpine watching the construction of Wembley Stadium in 1924 (bottom left); and Sir Robert McAlpine and his daughter Agnes, the Baroness de Belabre, on his yacht the *Naida*

family background was strictly Presbyterian. Robert's first wife, Agnes Hepburn, was the daughter of a stonemason who was an elder of his local church. The young couple met at church, both being teachers in the Sunday School. There was a McAlpine tradition of austerity. Sir Robert was teetotal for most of his early life and later became a vegetarian. The partners of the firm sternly discouraged drinking amongst McAlpine employees. Nevertheless this was the family that built what it proudly described as 'the most Modern and Beautiful Hotel in the World', an extravaganza using 140,000 square feet of polished marble, 160 miles of cable, 20 miles of pipes, 20,000 cork slabs (for soundproofing), 50,000 tons of gravel and sand, 2,000 miles of steel rods, 2,500 doors and half an acre of glass. In autumn 1930 this outrageously sophisticated building was rising at the rate of a floor every week. An inaugural lunch – a so-called 'House Warming' – was held in the ballroom on 18 April 1931 to encourage London's social elite and diplomatic fraternity to make use of the Dorchester's glamorous facilities. My mother's and my grandmother's names are amongst the 1,700 people on the guest list. An original short story – 'A Young Man Comes to London' – was commissioned from Michael Arlen, author of the fashionable novel *The Green Hat*. I still have my mother's copy of Arlen's wistful Mayfair romance written for the Dorchester, its zigzag Art Deco binding coloured soft grey and pink.

The planning of my dance at the Dorchester was by no means a straightforward commercial transaction. It was not like hiring the Hyde Park Hotel. There was just so much family history involved. For me the whole vast building was suffused with childhood memories, imprinted with the personalities of my McAlpine relations, in particular my grandmother. Though small in stature she was very imperious indeed. I can see her now in what she called her 'coat of many colours', a beautifully soft and hairy cashmere plaid, laying down the law to her companions and grandchildren and especially my mother whom she terrorised with her instructions, not even allowing her to drive a car. Agnes, the baroness, was the oldest daughter of Sir Robert, one of eleven of his surviving children, two others having died in infancy. After the death of her father's second wife and after her own divorce, she had acted as his hostess, living with him at Knott Park, his indescribably ugly country mansion at Oxshott in Surrey, and cruising around the Mediterranean on his yacht, the *Naida*. My mother's own coming-out ball had been held at Knott Park on 15 June 1925. The day after the dance for 150 guests Sir Robert entertained all his employees. There were sports with prizes presented by the baroness. The marquee was in use again for 400 for supper. The scene was very feudal. The great contractor and his daughter with the exotic title had a good working relationship. It always seemed to me a pity that there was a ban on women in the boardroom of the McAlpine family firm. My formidable grandmother could have made as valid a contribution to the company as any of Sir Robert's many sons.

I can just remember the Dorchester in wartime. Sir Robert was then dead and my grandmother had moved into a suite on the seventh floor. The hotel from then on was her home. We were evacuated to the Dorchester in 1944 once a bomb had destroyed a house in Queen's Gate, Kensington, close to the block of flats in which we were then living. After my father's death the year before, my mother had been desperate to return to London to resume what little remained of her old life. But this could not have been worse timing since Hitler's V-1s or flying bombs were just beginning. That night of the near miss I was woken up by the bombing to find my bed had become a mound of shattered glass. The Dorchester was said to be impervious to bombs because of its reinforced concrete structure. It was widely believed that any bomb that hit the building would just bounce off again, presumably exploding over in Hyde Park. Was this true, I sometimes wonder, or masterly publicity? A number of government ministers moved into the reputed safety of the Dorchester, among them Lord Halifax, Duff Cooper, Oliver Lyttelton and even the Air Chief of Staff, Lord Portal. Once American forces joined the war the American Commander, General Eisenhower, having first tried out Claridge's, transferred to the Dorchester, occupying what is now the Eisenhower Suite on the first floor. He preferred the decor of the Dorchester to that of Claridge's, where he had objected to the 'whorehouse pink' colour scheme of the bedroom and a black and gold sitting room that reminded him of 'a goddamned funeral parlour'. He found the Dorchester was more streamlined, shiny and reassuringly American.

The Dorchester had its own peculiar wartime nightlife. Some of the most famous society hostesses, evicted from their own homes, carried on their competitive grand style entertaining as best they could in the hotel. When Emerald, Lady Cunard's house in Grosvenor Square was damaged by bombs she took refuge in the Dorchester, moving into a suite with her own French antique furniture and *objets d'art*. Lady Sybil Colefax resurrected her pre-war dinner parties – known familiarly as Lady Colefax's 'ordinaries' – at the Dorchester. For a typical 'ordinary' she assembled T. S. Eliot, Edith Sitwell, Arthur Waley, Cyril Connolly and the 'Brains Trust' regular Professor Joad. Not everyone at these dinners was pleased to get a bill for 10s 6d the morning after, a charge which Lady Colefax put down to the exigencies of the war. Margaret Whigham, Deb of the Year in 1930, was another wartime resident. She was by this time married to Charles Sweeny and her son Brian was born there. When she discovered her husband was being repeatedly unfaithful she did not leave the Dorchester but simply took her own suite on another floor. The tempting loucheness of hotel life evidently suited her. Thomas Adès's opera *Powder Her Face*, with its brilliant libretto by Philip Hensher, is based on the imagined later life of Margaret Whigham, after she became the Duchess of Argyll. The scenes are set in a succcession of hotel rooms occupied by the pleasure-loving duchess. These are places where room service has no limitations.

A child of four was unaware of such overtones of scandal. But I did appreciate the marvellous surrealism of those war years at the Dorchester. The once decorous hotel had an air of improvisation. The official air-raid shelter was in the basement kitchen and in the cubicles of the ladies' Turkish baths and the gymnasium. But, as more London bomb refugees piled in, additional mattresses were strewn right down the corridors. People were sleeping all over the ballroom. The Dorchester was bursting at the seams. It was an extraordinary mélange of humanity, women in negligées, men still in their uniforms, over-excited chaos. Later I came upon Cecil Beaton's account of wartime dining at the Dorchester: 'What a mixed crew we are! Cabinet ministers and their self-consciously respectable wives; hatchet-jawed, iron-grey brigadiers; calf-like airmen off duty; tarts on duty, actresses . . . déclassé society people, cheap musicians and motor-car agents.'

The normal social demarcations were suspended. I recognised the scene.

Like Kay Thompson's Eloise at the Plaza I grew up as a hotel child, making the complex geography of the Dorchester my own, stalking around the vast green and gold foyer with its news-stand and a balcony terrace where the more sedate residents sat at little desks and wrote their letters on the writing paper headed 'The Dorchester Hotel'. From this balcony, which wound right around the entrance hall, I could spy on the comings and goings of guests with their piles of leather suitcases and hatboxes being carried through by porters to the lifts. The most important would get a special greeting from the manager. I liked exploring the huge-pillared lounge with its oriental lacquer chests and squashy sofas where tea was served with tiny sandwiches and Fullers' Walnut Cake. I would play in the lifts, getting out at every floor, no doubt to the intense annoyance of the liftman. From the top floor I discovered a little secret doorway that led up to the roof. On a good day you could see for miles across Hyde Park to Kensington Gardens. The scope for entertaining myself seemed almost endless. From my grandmother's suite I enjoyed ringing for room service. The page boys who would answer especially intrigued me. They must have been recruited for their dwarfish stature since some of them seemed almost as small as me. This luxury world had its own intense reality. I understood the hierarchy of the hotel and the smooth-running rhythms of its day focused on the sacred rites of breakfast, luncheon, tea, the cocktail hour, dinner and dancing, by which time the tables would be set again for breakfast the next morning. Where Kay Thompson's Eloise would say 'My mother knows the Owner', my own great-grandfather Sir Robert McAlpine *was* the owner. In my more bumptious moments I could be persuaded that I owned the Dorchester myself.

The Baroness de Belabre, Juju her companion, the enigmatic Captain Lovibond and a very tall friend on the putting green at Knott Park (top); and The Baroness de Belabre and Mrs Poulton, her ladies' maid, with her granddaughters Fiona and Karin MacCarthy at Seaview, Isle of Wight

My grandmother insisted we should call her Toto. She did not see herself as Granny. My grandmother's rooms were the hub of my hotel life. They were connected through to the rooms of her long-serving Belgian companion Juju, whose real name was Miss Lorraine. Juju was as tiny as my grandmother, though stout where she was slim. A strange symbiosis existed between Toto and Juju, as much sisterly as that of an employer and a servant. There would sometimes be explosions and Juju would walk out. Where did she go I wonder? After a few days she would return to the Dorchester and their old harmonious relations would resume. But because of these irregular absences of Juju's my grandmother, who imagined that she could never manage on her own, insisted on the insurance of a stand-in. Hence the changing population of professional ladies' maids, genteel widows in print dresses, exiled European countesses down on their luck, all recruited from the pages of the *Lady*, and installed in one of the Dorchester's small servant rooms. All were very soon found wanting and dismissed.

There were some memorably bizarre scenes at the Dorchester. The McAlpines as a family had an occult streak. Sir Robert, the chief, was said to be fey and claimed to have seen apparitions of his dead mother. My grandmother was clairvoyant. Visitors to Knott Park remembered her ensconced in a room with a pile of large glass balls which, according to one of her young nephews, gave the room 'the air of a witches' lair'. She had received a message from some spiritual contact telling her she was destined to die abroad with none of her kin near her. The result was she would never go abroad without my mother, who was then not allowed to stray out of Toto's sight. While living at the Dorchester she became obsessed with investigating possible life on other planets. A mystery colleague, a shabby little woman with strange eyes, whom my mother disapproved of, was sometimes imported to help with this research. Toto could be frightening, but I loved her and admired her for her strength of will, the asperity with which she dismissed those who attempted to bully or suck up to her. When she went to the most famous hairdresser in London, Raymond (better known as Mr Teasy-Weasy), he said to her, 'Just put yourself in my hands, my lady.' The baroness walked out.

John Betjeman's poem 'Christmas' includes a reference to:

> . . . *shining ones who dwell*
> *Safe in the Dorchester Hotel.*

I was convinced as a child he was referring to my grandmother and understood as I did the fascinating details of her life there. She had a delicate stomach and when the pair of waiters wheeled in the lunch trolley, laid as for a banquet with its white tablecloths and silver-plate hotel cutlery, all she ate was shredded lettuce and a dish of semolina. Her teeth had been extracted in her girlhood by a process which she would describe in ghoulish detail as involving slamming doors and bowls to hold the blood. Her false teeth sat in a glass of bicarbonate of soda beside her on the table. It used to worry me that the waiters would be startled or embarrassed by the baroness's dentures but no doubt they were attuned to far more outré sights. Sometimes her diet was varied with chicken broth made from black-market chickens smuggled into the Dorchester by a rather handsome raven-haired Jewess known as Mrs Snooks, a name presumably as fake as the leopard-skin coat she wore on these clandestine expeditions to Park Lane. Mrs Snooks (another visitor regarded by my mother with immense anxiety) would inveigle her way past the liftman with the suitcase she unloaded when she got to Toto's suite. She brought out poultry, eggs and once even a banana, the very first banana I had ever seen. The chickens were seized on by Juju and boiled down to make stock on the Baby Belling she kept in her apartment. No doubt the Dorchester kitchens, by fair means or illicit, could have made some chicken soup for my grandmother. But it would not have tasted like the soup from the chickens smuggled in by Mrs Snooks.

In the background to our lives at the Dorchester loomed the clan McAlpine, the cohort of descendants of Sir Robert, solid in its maleness, denigrating to its females, still clinging together with the family cohesiveness of the Highland ancestors who migrated south to the Lowlands to seek work after the Rebellion of 1745. They were portly, three-piece suited figures, Uncle Willie, Uncle Edwin and – largest of all – the Uncle who was known as 'Big Tom' and seemed a little simple-minded, though nobody quite said so. These McAlpine uncles had physical traits of the albino, with white pigmentation and pink guinea pig-like eyes. They inhabited a colony of neo-Georgian red-brick houses around Henley-on-Thames where the paintings, if not quite drinking cardinals, depicted Highland cattle wandering in purple heather. It was perhaps in a spirit of rebellion that my cousin Alistair McAlpine became a serious collector of modern abstract art. In the Dorchester days the McAlpine we saw most of was my grandmother's brother Malcolm, by this time Sir Malcolm. He had masterminded the Dorchester development and in the 1950s took up residence in one of the new suites commissioned from Oliver Messel. Uncle Malcolm was a martinet figure who would shame the hotel staff out of presumed indolence by setting an example of not using the hotel lift but walking down the nine flights of stairs and, as well as this, tramping the length of each long corridor past hundreds of hotel guests still slumbering in bed. We were taken on terrifying visits to the Adam Suite where Uncle Malcolm would go through the ritual of performing his favourite con-juring tricks. If Uncle Malcolm found it hard to be congenial to chil-dren still less cosy was his wife Aunt Maud, known to us as 'Aunt Mud', a woman so grimly superstitious that she forbade the hotel florists to use yellow roses or to mix red flowers with white. Reputedly she still haunts the Dorchester. Childhood fears never quite leave one. I would still find Aunt Mud intimidating if I met her as a ghost.

Politically the McAlpines were a prime example of a family who transformed themselves over a century from reforming liberals to extreme conservatives. The political cross-currents are remarkable. My great-grandfather Sir Robert had, as I have mentioned, started life in Scotland as a coal miner and a building-site labourer. It is interesting that one of his early employees on the construction site at Burnbank was Keir Hardie who was to become the first Labour MP. But Robert McAlpine's own political allegiances were never with the working class-es. He was upwardly mobile and by the 1870s had joined the Liberals. This was then the preferred party of the rising Scottish urban middle classes, in tune with my great-grandfather's belief in self-help, local self-government and temperance reform. But with success came increasing conservatism and dependence for the firm's contracts on the politics of power. Sir Robert McAlpine had become a staunch Tory by 1918 when his daughter Roberta, ironically enough, married the eldest son of Liberal Prime Minister Lloyd George. The McAlpines had by then left their Liberal antecedents far behind. Sir Robert's sons and grandsons were increasingly drawn into the inner circles of the Tories as the centu-ry progressed. My Uncle Edwin, a generous contributor to Tory Party funds, was ennobled in 1980, becoming Lord McAlpine of Moffat. His son Alistair, the adorer (and adored) of Margaret Thatcher, served as Treasurer of the Conservative Party from 1975 to 1990 and as Deputy Chairman from 1979 to 1983. He too was made a Lord, becoming Lord McAlpine of West Green in 1984. This was the first example of a father and son to be appointed to the House of Lords each in his own right. When Edwin died, his memorial service, in May 1990, took place in St Paul's Cathedral. The huge church was almost full, with Thatcher, Carrington and others of the Tory hierarchy all lined up to do him honour. The second half of the twentieth century has seen a great acceleration in social mobility. This is obviously one of the main themes of my book. Few debutante families were unaffected by it. But as I listened to the Dean of St Paul's delivering a eulogy about my Uncle Edwin in terms fulsome enough for a great hero of the nation I wondered if my own family experience had not been more extreme than most.

The Dorchester was our viewing point for the momentous public events of the early 1950s. From the balcony of my grandmother's suite high above Park Lane we watched the British Legion Victory Parade of 1951, when thousands upon thousands of men and women in their uniforms with their regimental banners snaked down Park Lane. On a dismal day in February 1952 we were gathered at this same vantage

The Dorchester Hotel elaborately decorated by Oliver Messel for the Coronation of Queen Elizabeth II in 1953

point to view the funeral procession for King George VI, his coffin borne on the same gun carriage that had carried the body of his father George V. The following summer my mother, sister, our nanny and many of our friends were at the Dorchester to celebrate Elizabeth II's Coronation, staying the night before at the hotel. The Dorchester had been decorated for the Coronation by Oliver Messel at his most neo-Romantic and loomed over Park Lane like a giant tiered wedding cake. On Coronation morning I rushed down as usual early to the news-stand in the hall. With exquisite timing the papers were announcing the recent ascent of Everest by the New Zealander Edmund Hillary and the Nepalese Sherpa Tensing, a feat that was nimbly transformed in the reporting to a personal triumph for the Queen.

The life of the London grand hotel was by its nature versatile, able to ring the changes from funereal to celebratory, the expressions on the faces of the staff altering accordingly. As we watched the Coronation ceremony in the abbey on my grandmother's black and white television set, the floor waiters in her suite stood to attention as we all did for the final triumphant 'God Save the Queen'. The hotel was a kind of production line of parties, built for marking all possible

Fiona MacCarthy's tenth birthday tea party at the Dorchester. Rose Dugdale's sister Caroline sits on her right. Elfrida Eden back left

occasions. For every national event celebrated at the Dorchester on a public scale there were a thousand smaller private parties held in the myriad entertaining suites. My deb dance was not in fact my first party at the Dorchester. I had held my tenth birthday party in one of the ground-floor reception rooms that face directly on the park. This was an all-girls tea party, the guests having been recruited from my day school, Miss Ironside's, and from my dancing classes. I sat at one of the long tables, looking solemn in my birthday crown. My sister, also crowned, presided at the other. All our nannies were in attendance, supervising the waiters as they poured our tea. Seen from this distance, the formality astonishes. We were little children in the guise of grown-up people. Some of these same children would curtsey to the Queen with me in 1958. Researching this book, I revisited these rooms, now used mainly for business meetings. I noticed David Beckham with a woman companion drinking in a corner of what is now a very glitzy bar and thought how much my grandmother would have disapproved of the incursions of celebrity. However, Beckham looked magnificent to me.

The date for my dance, 10 June, selected so carefully with Jennifer's approval, proved to be a good one. There were no rival deb dances on that night, although a super-critical deb's mother might have judged that it followed too closely on the high profile dance given at the Dorchester by Lady Rosemary Rubens for her daughter Davina Nutting only the week before. It had been decided that my dance would be held not in the ballroom but in the two smaller Orchid and Holford Rooms and that it would be a dinner dance which meant that all the guests would meet and dine at the Dorchester at 9 p.m. instead of first being farmed out to London dinner parties. I think this plan was meant to give my dance more intimacy and individuality, harking back to my mother's many nights of dancing and dining at the Dorchester when the hotel was new and she herself was young. The detailed organisation of the dance was in the hands of George Ronus who had worked for the hotel for more than twenty years and was now the ultra-confident managing director, adept at smoothing over the tantrums of the many Hollywood film stars who used the Dorchester as their London base, and even equal to Somerset Maugham when he complained that, at sixpence a minute, the Dorchester's charges for its luxury suites were exorbitant. No problem was insurmountable to Swiss-born Mr Ronus, who always wore a dark-blue pin-striped suit with a waistcoat and a watch chain and could move from professional bonhomie to deference with breathtaking efficiency. I am sure he was unfazed by my grandmother's death in the Dorchester in 1952. He was in his role of trusty family retainer as he received me and my mother in his office. I remember close discussion of the menus for the dinner and the breakfast. These were days before all-year-round availability of any food you cared to mention and there was anxious calculation about the likely ripeness of strawberries for the 10th of June.

Leonora Carrington's short story 'The Debutante' is about a young girl who became so nerve-racked at the prospect of her ball that she persuaded a hyena from the zoo to take her place at it, dressed in her dress and trained to walk in her high heels. The substitution was only discovered when the debutante emitted an unaccountably strong smell. I was not worried enough at the prospect of my debut to cast around for someone or something to replace me. But I can recall a succession of small agonies, beginning with the fittings for my dress at Worth. The House of Worth, which had originally been an offshoot of Worth in Paris, had its premises in Grosvenor Street. I had sometimes been there with my grandmother whose idea of an afternoon's entertainment was to walk around from the Dorchester to order a new dress. She would try on model after model. Then after the fitter had arrived to make adjustments to the model she had chosen, pinning up, altering waistlines, removing shoulder pads, my grandmother inevitably changed her mind and would sweep out again, back to the hotel. Perhaps it was the memory of these expeditions, which cast me into embarrassment and shame, that made me so much dislike the prolonged negotiations for my own ball dress, described in precise terms by the *Tatler* as 'a dark lilac satin dress with harem skirt'. Like many of that Season's coming out dresses this mauve satin evening gown was strapless with a boned bodice. One never felt completely confident that the bodice would stay up. The harem skirt, vaguely reminiscent of the costume of a temple dancer in *La Bayadère*, looked especially incongruous when worn with long white gloves.

My hair had been a further torture. Since early adolescence I had gone to my mother's hairdresser who worked in a salon in the street next door to Harrods. This hairdresser was called Albert, pronounced not in the English but the continental fashion, and he was genuinely Parisian. Like George Ronus at the Dorchester, Albert inhabited a treacherous terrain that needed very careful management, sometimes the employee, at other times the friend. Albert had a daughter about my age. This daughter Michelle was always given Christmas presents by my mother and was occasionally invited to tea at our flat in Queen's Gate. On the other hand my mother had no compunction in eventually leaving poor Albert for a younger and more dashing hair-dresser, an Italian, who worked at another Knightsbridge salon, Aldo Bruno. She did have the grace to feel disconcerted when some months later Albert himself turned up at Aldo Bruno, put out to grass with only very aged ladies as his clientèle. At the time of my debut Albert was still in favour. I hated my weekly visits to the salon, the agony of rollers and the hours under the drier, clamped down over your head like a horrible hot helmet. Even worse was the long-winded perfor-mance of the perm. Looking back at the picture of my dance my hairstyle – high off the forehead, set in corrugated waves – seems com-pletely inappropriate for a young girl's debut. I look aged and stilted far beyond my years.

It had been almost impossible arriving at a guest list that would please me and my mother and, most difficult, my nanny who was becoming an increasingly dominant figure in our house. Isa – full name Isabella Forrest Hughes – came from a Scottish family whose history revolved around the service of the rich. Her father had been

Their nanny Isabella Hughes with Fiona and Karin MacCarthy

The MacCarthy–Burness dance at the Dorchester. Petie and Kenneth Burness with Jennifer, Yolande MacCarthy with Fiona, just before the guests arrive

a gardener on the Calder Glen estate, Blantyre. Her elder sister went into service as a ladies' maid and Isa as a housemaid in one of the large McAlpine households in Scotland where, her talent being spotted, she had been upgraded as nanny to two small Bishop boys, my cousins. From there she was handed on to my own mother soon after I was born, looking after me and my sister with a fiercely protective devotion, staying with us through our schooldays and right up to my debut. We had become in effect her family at a time when smaller houses, more restricted living spaces and a post-war relaxation of the old formalities meant that domestic servants were becoming much more integrated with the households in which they were employed. This was only a few years before the film *The Servant*, Joseph Losey's sinister story of domestic role reversal in just the sort of Chelsea terraced house in which we ourselves lived. Even at Limerston Street there were moments when my nanny not my mother was the one in charge and Isa was relentless in her judgement of the friends from the deb scene I brought back to the house. 'She's not backwards in coming forwards' she would say of a girl she had diagnosed as sexually suspect. My old nanny was particularly critical of showiness without substance, of what she termed 'palaver'. She suspected this whole world of compulsive conversation, in which a gap of silence was tantamount to failure, and had found a good old Scots word 'bletherer' for many of my men. Isa was determined that no bletherer would be on my dance list. I fought hard in retaining one or two of the bletherers of whom I was, at the time, particularly fond.

As far as the girls went the guest list was a minefield since I had already used up most of my own quota of sixty or so girls by inviting those whose dances I had already either been to or accepted. No room at the Dorchester for debs who would be holding far-flung county dances later in the summer or indeed for girls with whom I had recently made friends. This caused me such anxieties I went so far as to send out some laborious letters of apology instead of invitations to, for instance, a deb whose August dance was in Northumberland. She was very sweet natured and she asked me anyway.

As the day approached my mother showed signs of a new panic. It has always been mysterious to me why, with all the McAlpine millions in the background, my mother had so little disposable income, but this is perhaps explained by the deeply entrenched view of this primitively patriarchal family that women were so incompetent with money they were better off without it. Female money was put into complicated trusts. I am also rather puzzled about why my mother was evidently being charged full price for a coming-out dance at her own family hotel. Had the deferential Mr Ronus not allowed a discount to the baroness's daughter? Whatever the financial arrangements they were clearly becoming a nightmare to my mother. By early June so tormented did she become about the prospect of not being able to pay the Dorchester account she decided she must sell some of her jewellery. Her diamond clips were selected as the sacrifice. We took a taxi from Chelsea to her usual jeweller, Richard Ogden in Burlington Arcade, the two clips in their little leather case in Mummy's handbag. The jewels were examined in a discreet inner office, sums were named in a hushed tone. I found the whole episode desperately worrying. The deal done, we left the clips and took another taxi. It did not occur to my mother that, in these circumstances, it might have been more appropriate to travel home by bus.

Every little girl would like to be
The fairy on the Christmas tree –
High above the party
Dressed in white
Shining in the candlelight.

This is what we used to sing at Miss Ballantine's, pointing our toes in our little white tulle tutus. The downside of my dance at the Dorchester was that I was not the only fairy on the tree. But at least there was just one other fairy not the two or even three at some economy deb dances. And at least Jenny Burness and I were reasonably friendly, unlike two famously incompatible debutantes who scowled and snarled at one another through their shared dance at the Hyde Park Hotel.

The details of the evening are still clear in my mind. It was a coming together, in that familiar setting, of my childhood past and an already fleeting present of myself as debutante. I had carefully arranged the seating plan to place myself between two handsome debs' delights, both of whom would have rated high on Isa's list of bletherers and the

The MacCarthy–Burness dance going with a swing

debs' mothers' blacklists of NSITs. The bandleader Ian Stewart, ineffably distinguished with his silver grey hair and his exquisite ex-RAF moustache, began to play the piano – 'Cheek to Cheek', 'Night and Day', 'These Foolish Things', the period tunes we had known since we were children. Easy-going upper-class emotion. Everyone joined in. The party started moving. Later in the evening came the stronger rhythms of Russ Henderson and his West Indians, a brief glance of recognition in that summer of 1958 towards the multiculturalism just beginning as immigrants arrived in London from Africa and the Caribbean. 'Coloured folk', my mother called them, patronising though well meaning. Few London balls that summer were without a newly fashionable calypso band. We also had a fortune teller. Estelle, professional clairvoyant, who set up her little booth at the Dorchester. This small, stooped, croaky voiced old woman had been telling young girls' fortunes, she assured us, since Edward VII was on the throne. She examined our hands through a magnifying glass and gazed into a crystal ball. Over the decades Estelle had learned to speak to please, tailoring her predictions to old-time society's conventional expectations. Every deb at my dance was told she would be married within the next two years.

This was the summer in which the musical *My Fair Lady* came to London, starring Julie Andrews, Rex Harrison and Stanley Holloway as the lovable cockney rascal of a dustman. The show had opened in New York two years earlier. *My Fair Lady* became the craze of my deb summer. Many of us had been at the Gala performance whose Chairman Lady Dalrymple-Champneys, Deputy Chairman Mrs Reynolds-Veitch and committee of predominantly double-barrelled names were just the sort of people George Bernard Shaw was satirising as the Eynsford-Hills in *Pygmalion*, the play on which the musical was based. Jennifer, who went to both the preview and first night, said she could easily have seen it three nights running. I must have seen the musical six or seven times. Night after night debs and debs' delights made up parties to go to *My Fair Lady*, starting with drinks at the Cavalry Club, winding up with after-theatre supper at the Savoy. Desperate pleas for tickets were made in the Personal Column of *The Times* and seats were sold on the black market at racketeering prices. What was the attraction? Not just the sumptuous Cecil Beaton costumes, nor the infinitely hummable Lerner and Loewe music – 'I could have danced all night' being especially appealing to a debutante. Not even the thrill of recognising an ex-deb, Fiona Sprot, in the Ascot Gavotte chorus. I think the popularity of *My Fair Lady* sprang from something deeper: the sense of insecurity amongst the upper classes in the later 1950s. Shaw's plot hinges upon the transformation of the flower girl. Can she be groomed to pass in high society? Her triumph shows the upper classes to be gullible. Those who clapped and cheered the musical in 1958 saw this less as a critique, more as a comfort and a reassurance for the future – as if Bernard Shaw, by mocking it, affirmed the status quo.

In mid-June we assembled for our own Ascot Gavotte. Royal Ascot was held over four days, from the 17th to 20th of June. We had been through the hurdle of applying for entrance tickets for the Royal Enclosure from Her Majesty's Representative at the Ascot Office in St James's Palace. As with applications for presentations the rules were elaborate, each application needing the signature of a sponsor who had been granted vouchers for the Royal Enclosure on at least four occasions in recent years, unless the applicant was personally known to the Queen's Representative. This vetting was surely an unreliable method of preventing a woman of doubtful virtue from straying into the vicinity of our gracious Queen. It gave an aura of exclusivity to the enclosure in which, on the first day of the Royal Ascot racing, 7,000 chosen people in their stipulated livery – day dress with hats for ladies, morning dress or service dress for gentlemen – huddled under their umbrellas. It had rained the previous week for Trooping the Colour, drenching the Queen as she rode in her birthday procession on Horse Guards Parade. Now it was wet again for Royal Ascot. It had so far been a deluging June.

The top debs had been snapped as they left their homes for Ascot. Melanie Lowson in her dazzling white dress printed with blue carnations and her cornflower-blue hat. Davina Nutting in an off-the-peg beige cotton trapeze which had cost £6. Amazing! Any triviality of deb life was then newsworthy. Debs were still the celebrities in 1958. But for how much longer? Beyond the Royal Enclosure the crowds massed behind the railings gaped through at the parade of the beautifully dressed and over-privileged. This was class confrontation as dramatic as a scene in a Lindsay Anderson film. Such social demarcations were already fragile. A commentator in *Queen* magazine lamented that 'Discipline has declined in the Royal Enclosure at Ascot', observing that women were now brazenly going to the rails and placing their own bets and that men were daring to appear without their bowler hats. Exclusivity was ending and only the real diehards could regret it as one sort of overdressing gave way to another and Royal Ascot became a parade ground for a colourful elite with quite another set of values. The signs were that very soon celebrities and self-publicists, television personalities, Euro trash and wives of footballers would be breaking in.

CHAPTER SIX

Country Dances

1958 was a terribly wet Season. Floods followed the heavy June rainfall. By 1 July the town centre of Market Harborough, in the heart of hunting country, was reported to have turned into a lake. On 2 July Henley Royal Regatta opened in a downpour. The *Tatler* published a full-page photograph of rows of empty deckchairs on the banks of the river in the Steward's Enclosure. The implied moral was never say die.

The Thames's most social regatta suggests sunshine, parasols and gay summer fashions. The reality is a British July. This scene of desolation shows what the rain did to Henley on the first day. But the British are used to holding their outdoor entertainments with mud underfoot, and though the banks never became fit for high heels the regatta went on regardless.

It was an end of Empire scene, heroic and yet hopeless. In the deluge, aged members of Henley's exclusive Leander Club, in their salmon-pink ties, their matching socks and blazers, caps rammed on their heads like Lewis Carroll's Tweedledum and Tweedledee, looked more and more absurd.

There were many scenes that summer of a rather desperate insouciance in the face of adversity. Drinks parties in the garden were quickly shunted indoors, village cricket matches were called off and marquees erected for deb dances became waterlogged as the night wore on. As Jennifer reported of the 'lovely ball' held at the Hurlingham Club by the Dowager Countess of Lauderdale for her granddaughters Lady Anne Maitland and the Hon. Diana Connolly-Carew, 'Like so many evenings this summer it was raining, so guests could not stroll about the floodlit grounds in Hurlingham (though, as I left, I did see one intrepid couple slowly walking about under a large umbrella!). Hence the ballroom was perhaps gayer than usual and

always full of energetic young dancers.' What gave Jennifer her invio-
lable reputation as the trusted confidante of the upper classes was just
this ability to make the best of things. She upheld stable values –
resourcefulness and cheerfulness, residual nobility – in an increasingly
uncertain world.

Even now old debs remember, with a kind of smiling courage, the
night that the rains came to ruin their deb dance. For the men it was
quite different. With their traditional affinity for water it could be said
the debs' delights were in their element. In a famous episode of 1955
a twenty-one-year-old Oxford undergraduate, the Hon. Richard
Bigham, Master of Nairne, son of Baroness Nairne (a peeress in her
own right), made a bet at a deb's dance at the Savoy that he would
swim the Thames. An admiring gathering of debs in their summery
evening dresses watched him as he stripped to his underpants and
swam through the strong current from the Embankment to the South
Bank. Osbert Lancaster based one of his Pocket Cartoons on the
episode, showing two moustached old clubmen standing by the river,
one saying to the other, 'In my young days a gentleman swam the
Thames fully dressed or not at all.' In deb circles immersion of their
fellow guests in water was an accepted amusement, a symbolic ritual
of upper-class inclusiveness, enjoyed both by the perpetrators and the
victims. For young men about London one of the main pleasures of
attending dances at the Anglo-Belgian Club in Belgrave Square was
the likelihood of a drenching in the fountain. At dances in the country,
where the scope was greater, being flung into the lake or dunked in a
dank fishpool was part of the whole gentlemanly sport of mobbing up.
As I remember that summer the popping of champagne corks made a
bizarre cacophony with the yells and splashes of debs' delights being
forcibly heaved into the swimming pool. Nothing malevolent or savage: in the code of our upbringing this was all good fun.

Of the 118 dances in the *Tatler*'s preview listing for 1958, 70 were
in the country, the majority scheduled for June and July when country-
house gardens could be expected to be at their best. Besides balls in
country houses there were a number of midsummer dances in riverside
hotels and clubs such as the Café de Paris at Bray, the Guards Boat
Club at Maidenhead and Phyllis Court at Henley-on-Thames where as
well as dancing there was punting on the river and flirting in the swing
seats on the lawns. Debs' mothers carefully synchronised their dances
with the Season's events in the locality: there was a clutch of dances in

Bucolic scene at Belinda Bucknill and Sara Barnett's dance in Windsor Forest

the south-western Home Counties in the week of Royal Ascot; dances around Henley at the time of the Regatta; dances in Sussex in the last days of July coinciding with Cowdray Park Polo week and the racing at Goodwood, the traditional finale of the London summer Season, attended by the Queen. No one would have been seen dead in London after Goodwood. It was still as if Wilde's Lady Bracknell were in charge.

The dances with most kudos were the ones held in a debutante's own house in the country, a stately home which had been in her family through the generations. The legendary example was the great ball held at Blenheim Palace on 7 July 1939, in that final Season before the Second World War. It was given by the Duchess of Marlborough for her seventeen-year-old daughter, Lady Sarah Spencer-Churchill. Lady Sarah's grandmother Madame Jacques Balsan, formerly the American heiress Consuelo Vanderbilt who had married the future 9th Duke of Marlborough, was amongst the thousand or so guests. Winston Churchill and Anthony Eden were to be seen deep in conversation together on the terrace. The wonder of the evening, as described by many of the participants, has to be seen in context as a kind of final flowering of country-house luxuriance, almost a throwback to Edwardian ways of doing things. Blenheim Palace was decorated throughout with malmaisons, colossal pink carnations grown by the estate gardeners especially for the ball. The footmen, in their scarlet Marlborough livery and knee breeches, wore powdered wigs; apparently the last time that powdered wigs were seen at an English private ball. Guests waltzed in Vanbrugh's long library. The formal terraces with their classical ornamentations were beautifully illuminated for the evening, as was the famous lake. A dance floor had been put up in the garden but torrents of rain halfway through the ball meant that plans for outdoor dancing had to be abandoned, in 1939 as so frequently in 1958. But the ball at Blenheim remained a kind of symbol of perfection in the minds of many of my parents' generation. Chips Channon was, as usual, the most gushing, writing in his diary:

I have seen much, travelled far, and am accustomed to splendour, but there has never been anything like tonight. The Palace was floodlit, and its grand baroque beauty could be seen for miles . . . I was loathe to leave, but did so at about 4.30 and took one last look at the Baroque terraces with the lake below, and the golden statues and the great palace. Shall we ever see the like again?

No post-war balls were on the scale of that night of spectacular extravagance at Blenheim where, according to Channon, 'there were literally rivers of champagne'. No one quite had the stomach – or indeed the funds – for such conspicuous consumption in an age of continuing post-war austerity. But some 1958 dances, though less lavish, followed the old formula. These were aristocratic English families with long and complex genealogies entertaining for their daughters in historic English country homes. Carolyn Townshend's ball was at Raynham Hall, the red-brick mansion built for her ancestor Sir Roger Townshend by William Edge (or perhaps Inigo Jones), an exquisite small stately home described by Nikolaus Pevsner in his *Buildings of England* as 'the paramount house of its date in Norfolk', with a wonderful interior designed for the famous second Viscount, 'Turnip' Townshend, by William Kent. Bramham Park, West Yorkshire, was the setting for Marcia Lane Fox's debut. The house was built in 1698 by Robert Benson, 1st Lord Bingley, who spent thirty years developing its French-style pleasure gardens. Bramham had been in the Lane Fox family ever since. Katherine Courtenay's coming out took place at Powderham Castle, the medieval stronghold built by her ancestors, the Earls of Devon, and set in an ancient deer park alongside the estuary of the River Exe. Family continuity, romance of ancient lineage, beauty of old buildings even when a bit decaying: these were invitations to be angled for and vied for by the upwardly mobile debs' mothers of our year.

Bramham Park, West Yorkshire, where Marcia Lane Fox's coming out ball was held

One of the most successful summer dances of that Season was Miranda Smiley's, held at Parham Park in Sussex, one of the finest Elizabethan houses in the country, a grey stone building set in its own great estate and deer park on the edge of the South Downs. With its gables and its turrets, its unassuming, very English architectural rightness, Parham is a house that William Morris would have loved. The house was floodlit for the evening. As they drove up the drive towards the entrance court the guests could see the deer silhouetted in the park. Everything about the evening radiated ancient history: the panelled reception rooms hung with ancestral portraits, the mouldings and the carvings, period furniture and tapestries. A long buffet had been set out down the whole length of the Elizabethan banqueting hall. A large marquee for dancing had been built out from one side of the house. For non-dancers, bridge tables and a chessboard were laid out in the Great Chamber which contained a vast four poster with embroidered hangings reputed (like so many beds in England) to have been used by Queen Elizabeth I. A second smaller dance floor had been erected in the garden and guests wandered out through the pleasure grounds and orchards to continue dancing under a cedar tree. In the distance beyond the house stood the small grey stone church of St Peter, dating back to the twelfth century. In this church the private pew kept for the family showed clearly the inter-dependence of the church and local landowner. The private pew was even equipped with its own fireplace, to keep the aristocrats warm while the rector gave his sermons. The

Miranda Smiley on the night of her dance at Parham Park

whole scene was, or appeared to be, a glorious amalgam of time-honoured traditions, long centuries of quintessential Englishness.

Except that the Pearsons, Miranda Smiley's grandparents, only came to Parham in 1922. The house and its 3,733-acre estate had been purchased for his second son, Clive Pearson, by the 1st Lord Cowdray, the entrepreneur who had made a fortune from the family engineering firm S. Pearson and Sons. He bought Parham from the 17th Baroness Zouche of Haryngworth whose ancestors had lived there since 1598. The house was then dilapidated, without water, drains or electricity; the roof leaked badly; previous owners had made crass alterations to the structure. By the time Clive Pearson and his wife, Alicia, acquired Parham, most of the original furnishings, family paintings and armour in the house had been dispersed. Through a process of gradual and careful restoration over several decades the house was returned to its original architectural pattern. All the panelling had been removed, repaired and put back in place. The plaster ceilings, friezes and heraldic decorations had been redesigned and restored in the early 1930s. The house, more or less empty when Lord Cowdray purchased it, had filled up slowly with the pictures, antique furniture, needlework and hangings collected astutely and knowledgeably by the Pearsons, many of which had historical connections with the house. A large collection of portraits, mainly of people associated with Parham, was acquired from Lady Zouche and augmented by portraits that belonged to Alicia Pearson's family, the Brabournes. The Pearsons also built up a library at Parham, reflecting Clive's own interests in history and topography, Alicia's in natural history and heraldry: the revival of Parham was not so much a pastiche of an Elizabethan building as a superlatively convincing reconstruction carried out with all the taste and money that the mid-twentieth century could supply. Few people at Miranda's dance would have been conscious that Parham had not been in her family for many centuries.

There are multiple examples of new money buying into history. My own great-grandfather Sir Robert McAlpine had done it with much less discrimination than the Pearsons when, having risen in the world, he moved into Knott Park, his sprawling Tudorbethan mansion. Another of the major country dances of that summer of 1958 was held for Christa Slater at Ladbroke Hall near Leamington Spa in Warwickshire, a fine eighteenth-century house owned by Christa's stepfather, Geoffrey Rootes, eldest son of William Rootes, the motor manufacturer. He was to succeed his father as the 2nd Baron Rootes in 1964. At the time it took a wealthy industrialist to maintain a major country house in the condition it deserved with the specialist staff to service and maintain it. Many of the more traditional landowning families were floundering, short of cash, lacking the means of sustaining the inheritance they had been brought up to regard as their birthright and their lifelong responsibility.

The stately homes of England
How beautiful they stand
To prove the upper classes

Have still the upper hand.
Though the fact that they have to be rebuilt
And frequently mortgaged to the hilt
Is inclined to take the gilt
Off the gingerbread –
And certainly damps the fun
Of the eldest son.
But still we won't be beaten,
We'll scrimp and screw and save.
The playing fields of Eton
Have made us frightfully brave –
And though if the Van Dycks have to go
And we pawn the Bechstein grand,
We'll stand by the stately homes of England.

As Noël Coward pointed out in his tragi-comic song 'The Stately Homes of England', a great favourite with the beleaguered upper classes, the post-war stately homes were 'rather in the lurch'. Many had been requisitioned in the war, invaded by evacuees from London and the big industrial cities, occupied by schoolchildren transferred from public boarding schools in vulnerable areas, used as military headquarters and hospitals and finally, towards the end of the fighting, taken over as billets for the foreign troops temporarily based in Britain. Longleat, Blenheim, Castle Howard, Knebworth, Chatsworth: these and many other great houses in the English countryside were transformed to new uses. Parham Park was typical in giving shelter, in the early war years, to many bombed-out members of the family and friends. It then became the temporary home of thirty small boy evacuees from Peckham, before being requisitioned for three companies of troops of the Canadian Third Corps in training for the eventual invasion of Europe. The main house was taken over as the regimental headquarters, the officers occupying the Great Hall and all rooms to the west. Canadian troops remained at Parham until late 1946. Such long-term and large-scale occupation took its inevitable toll on the fabric of the building. Requisitioned country houses were always knocked about a bit. Judging by the horror stories circulating in the fifties of Van Dycks used as dartboards, Grinling Gibbons carvings ripped out and burned for firewood, Parham was relatively lucky. The wartime depredations in many other English country houses had been even worse.

The plight of these country-house owners comes over graphically in the diaries of James Lees-Milne, written during the war and over the next decade while he travelled from crumbling castle to disintegrating manor as a member of the staff of the National Trust. What was the future for these tragic houses with their disillusioned owners rattling around in their twenty (or two hundred) freezing rooms without the servants they used to depend on not just for their own comforts but the basic upkeep of the place? Lees-Milne's own considered view was unequivocal: 'One thing is quite certain. The country-house way of life as some of us have known it, will never be revived.' The problem was addressed officially by the Gowers Committee on Houses of Outstanding Historic or Architectural Interest which reported to the government in 1950. It is interesting that the report had been commissioned by a socialist government, which recognised the problem as being one of national significance, not simply the selfish concern of the elite. But official recognition did little to solve the immediate dilemma of the owners of large English country houses, increasingly impractical and financially draining in a post-war period of high taxation and low agricultural rents. It was not always possible, even if one could afford it, to carry out repairs on houses damaged in the war since building licences, which put strict restraints on building, had been mandatory up to 1953.

Many of these anxieties impinged directly on the families of the girls that I came out with. Some were resilient and able to diversify in such a way as to keep their houses and estates viable. Annabella Loudon's father, Francis Loudon, ran a market garden at Olantigh near Wye, the house in Kent where Annabella had her dance that autumn. The decor included his home-grown chrysanthemums. There were other fathers who lent their ancient titles to modern business ventures. The 7th Marquess Townshend, who in 1958 owned 7,000 acres, helped sustain his large estate and Raynham Hall, where Carolyn had made her 'sparkling debut' in the summer, by his directorship of Anglia Television from its very early days and his active involvement in other public companies. Carolyn's father is a very good example of mid-twentieth century aristocrat turned entrepreneur.

But many families lacked a comparable enterprise. As Giles Worsley indicates in his professionally expert study *England's Lost Houses*, the 1950s were years of extreme crisis for the nation's country houses. Almost three hundred substantial and architecturally important English houses were recorded as having been demolished in that decade. The many demolitions unrecorded could lift that startling total even higher. Family houses not in line for actual demolition were being frequently sold off and adapted in their usage, turned into flats and schools, offices and institutions. Even girls of my own age were well aware of the heart-searching that could lie behind the decision to abandon buildings that were often regarded by their owners as a sacred charge. 1958 was a year of frantic downsizing among the upper classes. A typical announcement appeared in *The Times* Court Circular for 26 April 1958: 'The Countess of Gosford and her daughter Lady Caroline Acheson have left Gosford Castle, Co. Armagh and their permanent address is now Stone Hall Cottage, Oxted, Surrey.' From castle to cottage, like a novel by Jane Austen: Caroline Acheson was a fellow deb of mine. Caroline Butler's dance in June was held at the Café de Paris in Bray rather than at nearby Taplow House, her father's former home. Her father had just sold it. He arrived at the Café de Paris bearing 5,000 flowers, the last raid on his garden, to decorate the ballroom. A poignant incident that sums up the whole impermanent feeling of the time.

The alternative to selling a house of course was opening it to a paying public. Ragley Hall, the Warwickshire home of the Marquess and Marchioness of Hertford, opened for the first time in March 1958, in the week after the final presentations. It had now been renovated after its use as a hospital in wartime. In April, Burghley House, near Stamford in Northamptonshire, was also opened. This was the palatial Elizabethan house built for the first Lord Burghley, Lord High Treasurer to Queen Elizabeth I, and lived in ever since by the Cecils and the Exeters. These were two of the forty British country houses which opened to the public in the year of the last curtseys. Woburn, Chatsworth, Blenheim, Longleat, Hatfield, Harewood and others were already open, the most popular attracting a quarter of a million visitors a year. None of this was achieved without misgivings. There was an obvious reluctance to surrender privacy, to relax the social boundaries. It was widely felt that you were letting down your ancestors by allowing the hoi polloi to come surging in. The Duke of Bedford's showmanship in pushing Woburn to the top of the stately homes league table was unpopular: he became a byword for betrayal of his class by bringing in such vulgar attractions as a zoo, a children's playground, a milk bar and a jukebox. He was even to be seen guiding tours around himself. In 1958 a certain shame still attached to opening your house up. I remember a weekend house party in which we stayed cowering indoors in the rooms kept private for the family while the paying public thronged around the grounds.

But some families' attitudes were much more positive. Miranda Smiley's grandparents, Clive and Alicia Pearson, had been pioneers in the opening of country houses at the suggestion of a visionary art consultant Rupert Gunnis, seeing this as the only means of repairing and refurbishing the recently de-requisitioned Parham and giving it a role in a more democratic age. By the time of Miranda's ball in 1958 Parham Park had been open to the public for ten years. Rupert Gunnis was also to advise the Howards on the opening of Castle Howard. George Howard wrote to Alicia Pearson saying 'You were our godparent' when Castle Howard first opened in 1952.

The sense of so many changes happening so fast gave that Season its sometimes surreal quality. An alternative solution to selling up or opening their houses to the public was the National Trust Country Houses Scheme, a temptingly convenient arrangement which enabled families to hand over their houses to the National Trust with an endowment and, in many cases, to continue living there. The Trust acquired twenty-one houses between 1956 and 1960, more than ever

Clandon Park, where the Countess of Iveagh, daughter of the 4th Earl of Onslow, held her dance

before. One of these acquisitions was Clandon Park in Surrey, the early eighteenth-century house where the Countess of Iveagh held a dance for her granddaughter the Hon. Eliza Guinness and her grand-niece Lady Teresa Onslow in the summer of 1958. The family was no longer living in the big house, which had been donated to the National Trust by Lady Iveagh two years earlier, but in a smaller house within the park. Clandon was opened up especially for the occasion. At the time it was still a kind of ghost house, sparsely furnished and shabby after its wartime requisition by the Public Record Office as a store for important state papers. Clandon's flamboyant redecoration by John Fowler and its splendid augmentation with the fine collection of eighteenth-century furniture, porcelain and textiles bequeathed to the Trust by the famously discerning Mrs Gubbay was still to come. In 1958 it was a sad house, half abandoned. The young dancers waltzing, fox-trotting and Charlestoning through those wonderful paved marble halls at Clandon brought the building strangely, temporarily to life.

Elisabeth Hyde Parker's coming out was at Melford Hall near Sudbury in Suffolk, a joint celebration for Beth and for her brother Sir Richard Hyde Parker, 12th Baronet, who was twenty-one that year. The faded red-brick house, with its cupolas and turrets, is one of the most romantic of all English country houses, mainly dating from the mid-sixteenth century. When Queen Elizabeth I made her progress around Suffolk in 1578 she was entertained at Melford. According to contemporary records:

There were 200 young gentlemen cladde alle in white velvet, and 300 of the graver sort apparelled in black velvet coates and with faire chaines . . . with 1,500 servying men all on horsebacke, well and bravelie mounted, to receive the Queen's Highnesse into Suffolke . . . and there was in Suffolke suche sumptuous feastinges and bankets as seldom in anie parte of the worlde there hath been seene afore.

In the eighteenth century the hall was bought by Sir Harry Parker, 6th Baronet. The Parkers were a great naval family, producing a succession of three distinguished admirals, all of them called Hyde. It was the second Admiral Hyde Parker who, at the Battle of Copenhagen, gave the signal to withdraw which provoked Nelson to put the telescope to his blind eye. The third of these illustrious Admiral Hyde Parkers fought in the Napoleonic Wars, finally becoming First Sea Lord. Portraits of the admirals and the spoils they acquired give the house its particular historic atmosphere. Later Parkers were keen antiquarians and collectors. By the time of Beth Hyde Parker's coming out, Melford Hall had been in the family for almost two centuries. But their tenure was now coming to an end. On the death of her father in 1951 the house, which had been badly damaged during military occupation in the war, had been accepted by the Treasury in lieu of death duties, together with some of the principal contents and a hundred and thirty acres of park. Two years after her party in that memorable setting Melford Hall too had been transferred to the National Trust.

Sarah Norman's dance was held at Sutton Place in Surrey, the vast country house where in the 1930s the Duke and Duchess of Sutherland frequently entertained the Prince of Wales. The dance was given by her mother, the Hon. Mrs Willoughby Norman with the duchess as co-hostess. Jennifer of course was there: 'I join 800 at a duchess's ball,' she reported in the *Tatler*, rather breathlessly. 'The lovely house of the Duke and Duchess of Sutherland is a superb setting for a ball, and each one I have been to here has been outstanding.' She praised the duchess, 'enchanting in a rose and white printed taffeta dress', who had personally arranged the exquisite flowers throughout the house. The duchess was apparently 'in no way perturbed' at having a party for more than thirty friends staying in the house, and a dinner party of eighty guests before the dance. She praised the duke, 'always a charming host', seen quietly going round chatting to his many guests. Jennifer was a thrilled spectator of the dancing in the long panelled library and out on the small dance floor beside 'one of the best designed and prettiest swimming pools in the country'. The scene reminded her of fairyland. But this was not to last. Only two years later Sutton Place had been sold to the multi-millionaire Paul Getty. In her memoirs, describing a party held in 1960, Jennifer expresses deep displeasure at the transformation:

I have been to many gracious parties in this house: this was a complete contrast. Firstly it was far too crowded. Secondly, around the swimming pool that evening were stalls with milk shakes, soft drinks and a variety of other items, all advertising their wares – it looked like a market. Thirdly, the ladies' cloakroom was a row of creosoted loos in creosoted huts such as you had at point-to-points in the old days, which the ladies in their often very pale silks and satins were afraid to use, as Mr Getty had had all the luxurious bathrooms locked!

Milkshakes at Sutton Place. Portaloos out in the garden. To Jennifer this signified the coming of the barbarians.

Unlike the London dances, deb dances in the country were completely unpredictable. Every weekend through the summer you would
set off on this magical mystery tour, travelling on Friday afternoon,
usually by train, to a probably unfamiliar part of England to stay with
people you most likely had never met before. Week by week you were
landed in new social situations with little possibility of rescue or
escape. Not easy in, say, Warwickshire to take a taxi home as you
could do if an evening in London proved disastrous. In this respect,
upper-class parents had always been hard-hearted. Being sent off into
the blue without compunction had been an element, I think, in all our
upbringings: the children had to be taught to be socially adaptable, to
stand on their own feet.

My sister and I had started young with house parties, having been
invited at the age of seven and ten respectively to stay with some distant friends of my mother's, the D'Avigdor-Goldsmids. Looking back
I imagine the idea originated with my lounge-lizard of a godfather,
Colonel 'Dicky' Pembroke, who was the close companion of Rosie
D'Avigdor-Goldsmid at the time. The invitation was for a children's
dance at Somerhill, the Goldsmids' country house near Tonbridge in
Kent. Slightly in trepidation, the two small girls, as we then were,
wearing our identical gingham cotton dresses with rick-rack round the
hem, travelled alone by train from Victoria having been given strict
instructions to get out at Tonbridge, where the Goldsmids' chauffeur
would be meeting us. In the car we caught a first breathtaking view of
Somerhill, the dramatic Jacobean building standing high on a ridge
above the lake and forest, as Turner had painted it in the early nineteenth century. We were led in through the entrance porch and hall-
way, through reception rooms and library, which we were informed by
the parlour maid was the longest room in Kent, to an upstairs drawing room where a tea party was in progress with a greater choice of
sandwiches and cakes than I had seen in my whole lifetime, far outdo-
ing the selection in the tea lounge at the Dorchester. I was accustomed
to middling rich families but it was obvious even to a ten-year-old that
the D'Avigdor-Goldsmids were in a different league.

Sir Harry was a bullion broker and came from a famous Anglo-
Jewish banking dynasty. At the time we went to Somerhill he was also
on the brink of a political career. In 1955 he entered Parliament,
becoming Parliamentary Private Secretary to Duncan Sandys when
Sandys was Minister of Housing, a post for which Sir Harry's owner-

ship of a 270-room Kent mansion gave him a particular expertise. The regime at Somerhill was famously hospitable. Rosie herself, the china-doll-like chatelaine who chain-smoked small cigars, compared her house to a hotel, 'except that the guests never paid'. Writers, artists, politicians, royalty, John Betjeman, Hugh Casson, David Niven, Enoch Powell, a fashionably eclectic mix, sat down to banquets so gargantuan that, according to Violet Powell, a frequent visitor, 'stiff sets of tennis were a necessity between meals'. The Goldsmids' effusive hospitality extended to the children. As friends of their daughters, Sarah and Chloë, the little girls from South Kensington were cosseted. For the dance in the evening we were bathed and changed and our hair was brushed to shimmering point by a succession of maids. Local children and bashful teenagers were ushered in to join us in Sir Roger de Coverley, Strip the Willow, the Dashing White Sergeant and other such galumphing performances, the staple of all Pony Club dances in the country, while the grown-ups in their evening clothes drifted in and out, smiling indulgently at the scene. At breakfast in the morning footmen stood behind our chairs in the dining room hung with Brussels tapestries. After breakfast a line of little ponies was led out by the grooms for the children to take a morning ride. When we got back to London I wrote an account of the stay in a wide-eyed style reminiscent of Daisy Ashford's *The Young Visiters*. It was useful childhood training. If you could cope with a weekend at Somerhill you would be equipped for whatever life might bring.

In 1958 the first dance I went to in the country was Davina Griffiths' at Orlingbury Hall, her family house near Kettering in Leicestershire. This was in mid-May. Over the next four months I danced in Hampshire, Surrey, Sussex, Warwickshire, Norfolk, Buckinghamshire, Cheshire, Gloucestershire, Kent, Oxfordshire and Somerset before proceeding onwards to Dublin and to Scotland in August and September. When country invitations clashed, logistics meant that you must settle for one dance or another, unlike in London where with ingenuity several parties could be managed in one night. However, country hostesses would often cooperate to ensure maximum attendance at their balls by running them together. There would be a sudden glut of parties in, say, Hampshire, one on Friday, one on Saturday. If you were an especial crony of the deb for whom the dance was being held you would be asked to join her house party: there was a certain kudos in staying in the house. Otherwise debs and young men would be farmed out around the other large houses in the neighbourhood, which could in practice be as much as forty miles away.

The country house routine began with the letter of invitation from your house party hostess. Generally this letter would be addressed to you, but more old-fashioned country people would send it to your mother. For instance, in the wonderfully comprehensive collection of invitations relating to our Season kept by Margaret McKay, as she then was, I found one of those letters sent on deep blue paper from a good address in Shropshire to her mother saying: 'Mrs. Wenger has asked me to have Margaret to stay for her dance on May 10th and this I am very pleased to do.' Usually, especially in far-flung counties, the prospective hostess would be a total stranger, probably belonging in the 'up-from-the-country' category my Londonised mother so despised. Your hostess's directions for the journey could be complex. To quote another letter sent to Margaret McKay, this time an invitation to Bembridge, Isle of Wight:

This is just to tell you you are staying with us for the dance on 21st June. These are the plans: Waterloo–Portsmouth Harbour *fast* train 1.50 and 2.50. These are being met by private launches which leave on the Gosport Ferry pontoon. Should you not be on either of these trains you will have to come over on the ordinary ferry boat to Ryde – share a taxi or come out by a No. 8 bus – it stops at the post office and this house is very easy to find, anyone will tell you.

Not surprisingly these optimistic travel plans very often went awry. One summer evening I thought I had caught a train to Newbury but discovered when I got to Reading that I was on the Didcot–Oxford line. I shot off the train and travelled on by taxi, panic-stricken, to find the whole house party just sitting down to dinner. I had somehow scrambled into my evening dress en route. In an age long before the mobile phone these ventures into unknown territory – geographical and social – could be testing to a deb's initiative.

In our mother's generation house parties in the country were quite formal, very laboured. Robert Altman caught the mood precisely in his movie *Gosford Park*. A young girl would often be sent with her own maid who would unpack for her and dress her and also discreetly act as chaperone. If she did not bring a servant then a housemaid would unpack for her. In our own more makeshift days this was no longer usual. The lavish style of entertaining my sister and I had been startled by at Somerhill had become exceptional by 1958. You would not necessarily be going to a grand house. A private drive, even a short one, was more or less *de rigueur*: there were only rare occasions, a desperation billet, when debs found themselves staying in houses in a road. But the substantial halls and manors in which we mainly found ourselves were often a bit shabby, bashed around and dog-haired, in the days before 'shabby chic' became a style to aim for. In post-war Britain this was the real thing.

House party guests would be instructed to arrive in early evening: late tea or early drinks time, according to the strictly timed rituals of consumption in such households. Sometimes there would be a little throng of you together since, as so helpfully suggested by your hostess, you had met up at the ticket office before travelling or located one another on the train. These were not always people you would ideally have chosen to spend a whole weekend with. 'The other people who are coming to stop with us are Caroline Butler, Brian Dykes and Philip Fazil': sometimes the heart sank. As soon as you arrived you were shown up to your room. You never knew whether you would be assigned a draped four poster or a camp bed in the now abandoned nursery. As a child, at children's parties or church fêtes, I had loved the tense exhilaration of the lucky dip: pushing my hand down through the sawdust in the dustbin to extract a surprise package that might be a dud but might equally well be the thing I had most wanted. The charm or, to some, the nerve-racking quality of these country-house weekends was that they were always a total lucky dip.

Though often architecturally fine and stacked with the inherited treasures of the ancestors, few of these houses were up to date in their equipment. There was a striking shortage of mod cons. In the hours before the dance the girls in the house party fought for the hot water for the bath, which was almost always dauntingly old world, freestanding on claw feet in a large unheated bathroom. The enamel would be chipping, with suspicious brown stains. The lavatory was enclosed in a mahogany surround, like a lumbering piece of furniture itself. The lavatory paper would be sitting there beside you, not on a toilet roll (perish the thought) but laid out neatly sheet by sheet on a china, often a willow-pattern, plate. Washed and dressed for dinner, the house party assembled in the drawing room, downed a lukewarm gin and tonic and moved through to the dining room. Country house food in those days was unexperimental, a formulaic matter of tinned consommé enlivened with a dash of Tio Pepe, chicken casserole and lemon rice pudding. Nor was it always even plentiful. Sometimes the guests got hungry. Night-time raids on the kitchen were not unknown. We could not blame the hosts and hostesses on whom we had been foisted, most of whom accepted the burden of a sudden houseful of quite unknown young people with extraordinary cheerfulness.

The dances themselves were the point of it, the glory of the Season as far as I and many others were concerned. There was an extreme excitement, tinged with nervousness, in arriving late at night, after dinner, at the house in the country where the ball was being held. Driving slowly past the gatehouses, up the drive and through the parkland to arrive at the brightly lit façade of what was very often a marvellous old house set in its own great gardens, part and parcel of England, resonant with history. The Brideshead factor, absorbed from Evelyn Waugh's novel, was a strong one in 1958. Even when the dance was not in an ancestral home the English country setting gave it a special quality. In a sense the Season only came alive out in the country. People dressed less formally, more colourfully than at the London balls: the girls in their Frank Usher floral-printed dresses; the young men in dinner jackets with coloured cummerbunds, sometimes even white tuxedos, though these were regarded as just a little suspect, as my mother would have put it 'Very Sunningdale'. Some of the dances held in old farm buildings in the country had a kind of timeless bucolic quality in contrast to the urban smartness of a dance held at the Dorchester or Claridge's. The character of the evening was more local, the gathering more socially mixed, like a country party in a D.H.

Barn dance given for Mary Groves and Eliza Buckingham at Speen Farm, Buckinghamshire (left); and the two debutantes Eliza Buckingham (left); and Mary Groves (right) with their parents at the barn dance

Lawrence novel or the dance that forms the climax of Rosamond Lehmann's *Invitation to the Waltz*. These were parties which easily contained a lot of oddities, fringe figures: country doctors, inebriated clergymen, gawky second cousins once removed. The rather ramshackle marquees erected in the gardens gave the dances held within them a curious, and pleasing, improvisatory air. The debs' delights' rowdyism, so crass in central London, seemed acceptable, amusing even, far out in the country. The night when three young men drove a vintage car into the marquee of a coming out in Berkshire, scattering the dancers, overturning the drinks tables, seemed more like a scene from a gentle Ealing comedy than proof of the viciousness of the upper classes. Everybody cheered. At these dances there was often an atmosphere of happiness hard to describe exactly, an innocent exuberance that disappeared completely over the next decade. In the last hour or two of a good party in the country, as dawn rose on dancing partners sleepily entwined on the dance floor in the garden, even girls who had their reservations about the Season felt fortunate indeed.

These were the pleasures. But there were particular drawbacks attached to dances in the country. Because the guest list was more family and local there were likely to be fewer people that you knew than at London hotel dances. The young men could be gaucher and less practised on the dance floor. 'The trouble with deb dances is that the men don't dance very well' as Elfrida Eden, a superlative ballroom as well as ballet dancer, acidly remarked. Nor were they always very entertaining talkers; obsessive interest in hunting, shooting and fishing was more to be expected in rural locations. It was all too easy to be landed for the evening with a clumsy-footed, non-rhythmic dance partner with a one-track mind. If your partner disappeared, as men did without compunction, there was a relatively smaller pool of male friends and acquaintances from which to find another. A girl without a partner could, albeit tearfully, take refuge with some dignity in the large impersonal Ladies' Retiring Room of a London grand hotel, but your plight would be quite obvious in the more domestic setting of the first-floor bedroom which served as ladies' cloakroom in an English country house.

The journey back from the dance to the house where you were staying was a nagging worry. How would you ever again find the driver that you came with in the vast acreage of parkland, perhaps by this time secreted with a partner in the undergrowth? And, even once located, would he want to leave when you did? The other burning question was just how drunk would he be. At the time there were no strict rules against drinking and driving. Most debs' escorts drove their cars when they were very drunk indeed. Dangerous driving was indeed regarded as a kind of badge of honour. One young man, his reckless left arm around my shoulder, told me as we skirted at top speed around Hyde Park Corner in the middle of the night that he had once killed a man while driving: hardly a confession to inspire my confidence. Such hazards were multiplied tenfold in the country; '. . . deb escorts drive at breakneck speed through the twisting lanes of Buckinghamshire', the *Evening Standard* reported after Caroline Butler and Harriet Nares's party at the Café de Paris in Bray. There were numerous reports of injuries that summer. Sandra Farley, at her dance, had a black eye and a cracked cheekbone sustained in a car crash only a few days earlier. Gay Foster's dance, planned for June at Claridge's, was postponed till the autumn since Gay was then in hospital, having been extracted from the wreckage of an escort's car. Jennifer thought it worth telling the story in the *Tatler* that 'After Sarah Norman's ball at Sutton Place, the Hon. Shaun Plunket rescued Mr. John Hignett and his passenger Miss Sally Croker-Poole when Mr. Hignett's car hit a lamp standard on the way home.' So alarmed did the debs' mothers become at all these accidents that Mrs Frederick Versen laid on a coach to return girls safely after the dance she gave for Alexandra at a house borrowed from friends at Englefield Green. How many girls availed themselves of Mrs Versen's charabanc I do not know exactly, but it would have seemed a very tame end to the evening. I feel certain most debutantes would have preferred the risks.

The other homeward hazard, besides drunkenness, was lustfulness. Men not safe in taxis were very much unsafer when driving their own vehicles very late at night on a lonely country road. 'Shall we stop the car?' was the inevitable question, either to be welcomed or definitely otherwise, according to one's mood. Refusal could result in a hostile atmosphere. I was never actually ejected from the car of a drunken debs' delight whose overtures I had rejected but it remained a possibility. Even back at the house there could be no relaxation. Two of my fellow debs, staying at Highclere Castle, took to sharing a state bed as mutual protection against the attentions of the marauding earl known to tramp his corridors in search of succulent young girls.

These mid-twentieth century travels through the country, from house party to house party, from dance to dance, added up to an extraordinary new experience, gathering significance in retrospect. I was mostly in a haze of tiredness at the time. There was the basic human interest, to anybody curious, of arriving in strange households, identifying the members of the family and the often multiple hangers-on, gauging the relationships and emotional cross-currents, observing the ineffably peculiar ways in which people choose to live their lives. I have sometimes wondered whether it was this early, forcible immersion into the lives of others that made me a biographer. I loved the unexpected scenes, the often bizarre connections. There was a certain frisson, for a girl who had just curtsied, in sleeping in a bed the Queen herself had vacated only the week before.

Beyond the domestic detail there was the broader pattern. Out in the country there was a sharper sense of the old feudal way of life than I had known in London. What emerged was a whole picture of a certain sort of Britain, a way of life enduring in the section of society which could roughly be termed 'county', still in 1958 with its framework of behaviour and accepted rural values more or less intact. Official records for that year show 966 hereditary peers, most with country estates, 25 peeresses, upwards of 1,000 baronets, plus a further 1,000 or so landed gentry with estates substantial enough to give them a position of local influence. The networks in the counties still kept to the old hierarchies, starting with the Lord Lieutenant in his role of the Queen's local representative, organising royal tours and supervising the Territorial Army. Then came the high sheriffs, the masters of foxhounds, the bishops, the chairmen of the quarter sessions, the JPs. It was a network in which the aristocracy connected with the local country gentry and the largest of the landowners or farmers, the more presentable of whom might be invited to dinner at the Big House (but not often). This was a static and unquestioning society in which certain country landowners retained the hereditary right to choose the vicar and in which peers took part in the law-making processes of the country simply by right of birth.

In 1873, an anxious Lady Minto wrote a letter remonstrating with her son Bertie, Viscount Melgund, who at the age of twenty-eight was not behaving in a manner fitting for an heir to an earldom: '. . . you are at the head of a family which has *ties to the soil* – traditions – and a reputation. . . . You can't live a life of mere personal gratification much longer without doing yourself harm.'

Well into the next century I was aware of such attitudes enduring. Your territorial privilege brought certain obligations of moral leadership. Whatever the temptations you did not let the side down. Even a failing marriage must, if at all possible, be endlessly patched up not just for the sake of the children. The likely effect on the few remaining servants, the gamekeepers and tenants, even the dogs and horses, came into the equation. This was an enclosed world in which the stiff upper lip ruled to an extent which would these days seem absurd. There was no talking things through. Excretion, menstruation and especially sex remained completely no-go subjects. These were people who faced death rather than endure a talking cure, a resistance which was as much social as psychological: the whole paraphernalia of professional unburdening to shrinks with foreign accents seemed impossibly embarrassing and very middle class. But this is not to say that English county people were emotionally deficient, as has often been assumed. My own Uncle Justin was a very good example of the man of hidden feelings. Justin, my father's brother, was the almost archetypal retired army colonel who farmed in Wiltshire, upright and moustached. He was reticent in conversation. But with him as with so many of his contemporaries a strain of strong emotion underlay the silences. They felt deep loves and loyalties to their houses and their gardens, the tracts of land they owned, to the hunt, to their old regiments, and most of all their children. These were things that could easily move strong men to tears.

With love of the land went lineage. It seemed to me the county set drew a measure of security, in those uncertain times, in placing themselves and placing others. There was an obsessive preoccupation with genealogy. Arriving in a strange house you would be cross-examined about your father, your mother, grandparents, distant ancestors. Where was your father at school? What was his regiment? They were desperate to define you – in such terms as 'Oh her grandmother was one of the McAlpines' – as if family and lineage explained it all. In many of these households, other people that you knew, other houses you had stayed in, other dances you were going to, provided the main topics of conversation. There was an enormous expertise attached to it, an intimate knowledge of spellings, hyphenations and correct modes of address. Was it Fitzgerald with a small 'g' or a big one? Did Montagu-Douglas-Scott have two hyphens or none? And what about those terrible tongue-twisters of nomenclature Craven-Smith-Milnes and Twistleton-Wykeham-Fiennes? Why was Fiona's grandmother the Marchioness of

Bute whereas Carolyn's mother was Marchioness Townshend? Where had the 'of' gone to? Such niceties, annoyingly mysterious to people on the outer fringes of society, were second nature here.

The routines in these country houses were quite strict ones, rather as I imagine in a military barracks. Gongs sounded, bells were rung and the house party was expected to assemble. One of the recurring bones of contention between the hosts and guests was the young people's attendance at breakfast, scheduled sharp at 8.30, when they might only have got to bed at 5.00. Was it better to turn up bleary-eyed or risk a cross host's reprimand, which I can still remember with a shudder, if you simply stayed in bed? Even in those austere years breakfast retained some splendour with porridge on the sideboard, sausage, bacon, eggs and mushrooms kept hot in silver dishes set on little spirit stoves; toast, marmalade, honey, coffee, tea. No croissants, which at that time still bore the stigma of fancy foreign food. At 12.30 the house party would collect in the hall and a glass of sherry would be issued. Lunch was served at 1.00. At 4.30 tea would be pushed into the hall on a two-tier wooden trolley bearing sandwiches and cakes. Henry Blofeld, in his memoirs of his upbringing in Norfolk, describes how the old cake had to be used up before a new cake could be started. This figures: in such households there was a certain stinginess, a multitude of rules. In early evening, even when it was not a dance night, the whole family dispersed to bathe and change for dinner, men putting on a green or plum-coloured velvet smoking jacket and black tie, women usually wearing a long dress or long skirt worn with a blouse and long silk cardigan. Blofeld points out that this formality of dress persisted over the decades even when his then aged parents sat down to a small supper warmed up on the Aga and served on a yellow Formica kitchen table: the instinct for keeping up appearances died hard.

It has always been a mystery how, in so tightly regimented a regime with every hour spoken for, the time went by so slowly. I have only to think back to those weekends in the country for the cloud of lassitude to redescend. In *Hons and Rebels* Jessica Mitford identifies this sense of being out of time, as she became aware of it during her own upbringing at Swinbrook, the Redesdales' house in Oxfordshire: 'Growing up in the English countryside seemed an interminable process . . . We were as though caught in a time-proofed corner of the world, foster-children, if not exactly of silence, at least of slow time.'

This feeling of floating somewhere where the deadlines of ordinary

human life did not apply was not simply a question of the physical isolation of these houses, often miles from the next village. It was even
more a matter of the mental separation of their occupants from the
workaday timetables of industry, commerce, the life of the big cities.
There was a fastidious avoidance of such topics. Debutantes had little
concept of how their friends' fathers occupied their lives. Though
many of our house party hosts had business interests, owned a facto-
ry, a local engineering works, one turning out to be a tycoon of toilet
paper, these exploits were rarely mentioned. There was total concen-
tration on country pursuits, breeding animals and birds, riding, hunting, shooting, fishing. These were the things which were regarded with
the utmost seriousness, dominating conversation and imposing their
own gentlemanly disciplines and deadlines, as if living in the country
was itself the work.

These were people who saw a virtue in recurrence. The routines of
the household linked in closely to the cycle of the Seasons, from the
winter to the summer, from the short days to the long days, from seed
time to the harvest, as it was and as they hoped against hope it always
would be, the rich man in his castle, the poor man at his gate. They put
their faith in same old things. The same old cut-crystal salad bowl containing the same salad made of lettuce, tomatoes cut in quarters,
spring onions and radishes shaped like water lilies, served not with
vinaigrette – oh no – but bottles of Heinz Salad Cream. The comforting dowdy decor of the gentry: the same old chintzy chairs and sofas
in the drawing room, velvet curtains, fringed silk lampshades; the
reassuring clutter of the downstairs cloakroom with its fishing rods
and field glasses, cartridge bags and deerstalkers, shooting sticks and
Barbours, accumulated through the generations. Men's clothes could
last for centuries, till practically threadbare. Our hosts in the country
wore old tweeds and dinner jackets they boasted of inheriting from
fathers or from grandfathers. New clothes were always suspect and
modern design anathema. June and Teddy Heywood-Lonsdale were
the only people amongst my mother's fairly widespread group of
friends who showed any enthusiasm for the streamlined, actually com-
missioning a flat from Serge Chermayeff. The madly modern Junie
was the one glorious equivalent of Evelyn Waugh's Margot Best-
Chetwynde, admirer of the Bauhaus, whom I had ever met. In his survey
Industrial Art in England the German art historian Nikolaus Pevsner
attempted to explain England's deeply engrained conservatism of taste in

terms of social hierarchy: the middle classes aped the upper who had in their turn adopted the traditionalism of the royal family. Progress around these country houses could be disorientating, each new set of rooms so precisely resembling in the detail of their décor, down to the exact position of the sofa table bearing the Lenare portrait of your hostess, the one you had just left.

The humour too followed a formula. No one minded repeating a successful joke once made. People dined out on their anecdotes. At these country dinner parties funny stories would be reconstituted, details slightly altered, polished and embellished, until the cows came home. A very good example is the military anecdote recounted by Ludovic Kennedy at the funeral service for Sonia Heathcoat-Amory whose marriage to not one but two successive men named Heathcoat-Amory might be considered a funny story in itself. The story, often told by Roddy Heathcoat-Amory, Sonia's second husband and now revived by Kennedy, concerns a telephone call taken by Heathcoat-Amory while serving with the British Army on the Rhine:

In his office one day the telephone rang and Roddy answered it. The caller seemed particularly obtuse and Roddy gave as good as he got. Finally the caller said, 'Do you know who you're talking to?' Roddy replied he didn't and the voice said, 'Well, I'll tell you. It's Philip Knightley, the Commander in Chief.' 'Oh,' said Roddy, taken aback, 'do you know who you're talking to?' 'No,' said Knightley, 'can't say I do.' 'Thank God for that,' said Roddy, and slammed the phone down.

It could be guaranteed that most of the congregation at Sonia's service of thanksgiving had heard the story many times before and in a way this was the point of it. Such jokes, faintly anarchic and by their nature extremely upper class, comforted through repetition: they gave you confirmation of who and what you were.

Likewise the tribal legends. In my recent re-encounters with the men with whom I danced half a century ago it has been startling to discover some old tales still circulating with a vigour that reminds me of the way in which the story of Jimmy Stripling's attempt to put a po, a white earthenware chamber pot, in Sunny Farebrother's hatbox keeps recurring in Powell's *Hearing Secret Harmonies*. In 1958 our equivalents were these. The night when Johnnie Encombe killed a deer from the herd in the park at Magdalen College, Oxford, barbecuing it on the banks of the Cherwell. He was sent down from Oxford after the episode. The weekend Nigel Dempster, irritated by his hosts, stole the family silver and buried it beneath a tree on the estate. 'I know you've got it somewhere,' said the butler as they left.

With their jokes and chat and rituals, there was a kind of lunatic valour in these households in which we landed so strangely and arbitrarily that summer. They were resilient, proud people and they were holding on. But even I, the young London visitor, was conscious of an underlying disquietude, deep fears for the future. How long could this antiquated way of life survive? When he succeeded Anthony Eden as Prime Minister in 1956, Harold Macmillan, with his grouse moors persona and his grand laconic manner, had appeared to be the saviour of the county set. But by 1958 disillusion had set in. There had been the recent cuts in subsidies to farmers and even a tax on racing prize-money, about which my Uncle Malcolm, as President of the Racehorse Owners' Association, protested vigorously. It was becoming clear that Macmillan's political agenda was much wider, and much wilier, than mere protection of the people whom he resembled superficially in style. The debutante Season in its origins was territorial, to do with marriage treaties and the continuity of power through the landowners and monarchy. I was in at the tail end of it, as territories dwindled, as housing estates encroached upon old parklands, as great houses were either opened to the public or divided up and marketed as the most desirable of residences. Live like a lord! The land was all too visibly returning to the people and the landowners suffered the humiliation.

By the end of July the London Season was petering out. The debs were deadbeat, and for many of the mothers it was a time of reckoning. What had been achieved with all this effort and expenditure? I find my own name in the *Sketch*'s round-up list of 'the well known girls' of 1958, though I suspect that Gladys Boyd, the social editor, only included me to please my mother. In fact by July there was only one name worth mentioning and that was Sally Croker-Poole or Sally Poole as she now preferred to call herself, someone having perhaps told her that the 'Croker' was a joke. Lola Wigan, the Pre-Raphaelite beauty who had looked like the front runner early in the Season, lacked the stamina and will to follow through the adulation. She did not see the point of it. The publicity alarmed her. She drifted off to art school in her Chelsea Set black stockings and her Paris Left Bank polo necks. By the standards of the Season she became a bit eccentric, lavishing attention on pet ferrets in preference to dinner-jacketed young men.

Sally Poole, made of sterner stuff, slimmed, groomed herself, invested in expensive clothes, acquired an aura. We, her neighbours across Limerston Street, watched this transformation in the course of a few weeks from the pretty, over-eager, horse-loving girl from Berkshire to the *soignée* and self-confident woman of the world. Before our very eyes Sally became a beauty, her looks blossoming into an Edwardian lushness. She was photographed at every dance, including mine, her presence adding lustre. She was pictured in the arms of the difficult-to-pin-down Duke of Kent. At Cecil Beaton's own party, laden with famous faces, she was picked out by her host as 'one of the four most beautiful women in the room'. Her own dance had been aggrandised from the small dance in the country, as announced at the beginning of the Season, to a London ball in the large and glamorous new ballroom at Quaglino's. By the end of the summer Sally Poole was established as incontrovertible winner of the contest for 1958 Top Deb. There was the inevitable gossip and tut-tutting over the triumph of such naked ambitiousness shown by Sally and especially her cleverly calculating mother. At the same time most of us managed to be pleased for her. We basked in her reflected glory and we feared for her, with that instinctive solidarity of debs.

Sally Croker-Poole being given a word of advice by her mother before her dance at Quaglino's, shared with Julie Stratford

CHAPTER SEVEN

The Dublin Horse Show

Early in August, as London emptied out, the Season had a burst of new activity in Dublin. Many of the debs travelled over for the Horse Show and the succession of hunt balls and private parties surrounding the official equestrian events. In 1958 the Season in London was still relatively decorous. Dublin Horse Show week was a great deal more rampageous. Perhaps it was the unremitting horsiness of Dublin, the reminder – ever-present – of the primitive relationship of man and beast, that released the inhibitions, encouraged bad behaviour of a flair and thoroughgoingness peculiar to Ireland. Nigel Dempster, debs' delight turned social commentator, a poacher become gamekeeper, described the Dublin Horse Show as 'a wild Rabelaisian week of total drunkenness'.

I had been invited over to a house party for Horse Show Week. The travel instructions given by my Irish hostess were, for once, quite simple and allowed no argument. Take a plane from Heathrow to Dublin where the chauffeur will collect you. Travel in your evening dress since we will be going to a drinks party in Dun Laoghaire before that evening's ball. I remember the dress well: it was white satin, strapless, with very big red flowers that must have looked conspicuous on the mid-afternoon Aer Lingus flight. When I got to the drinks party there was nobody I knew. My father's family, the MacCarthys, originally Catholic, had come from County Cork. But this was a completely different kind of Ireland, the Anglo-Irish landowners, the racing and hunting set. To me, coming from London, they looked open-air and leathery. They spoke another language, the Jelletts, the Connolly-Carews, the hunting dynasties. The upper-class accents had a little Irish lilt. The son of the house, David Stapleton, loomed up, tall, dark, preposterously handsome, potentially brutal, Irish version of Clark Gable as Rhett Butler. I felt in a strange land.

I had never been to Ireland. Southern Ireland in the fifties was as yet unmodernised. Dublin itself had a small town feel, shabby, still almost rural. Lugubrious old men sat around in dingy pubs. The countryside, with its straggling ugly villages, seemed desolate and raw. The roads were bumpy, rough and dusty, with very little traffic: you hardly met another car. In my debutante haze I was not of course aware of the extent of Southern Ireland's social problems in this early post-war period: the problems of poverty, large families, poor housing, high infant mortality rates, excess drinking, excess smoking, alarming rates of suicides and mental illness, the ostracisation of single mothers and the disgrace surrounding bastard children. But a sense of the church-dominated culture of secrecy percolated through to me, even on that brief visit, and the desperation of many people's lives. Meanwhile the Anglo-Irish gentry in their great romantic houses were going to the races, playing polo, breeding horses and, as Elizabeth Bowen, the Anglo-Irish writer, so perfectly expressed it, 'closing their doors each evening and shutting Ireland out'. It was almost as if there were two separate nations. There was little of the nerviness, the social defensiveness, among the upper classes that had just begun in England. Class distinctions in Ireland were as extreme as they had been a century before.

Beaulieu, the Waddingtons' house at Drogheda, Co. Louth

I stayed for Horse Show Week at Beaulieu, Drogheda, Co. Louth. The coming-out dance for Gabriel Waddington, whose parents owned Beaulieu, was one of the week's events. Gabriel had been at my Paris finishing school, Madame Boués Study-Home. Besides some debs from England the house party included five alumnae of the Study-Home, so this was a finishing school reunion. There we perch in our twinsets and blue jeans in the girls' group photograph taken in the drawing room at Beaulieu, a little more sophisticated than when we were last together in Paris in the spring. Gabriel is the one resting her arm upon the poodle, a high-spirited and reckless Anglo-Irish girl.

We were fortunate in the house we had arrived at. Beaulieu is a building which sends the architectural historians into raptures. Mark Bence-Jones has described it as 'the finest and best-preserved country house of the second half of the seventeenth century in Ireland'. Hugh Montgomery-Massingberd pronounces this 'singularly satisfying house' to be 'the supreme example in Ireland of that delectable style of architecture which blended Dutch and Classical influence'. The beauty and coherence of the building in its setting with the church, trees, old walled gardens, lawns gently sloping down to the Boyne estuary, was obvious even to my then quite untrained eye. Drogheda was built

The girls in the Beaulieu House party. From left: Sally Nelson, Zia Foxwell, Fiona MacCarthy, Penny Graham, Coral Knowles, unknown, Gabriel Waddington, unknown, Jane Holden

from 1660 onwards by Sir William Tichborne whose father, Sir Henry, was a prominent Royalist military commander, famous for his exploits in the Siege of Drogheda. It had stayed in the same family from then on, descending to Gabriel's mother, who was born Sidney Montgomery. The painting of an earlier Sidney Montgomery hung amongst the many family portraits in the hall.

Staying with the Waddingtons I was in the heart of horsiness. Gabriel's mother had married Nesbit Waddington, for many years manager of the Aga Khan's stud farms in Ireland and himself a well-known rider. Nesbit was a grizzled, keen-eyed man, rather Regency in tone, dressing up for dinner in his velvet smoking jacket, debonair with all the debutantes, taking us on tours of the stables one by one. The house was run quite formally, more grandly than in many English houses I had stayed in: a maid had been instructed to unpack for us, did washing and ironing, laid our clothes out for the dances. At the same time there was an underlying sense of strain, as if the household were stretched to its limits by the influx of twenty or so self-centred and boisterous young people. It never occurred to anyone to offer to help with the bed-making or the washing-up. Sometimes, in desperation, the whole house party would be sent off into Dublin in the horsebox, jostled up against each other and singing bawdy choruses en route.

The dance for Gabriel took place the night after we arrived. 'V. nervous but tremendous fun', writes Penny Graham, one of the visitors from London, in her diary. The ball was held in the two-storey hall, the central

Nesbit Waddington with Lady Ainsworth at the Irish Grand National in 1958

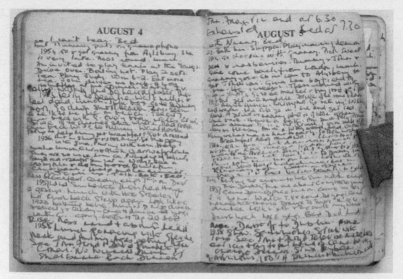

Penny Graham's five-year diary, including her account of Dublin Horse Show Week in 1958

room at Beaulieu, architecturally splendid, carved, moulded and adorned with coats of arms, the spoils of war and sporting trophies which included the huge horns of an ancient Irish elk. We as house guests could spy down from windows placed along the first-floor corridor as the party gradually assembled in the hall below. Like all Anglo-Irish parties this one had a tribal vigour. The portraits of the ancestors looked down as if admiring its abandon. It ended with us going out to paddle in the river at 5.30 in the morning. Irish dances were apt to end like that.

The rhythm of those days of the debutantes in Ireland, peaks of frenzied activity and troughs of indolence, emerges vividly from Penny Graham's small handwritten diary of that Dublin Horse Show Week.

August 3. 'Sleep till lunch. Rise in jeans. Mess around and read and listen to records. Some go to caves. Tea. Put on red sack dress. Drinks with the Meath MFH.'

August 4. 'Mess around and about. Read. Go racing with Greville*, Mark and Antony. Ages getting there. No winners. Drinks at Shelbourne. Back for dinner.'

* Greville Howard, still an Eton schoolboy, now transformed into Baron Howard of Castle Rising.

August 5. 'Drive off to Dublin Horse Show. Sandwiches. Stick with Jane. See John and Floyd. Televise ourselves. Come back. Change. Dinner. Stux-Ryber party. Fabulous. 100s of princes and millionaires. Frantic end at 6.30. Exhausted. Back at 7.30.

August 6. 'Don't wake till 12.30. Go evening racing in horse box. Gt. Fun. Don't win. John, Floyd etc. Come back. Tell filthy stories. Antony – ug! – turns pea green.'

August 7. 'Rise and stagger down stairs. Lunch. Go to show on slow train! Sing filthy songs. Quite fun. Don't watch much. Eat ices with John. Come back for dinner. Play ping-pong and generally mess around.'

August 8. 'Zia departs crack of dawn. Foul day. Misery. Put on sack coat and white hat. Horse Show. Aga Khan Cup won by England. See John and Bill. Then change at Shelbourne. Dinner at Kildare St. Club. Louth Hunt Ball. Tremendous but boiled. Bed at 6.'

August 9. 'Rise leisurely. Dress. Horrid day. Racing at Phoenix Park. See John etc. Rather fun but no ruddy winners. Change at Shelbourne again. Dinner at Kildare St. Club. TREMENDOUS. John Browne-Swinburne, Johnny, Douglas. Oh heavens. Ends at 6.30. Bed at 7.30!'

August 10. 'Rise exhausted for lunch. Play ping-pong frantically. Tea. Mess around. Dinner. 8 of us leap into a small car and go to cinema. Then dance on beach. Tremendous. Come back. Creep to bed.'

The diaries are fascinating in the way they resurrect a late 1950s girl-ish quality of heedlessness. The style too is very period. She writes in Mitfordese. Reconsidering her diary Penny Graham feels embarrassed at the emphasis she places on the boys and not the girls in the house party at Drogheda. This she attributes to 'a mixture of years in the Convent and reading Georgette Heyer'. But surely she was showing a correct sense of priorities. Boys were in fact what a debutante was for. In its record of the details of a debutante's totally frivolous existence in a world now so remote as to tax our credibility Penny Graham's diary is a valuable social document.

The Dublin Horse Show, focus of the week's events, took place at Ballsbridge. It was, and it remains, the most famous of all horse shows, not just a competition but a means of selling horses, attracting the best riders and the finest horses on the international scene. In 1958 there were more than 1,100 entries, apparently the most since 1913. The competitions took place in a vast green turfed enclosure bordered with flower beds, spectators crowded round the rails. The champion hunter in 1958 was Tenerife, a heavyweight brown gelding bred by

Nat Galway-Greer, of Dunboyne, in Co. Meath. This was no surprise since Galway-Greer, a hero in horse circles, also produced the previous year's champion, Work of Art, a hunter described by Jennifer, whose *Tatler* diary encompassed elite animals as well as top-class people, as 'a beautiful mover and an outstanding horse'. The highlight of the week (mentioned in Penny Graham's narrative) was the Aga Khan Trophy, competed for by four international jumping teams, the USA, Portugal, Ireland and Great Britain. In 1958 the British riders won the trophy which was presented by the Begum Aga Khan.

Compared with the International Horse Show at White City, which many of the debs had attended in July, the nature of the horse show in Dublin was quite different. The scene in Ireland was more concentrated, much more esoteric. This was the Anglo-Irish at devotions, the cult of the horse pushed to the extremes of quasi-religious ritual. There was the protocol of the sacred enclosures: who was and who was not invited to have lunch in the Show Pavilion; who watched the proceedings from the sanctified interior of the president's box. There were the high priests, the executive committee, the judges and the stewards, almost all of them titled or of high military rank, descendants of the Irish landlord-breeders of the past. There was the singular costume of the votaries. Male aficionados, with their smooth brown trilbies pulled low over the brow at a rakish angle; the black-clad female judges of the ladies' hunter classes in their bowler hats and veils to keep the flies off, grim-faced with expertise. What was special about Dublin was the mix of the native Anglo-Irish with the foreign and exotic. Masters of foreign hunts from, for example, Rome, Milan and Philadelphia came with their wives to Dublin to choose themselves new horses. It was a week of professional solemnity that also, in the evenings, turned into a wild carnival. Nightly cocktail parties held in the foreign embassies in Dublin led on to the succession of riotous hunt balls.

Debs of 1958 had a personal connection with the horse show. One of our number, the Hon. Diana Connolly-Carew, was a star performer. Diana was the daughter of Lord and Lady Carew, owners of Castletown at Celbridge, Co. Kildare, the largest house in Ireland, lauded in the *Tatler* as 'possessing an estate of over 4,000 acres providing fine shooting and fishing as well as many coverts yielding foxes'. Although by the late 1950s there were signs of an emergent anti-hunting lobby there was no sense whatsoever amongst any of the

The Hon. Diana Connolly-Carew and her brother the
Hon. Patrick Connolly-Carew

horse-riding people I then mingled with that foxhunting could be
cruel. Castletown was at the centre of the Anglo-Irish riding fraternity, ex-military in bias. At the meets which were held there hunting lieutenant colonels would be out in force and children received an early
indoctrination. Diana saw her first meet from a pram at the age of six
months, started riding at four, went out hunting at seven. Still only
seventeen, in the year before her debut, Diana was appointed Joint
Master of the North Kildare Hounds, making her the youngest Master
of Foxhounds in the world. Her progress in the show ring had been
equally precocious. She was eight when she first rode in the Dublin
Horse Show and was well on the way to becoming a member of the
Irish jumping team by 1958. In the equally testing human contests of
the Season she had not been a natural, a shy self-conscious girl who
was apt to be referred to not entirely kindly as 'the Irish horse'. But in
the Dublin show ring she seemed quite another person, authoritative,
marvellous, a debutante transformed.

The public balls in Horse Show Week were all linked to Irish hunts:

the Louth, the Tipperary, the Kildare, the Galway Blazers. Many of the men wore hunting pink which brought a heightened intensity, a touch of latent violence, to the proceedings. As the night wore on the scene became semi-orgiastic: people dancing on the tables, men and women in formal evening dress pelting one another with champagne corks and bread rolls. It was the tradition that the men became absolutely blotto and sensationally puerile. Lemon and orange peel was cast on the dance floor and doused with champagne so that the dancers lost their footing. Class victimisation broke out towards the end of the Meath Hunt Ball at the Gresham Hotel in 1958, as reported in the *Daily Express*. A group of drunk, determined men grabbed the assistant head waiter, Bobby Purcell, and frogmarched him towards the garden fountain. 'His crime: he had remonstrated with them about their hooliganism through-out the night. They grabbed him as magnums of champagne spilled to the floor and hunting horns blared the end of the dance. Everyone stood back and watched as the struggling shouting Purcell was hustled to the fountain.' Their progress was halted by 'a pretty 22 year old Irish Society girl', Sarah Perry, who yelled, 'Leave that man alone. Stop it at once you damn fools.' Her intervention was reported under the headline SOCIETY GIRL DEFIES THE DEBS' DELIGHTS. An attempt was made to blame the English debutante contingent, the aliens: '. . . it was just another of those disgusting English deb stunts. They come over here and ruin our hunt balls.' But such violent behaviour was not typical of England where class confrontation at deb dances did not advance beyond a formulaic ribbing of the waiters. Manhandling was another matter, more endemic of an Ireland where widespread and bitter class warfare was part of recent history.

In that week of far too many celebrations of the horse one flushed and hectic party ran on into another. The night of the Tipperary Hunt Ball was also that of the ball at Luttrellstown Castle given by Mr and Mrs Valerian Stux-Rybar for the members of the international teams. The indefatigable Jennifer contrived to be at both, leaving the Tipperary Hunt Ball after the midnight cabaret and reaching Luttrellstown in time for the bacon and egg breakfast. Elsa Maxwell, the American society gossip columnist, 'the hostess with the mostest', was also at the ball. It was the first time I had seen this famous figure, America's top party giver in the years between the wars. Born in small-town Iowa, she left school at fourteen to work as a theatre pianist. By the 1920s she had become an entertainer on a lavish scale, hiring her-

The Kildare Hunt Club meet at Castletown, Lord and Lady Carew's house at Celbridge, Co. Kildare

self out as party giver *extraordinaire* for high society and royalty. She gave legendary transvestite costume parties and was the inventor of scavenger hunts, a craze in the thirties. My mother would tell stories of the scavenger hunts – motorised treasure hunts which followed obscure clues – she and her friends would go out on from Knott Park.

Elsa Maxwell's enormous range of contacts provided the material for her widely syndicated gossip columns which, even by today's standards, verged on the scurrilous. By the time of the ball at Luttrellstown La Maxwell was well into her seventies, holding court from a wheelchair, a decaying ancient glamour girl, her great mound of flesh bejewelled, her scant hair in corrugated waves. Did she and Jennifer converse? I wish I knew. The meeting of two such rival goddesses of gossip, oppositional in style, one so toughly transatlantic and flamboyant, one so English and correct, would have been as potentially explosive as a meeting between Queen Elizabeth I and Mary Queen of Scots. Maxwell's trademark was tactlessness on a heroic scale. She had already dismissed the debs of 1958 as 'off a production line', not a judgement to endear her to our mothers. She had made what was reported as a 'tempestuous outburst' on arriving in Dublin. Elsa Maxwell was role model for the new rude women emerging in the fifties: compulsive international scene-maker Lady Docker, such fearsome female columnists as Nancy Spain.

Luttrellstown House, Co. Dublin

Luttrellstown is an astonishingly beautiful romantic Gothic castle like a backdrop to a ballet, complete with an ornamental lake, a Doric temple and a shivery sham ruin. It had been a wedding present from her father Ernest Guinness, of the banking and brewing dynasties, to Aileen, eldest of the three so called 'Fabulous Guinness Girls', on her first marriage to the Hon. Brinsley Plunket. Aileen, recently remarried to the Yugoslavian interior decorator Valerian Stux-Ryber, was our hostess for that night. When Penny Graham noted in her diary the '100s of princes and millionaires' at Luttrellstown she was only exaggerating slightly. The Stux-Rybers entertained in the grandest post-war manner, on the cosmopolitan circuit of royalty, film stars and the very very rich. The ball that night had an atmosphere of international glamour that made most of the English country house dances look homespun. Aileen Stux-Ryber was in green and white printed chiffon with splendid emerald and diamond jewellery; the Begum Aga Khan wore a white mink stole (it was a chilly Irish evening) over a pale orchid silk sari. The members of the International Horse Show teams had come on to the ball from an official dinner given in their honour by the army at McKee Barracks, attended by the Irish Minister for Defence, and many of the officers were in uniform. There was dancing in the ornate ballroom lit by magnificent crystal chandeliers. A second dance floor had been made across the lawns, surrounded by great urns planted with pink convolvuluses and adorned with pink and yellow ribbons. The flowers for the dance had been flown in from Japan. Twice during the evening twenty or so pipers came and played outside the house before disappearing back into the trees. It was a night of immense splendour that contained a certain sadness, a mood of valediction, a little like the ball on the eve of Waterloo.

In the background lay the sense of the long tragedy of Ireland, bitterness to be intensified over the next decades, and the particular Anglo-Irish weirdness of the Guinness family itself. Our hostess Aileen Stux-Ryber with her penchant for crude practical jokes and scatological humour, apt to accost her male guests like a comic Irish servant pointing out the lavatory: 'D'ye want to *go*, Surr?' The second Guinness sister, Oonagh, who was also at the ball with Miguel Ferreras, the Cuban dress designer she had recently married in New York. For one sister to marry a bisexual designer of saturnine good looks is understandable if risky; for two sisters to do it looks like carelessness. Oonagh too had been given a house by her indulgent father, Ernest Guinness. This house, Luggala in the Wicklow mountains, had been destroyed by fire in 1956 but was rebuilt as an exact facsimile. The Guinness sisters had a whole long history of outré personal relationships, unexplained accidents, mysterious deaths of children; they lived at an extraordinary level of insouciance, charmingly, effusively neglectful of the rules of responsibility and common sense. The high-pitched horror that has lingered round the Guinness family has been maliciously captured by the writer Caroline Blackwood, daughter of Maureen, Marchioness of Dufferin and Ava, third of the 'Golden Guinness Girls'. Blackwood's short story 'How You Love Our Lady' and her bleakly comic novel *Great Granny Webster* draws on her own memories of growing up in a wildly hedonistic but fast declining Ireland, of which the ball at Luttrellstown provided a small glimpse.

Who did I dance with to the Cuban band under the floodlit cypress tree? No, not the Maharajah of Jaipur. I have explained the deb's essential strategy to find herself a partner she could count on for the evening. I had found myself an ally the first night I got to the Waddingtons at Beaulieu. Did the emotions follow practical necessity? In any case by the night of the ball at Luttrellstown we were tightly clasped together and I felt I was in love. Bill Montgomery was so young that he had only just left Eton. I think he was related to my hostess, brought in to even up the girls and boys. The Montgomerys

William Montgomery, Master of the Eton beagles in summer 1958

lived at Grey Abbey, Co. Down, an old Anglo-Irish family of landowners and clerics. I imagine Grey Abbey as a kind of northern Irish
Northanger Abbey, its architecture Gothic and high-pitched, and Bill
as a Jane Austen hero of the best intentions and most gentlemanly
aspect. He was handsome with an early nineteenth-century finesse. We
left the house party and went off on bicycles to Drogheda. We roamed
over the cliffs above the sea and kissed in caves. When Christy the
chauffeur came to take me to the airport for the return journey I was
desolate. A few scrawled letters arrived on azure blue Grey Abbey
writing paper. But we were just posh teenagers trying out the possibilities, not ready for commitment. Devotion petered out. A decade later,
by which time I was writing for the *Guardian* and thought of myself
as an acerbic left-wing critic, it seemed incredible that my first love
had been the Master of the Eton Beagles. But Bill was a sweet boy.

I have described the decline of the English country houses as I was
aware of it travelling from house party to house party in 1958. The

problems were the same in Ireland only more so. Up to the 1860s the Anglo-Irish landlords, installed in their fine houses, lived lavishly and confidently, managing the upkeep of their large estates. But since then, as Terence Dooley details in his comprehensive study *The Decline of the Big House in Ireland*, there had been an inexorable process of decay. From the late nineteenth century onwards Irish landlords' disposable incomes were diminished; the Land League put pressure on the old ways of land management, transferring tracts of land from the landowners to tenants; the extravagantly sociable life of the estate-owning Anglo-Irish families was destroyed for ever by the painful upheavals of the First World War. Nor must we forget that inherent Irish doominess, a heritage of melancholy that could transform an Irish mansion all too easily into a poetic ruin. 'All Irish houses are deeply romantic, and on the verge of disintegration even when splendid', wrote James Lees-Milne, an expert on the species. 'All are tragic, mournful, nostalgic. The atmosphere dead, breathless, green and dank.' Queen Alexandra, in signing the visitors' book at Mount Stewart, added her regal judgement, 'A beautiful place, but damp'.

The decline of Irish houses was of course exacerbated in a way that had no English parallel by the burning of big houses during the Irish 'Troubles': the violent struggles for independence from 1919 to 1921, followed by two years of Civil War. It has been estimated that 199 big houses were destroyed by Irish revolutionaries in just fifteen months from January 1922 to April 1923. These events were so traumatic since often the incendiarists were personally known to the victims. They could be neighbours, employees or tenants of the landowners. The horrors and the tragedies caused some Anglo-Irish to abandon their inheritance. For example, after the shooting of the daughter of Glenstall Castle's owner, Sir Charles Barrington, in an IRA ambush in 1921 the family left Ireland and four years later sold off the estate. The tensions of that time have been marvellously captured in William Trevor's novel *The Story of Lucy Gault*.

The emotional reverberations of the Troubles lingered. The ebullience of the Anglo-Irish landowners was ended. The memoirs of the Irish peer Lord Castletown, written in the early 1920s, dwell regretfully on the 'most cheery shooting parties' of his youth at Strattan, which combined 'the best of sport and the best of claret'; hearty gatherings at Castle Bernard 'one of the cheeriest houses in Ireland, where many a practical joke was played'; the heart-warming conviviality of well-remembered house parties at Glenart 'with its two kind hosts, great woodcock, shooting and high pheasants'. These joys made a stark contrast to the muted atmosphere of a much-changed Ireland of the years after the Troubles: 'Alas! Those jolly days are over, and many of those kind hosts have gone west, never to be replaced, and the lovely old houses are sold or shut up or burnt.'

By the late 1950s, when I first went to Ireland, the plight of the vast old Irish country houses was all too evidently worse than that of their counterparts in England. Southern Ireland had no equivalent to the National Trust in offering a safety net for historically or architecturally important Irish houses threatened with demolition. Nor could Ireland provide a ready audience for owners prepared to open houses to the public. There was still a residue of social divisiveness, resentment of the landowners. Ireland had no aspirational middle class. The particular dilemma of the remnants of the Anglo-Irish ascendancy was sensitively stated by Elizabeth Bowen in her book *Bowen's Court*, an account of the house built in the eighteenth century by her family near Kildorrery, Co. Cork. She felt a deep devotion for this house which also features in her novel *The Last September*. She provides a clear-eyed, though affectionate, analysis of the self-destructive nature of the Irish gentry into which she had been born: '. . . its isolations, what might be called its outlandishness, makes Anglo-Irish society microcosmic'. Their social isolation had made the Anglo-Irish unusually dependent on the property they owned, attached with a great passion of possessiveness to their ramifications of house, garden, farms and fields, their animals, their children. But in a modern world such degrees of isolation were not practically sustainable. By 1959 Bowen's Court was sold and soon afterwards demolished. This was a common story. The 1988 exhibition *Vanishing Houses of Ireland* was a melancholy record of some five hundred Irish houses, some of poignant beauty, lost in the course of the twentieth century.

In summer 1959, the year after the Season, I was back in Dublin for a re-run of the Horse Show. This time I was staying with Rosemary FitzGerald who, as attentive readers will remember, had escaped from the Season in some boredom and dismay. Rosemary lived at Borris, Co. Carlow, with her mother who had been married first to the Marquess of Kildare, Rosemary's father, and secondly to Lieutenant-Colonel Archibald Macalpine Downie. Mrs Macalpine Downie, now on her own again, had retreated to the house of her forebears, the

Borris House, Co. Carlow

princely Gaelic dynasty of McMorrough Kavanagh. Borris is an enormous and architecturally complicated house, originally built in the eighteenth century around the ancient tower house of the McMorrough Kavanaghs, partially destroyed in the 1798 Rebellion, rebuilt in early nineteenth century Tudoresque with a wonderful decorative classical interior. Its accretions of period and personality made Borris a peculiarly fascinating place.

In the mid-eighteenth century, before its restoration, it was part of the story of the 'ladies of Llangollen', the two cross-dressing women friends Lady Eleanor Butler and Sarah Ponsonby. Lady Eleanor was kept a virtual prisoner at Borris after they first attempted to run away together until, one night, she managed to escape and the ladies eventually set up house in Wales, objects of curiosity and speculation. A century later Borris was inherited by Arthur McMorrough Kavanagh who, in spite of the misfortune of having been born with only the stumps of arms and legs, lived a formidably energetic life, riding, fishing, shooting, travelling in Russia, Persia and India, returning to become MP for Co. Carlow and a member of the Irish Privy Council. There are many pleasing stories about the limbless Kavanagh, apparently a man not just of great courage but endearing innocence. The best concerns the visit he made to Lady de Vesci at Abbeyleix in Co. Laois. Arriving at the station he said, 'It is extraordinary. I have not been here for over ten years and yet the stationmaster still recognised me.'

In his early nineteenth century travelogue *The Beauties of Ireland*

J.N. Brewer made the comment that 'the estate of Borris would appear to be formed by the hand of nature for the site of a baronial mansion', citing the rich woodlands, the River Barrow flowing on the edge of the estate, the picturesque mountain stream, the Blackstairs mountains forming a background vista of unusual grandeur. 'Convenience', wrote Brewer, 'in this noble residence, is carefully blended with ornament.' To me too, when I first saw it, Borris seemed a kind of beau-ideal of Irish country houses. Except that by the 1950s it was becoming a little desolate. With its hundreds of rooms, its chapel and its library, the gardens, the outlying estate, Borris needed an army of servants and specialist workers to sustain it. There had once, for example, been four masons all called Kelly. But the expert Kellys were now dead and gone. Finances were not easily talked about in those days, money being a hidden subject much like sex, but even I could sense that finances at Borris were at constant crisis point. According to Terence Dooley's detailed survey of Irish country houses Rosemary's grandfather Arthur McMorrough Kavanagh left assets of only £23,000 when he died in 1953. As far as one could tell there was very little left. Rosemary's mother appeared to be receiving little in the way of support from her two ex-husbands. The dashing Marquess of Kildare, who had taken up flying, was setting up an aviation company in Dublin. Colonel Macalpine Downie had converted an old Brixham trawler into a twelve-berth luxury cruiser running between Oban and the Western Isles. These were typical of the hit-or-miss occupations to which the aristocracy resorted in the years after the war. Rosemary's mother was certainly not without resourcefulness. She made a little money training and selling horses. Indeed in retrospect one can feel only admiration for her courage in bringing up her family alone in that vast acreage. At least at Borris no mushrooms were growing on the drawing-room ceiling as apparently they were at Rossmore Park. But the house, for all its beauty, felt too huge, a little tragic, on the edge of decrepitude.

This was not the histrionic Irish narrative of Caroline Blackwood's *Great Granny Webster*. Life at Borris was much closer to the quietly declining Anglo-Irish life as described by Molly Keane in her novels, those brilliant black comedies based in the minutiae of keeping up appearances while the whole fabric of society disintegrates. If you keep on hunting, fishing, shooting in their proper seasons you scarcely notice the money pouring quietly away. Molly Keane had been born in Co. Kildare and was a friend of the family at Borris. In the novel *Good Behaviour* the central character of Aroon St Charles is based loosely but recognisably on Rosemary. The child pushed into horsiness. The young girl, 'fiercely shy', arriving at the unknown house party. The relief to find a partner, albeit an old drunk one. The horror and humiliation when even he disappears, leaving her stranded. The

Lady Rosemary FitzGerald, a prizewinner in the childrens' pony competition at the Dublin Spring Show, with her mother Mrs Macalpine Downie (top); and Lady Rosemary FitzGerald and Fiona MacCarthy at the Dublin Horse Show in 1959. Rosemary's sister, Lady Nesta FitzGerald, is on far left

protracted nightmare of the rowdy, lecherous Dublin Hunt Balls.

Rosemary was defiantly anti-deb, almost pathologically opposed to good behaviour. That summer in Dublin she used me as her ally. She had been brought up in the Anglo-Irish horse riding elite, hard training and competitive. She could have been another Diana Connolly-Carew. But when we went to the horse show it was with groans and jibes. We mooched about together in a partnership of dissidence, not looking at the riders but discussing Samuel Beckett and W.B. Yeats. A picture in her album shows the two of us together in a group of horsey girls, one of them her sister Nesta. We stand out from the others as self-consciously superior non-performers. Rosemary in her caption calls us 'amicable strangers'. I was a bona fide stranger at the horse show. Rosemary had come to count herself a stranger too.

Why had Rosemary been so resistant to the Season? I find it very difficult to write of Rosemary. Even for a professional biographer – perhaps especially for a biographer? – there are inhibitions in attempting to account for the feelings and behaviour of someone who is still a dearest friend. I look at the pictures: Rosemary at a debs' tea party early in the Season, sitting at a table exchanging desultory girlish chatter, looking ill at ease in her new-that-morning André Bernard hairdo. No one wanted her address since no dance was in the offing. Rosemary outside the palace, coming to make her curtsey, swathed in her blue silk dress and that awful flower-pot hat. I listen to her stories. One night she had reluctantly agreed to meet another deb, an old school friend Gina Ward, at a cocktail party at the House of Lords. She arrived. No sign of Gina. She knew no one. She was bored and miserable, making anguished conversation to a mass of total strangers. After an hour she left. She had failed to diagnose that she had arrived at the wrong party, this one being no worse an ordeal than the rest.

Part of the problem was that Rosemary, in practical terms, was ill equipped for the rigours of the Season. Her only dress, she now claims, was the one she was presented in. Besides, 'skirts were short that year and mine were long'. But there was obviously more to it than that. One can partly explain her resistance to the Season as a symptom of the time that we grew up in. We were on the edge of a new decade of rebellion and questioning in which even the children of the entrenched upper classes began to challenge the social conventions. Those were to be the years of dropping out and hippydom, student protests and feminist agendas. Rosemary was a 1960s girl unhappily in 1958 debs' clothing. She could not take the Season's rampant silliness and she understood the way in which it could corrupt. Having fun? What to some debutantes was 'fabulous', 'tremendous' could appear the exact opposite to others who still look back to that Season with a deep enduring horror after what is now almost half a century.

CHAPTER EIGHT

The Scottish Balls

For debutantes coming out in 1958, Scotland was the last stop, the absolutely final fling. There was separatism between Scotland and England in the matter of curtseys, as in so much else, and the very last curtseys to the Queen were made in Scotland by Scottish debutantes at a ceremony in the Throne Room at the Palace of Holyroodhouse in Edinburgh on 3 July. The ceremonial was different in that both presenters and presented made a curtsey. The mothers or female sponsors curtseyed first and then the daughters, adding up to a grand total of more than six hundred curtseys. The final Scottish debutante to 'pass the Presence' was Miss Fiona Macrae who lived in Edinburgh and was presented by Mrs David MacIntyre. Outside in the palace quadrangle light music, played under the colonnade by the Band of the 1st Battalion the Black Watch, wafted up to the Throne Room on that long and somewhat arduous summer afternoon.

The Duke of Edinburgh was back in his titular city seated beside a Queen who was dressed for the late afternoon presentation ceremony in a full-skirted dress of primrose yellow lace with matching straw hat. She wore a diamond brooch and four strands of pearls. The Duchess of Devonshire, the Countess of Errol and Mrs Alexander Abel Smith were in attendance. So was the High Constable of the Palace of Holyroodhouse, the Hereditary High Constable and the Hereditary Standard Bearer. The Queen's Bodyguard, the Royal Company of Archers, carried longbows with ferocious little bundles of arrows thrust into their belts.

There was a primitivism about the presentations at Holyroodhouse which made Buckingham Palace seem almost easygoing. Scotland in the 1950s was still a feudal country of intense conservatism. The landowners were enduring in what seemed very much the pre-war manner in their great baronial houses set in huge estates attended by a still forelock-tugging house staff and estate staff, gardeners and game-keepers. The rural population had remained relatively static, centred on these tracts of land which provided its employment. The sense of tribal loyalties was strong. The Season in Scotland was another world away from coming out in England. As the social commentator Nigel Dempster recollected it 'the Scottish Season was always very grand, with the Perth races and the eightsome reels'. My own memories are mainly very vivid visual ones of a solid and solemn but also garish place. Those fantastically turreted Scottish baronial castles seen across broad vistas rising from the murky hills; their warlike entrance halls hung with antique weaponry, stags' heads and curiously interlocking sets of antlers; the surprise of seeing tartan used not just for clothing but as decor, lengths and lengths of it covering the sofas, draped across the walls. Most of all what I remember are vast distances between the houses in which the debutantes were staying and those we were dining in or dancing in, and the terror – more acute than it had ever been in England – about how, having arrived in some strange castle down many miles of driveway, I would ever get back home.

Some of the Scottish debs who curtseyed to the Queen at Holyroodhouse had already been in London for the southern Season. There the Scottish debs, like say the Irish debs or the girls from East Anglia, were easily identifiable. Though most of them had other friends, there were tribal ties between them and they would stick together in a jam. They were out in full force for the Royal Caledonian Ball, annual gathering point for social Scots in London, held in mid-May at Grosvenor House. This was a Scottish ball in all the formal splendour of Highland evening dress: kilt worn with black broadcloth jacket for the men; for the ladies, full-length dresses with clan tartan sashes draped across the breast and pinned with a large round brooch on the left shoulder. It was further stipulated that tiaras, orders and decorations should be worn. The 10th Duke of Atholl, the eligible bachelor high on the lists of mothers of the Scottish debs, led the dancers for the set reels down the same processional staircase the girls had descended to make their massed curtseys at Queen Charlotte's Ball. The Caledonian Ball was organised according to strict rules both of dress and of performance. It had the beautiful exuberance, the bal-letic satisfaction, of Scottish dancing properly performed. For the

The 110th Royal Caledonian Ball held at Grosvenor House in May 1958. Leading the dancers down for the set reels: the young Duke of Atholl, one of the top deb escorts of 1958, with Lady Malvina Murray, Captain John and Lady Gillian Anderson, Major David Butter and Serena Murray (top); and 1958 deb Lady Carolyn Townshend with Alastair MacInnes of the Cameron Highlanders

Scottish debutantes it had served as a rehearsal for the formal balls in Scotland later in the year.

Early in August the debs were on the move again, some stopping for the dances in Northumberland en route. I was, at a guess, amongst thirty or forty debs from England who attended at least some of the Scottish balls. The crucial date that dominated all departures and arrivals was, as always in the Season, an important sporting fixture: the beginning of the grouse shooting season on the 12th August, the so-called 'Glorious Twelfth'. Harold Macmillan, the Prime Minister, was reported as among the first to travel north, photographed in the plus fours worn with brogues and heavy knee socks and carrying the shooting stick that became the political cartoonists' stock in trade. The Queen too had embarked from Southampton on the royal yacht *Britannia*, and was heading for north Scotland for a tour around the Isles. Cheering crowds were there to greet her at Fort William. She proceeded to Balmoral where the royal family habitually gathered to spend the summer holiday. Jennifer reported in the *Tatler* for 27 August: 'Much of London's social life has moved to Scotland, where grouse shooting opened very quietly on the Twelfth as birds are scarce this year owing to the bad weather during the nesting season.' The birds had suffered from the downpours as the debs had. All the same, Jennifer tells us, on opening day at Quaich in Invernessshire, Viscount Bearsted, his two brothers and a party of friends shot 90$^{1}/_{2}$ brace while the Earl of Inchcape and his party of five guns bagged 62 brace over Glenfernate. In 1958 sporting activities were sacrosanct. Three or four years later, in an age sharpened by satire, it would become impossible for grouse-shooting exploits to be reported in such non-ironic terms.

Coming out dances in Scotland were all held in private houses. In this ultra-traditional landowning society, where the home was very often literally a castle, it would have crossed no one's mind to hold a dance in a hotel. As in England the young guests who did not live near-by were allotted out to house parties. Some debs from the South were in Scotland already, staying with their families in rented shooting lodges or, in greater comfort, at Gleneagles, the luxury hotel in Perthshire. Gleneagles had been built in French chateau-style in 1924 by the Caledonian Railway Company who equipped the hotel with its own station. It was advertised as a 'Riviera in the Highlands' but really it was more of a Scottish Dorchester with two famous eighteen-hole golf courses attached. The hotel was only open in the summer months.

The same English, continental and especially American families returned to Gleneagles year after year for the golfing and the shooting, the tennis and the putting, the swimming pool, the squash court and the table tennis, then considered the essential components of an all-ages summer holiday at a period when people were still satisfied with fairly simple pleasures. The fathers stayed at Gleneagles for the days when they had no invitations to the grouse moors. The debs from England used it as a rest home between dances. I think it was the mothers who lost out at Gleneagles with little occupation besides having their hair done and varnishing their nails.

The Scottish Season lasted on right through August and September. One of the private dances which was typical of Scotland in 1958 was given for Tessa Prain and Ann Carington Smith at the Prains' own home, Mugdrum, near Newburgh in Fife, a long seventeenth-century house in a wonderful position overlooking the River Tay with farming land around. Tessa was a smiling vivacious debutante, a good skier and enthusiastic huntress, riding out with the Fife Foxhounds. She had been in London for the Season returning north to make her curtsey at Holyroodhouse. Her father was a member of Her Majesty's Bodyguard in Scotland. A piper of the Black Watch played outside as guests arrived at Mugdrum for Tessa's dance. There was a blue and white striped marquee, built out for dancing, and a small outdoor dance floor with a beer and iced coffee bar on the terrace that looked over the river. An iced coffee bar was high sophistication for Scotland at the time as was the decor of aquariums and fishing nets and lobster pots. It was a balmy late summer night with a full moon. There is a sense of time-warp in Jennifer's account of it: 'Tessa, dark and pretty, with exceptionally good manners, looked enchanting in a long full-skirted dress of sea green faille. Ann, who is fair, wore a beautiful white crinoline of lace and chiffon. Her young sister Miss Rose Carington Smith, who was home for the holidays, was allowed to come to the dance.' Good manners, lace crinolines, parental permissions: deb dances in the sixties would never be like this.

Holly Urquhart's coming out ball took place much further north, at Craigston Castle near Turriff, north of Aberdeen. Her ancestor John Urquhart had completed the rebuilding of Craigston in 1607, a spectacularly simple double tower house with two side wings. Another ancestor, Sir Thomas Urquhart, is famous as translator of the first three books of Rabelais and as author of the idiosyncratic treatise

Tessa Prain and Ann Carington Smith before their dance at Mugdrum in Fife; and Dancers at Tessa Prain and Ann Carington Smith's ball

Holly Urquhart with her parents before her dance at Craigston Castle

Ekskubalauron, known as *The Jewel*, published in 1651. The family antecedents were intellectual and literary. The receiving group at Holly's coming out – handsome father, *soignée* mother, golden-haired young daughter in a white dress like the girl in a Winterhalter portrait – appears as an ideal aristocratic Scottish family. But, like so many other family group pictures of that unsettled period, it was not as conventional as it first appears. The proud father, Bruce Urquhart, holder of what Holly now describes as 'semi-Socialist views', differed from the usual pattern of the Scottish laird in that he held a salaried job as a forester which helped to sustain his 'small, quite poor but very productive estate'. He was not available for grouse shooting on weekdays because he was at work. Holly's mother, more of a London socialite, friend of the *Vogue* journalist-photographer Lee Miller, was still slowly adjusting to the differently arduous demands of life in the north of Scotland in that post-war period. The early spring weeks she spent in London for her daughter's presentation, living in a rented houseboat on the Thames, had been a temporary return to the metropolitan life she had now left. Holly herself in fact had found the Season of very little relevance. To a girl who had lived in Rome and already acquired the Italian lover who followed her to Britain, the debs appeared a bit naive and the young men very callow. She got through the months in London by renting a room in a Catholic girls' club, working in an art gallery, enduring the pre-dance dinner parties (she needed to eat somewhere) and taking the bus back to the Catholic club, avoiding all the dances except those being given by friends of her mother's where her absence would be spotted. In these circumstances Holly's return to the ancestral castle in north Scotland, a scene in which her role was to play the lovely ingénue, had a certain underlying piquancy.

What gave the Scottish coming-out balls their special character? First of all, very often, the splendour of the setting. Craigston Castle is a place of beautiful complexity, sturdy and yet evanescent, like one of those dream buildings in a late nineteenth-century etching by Sir David Young Cameron. No need to bring in the decorators for a ball. In this and other Scottish castles the architecture was itself the decor, a constant entertainment of corbellings and gables, parapets and archways, grotesque carvings and gargoyle water spouts. At Scottish dances, compared with coming out in England, there tended to be more of a social mix in that local people, tenants and estate workers might be asked to join the dancing in the marquee after dinner. This custom belonged to the still-present feudal tradition, the concept of the largesse of the laird. At most private balls conventional ballroom dances alternated with the simpler of the Scottish country dances, for instance the Dashing White Sergeant and the Eightsome. As one Scottish deb remembers 'the bands were usually execrable, when attempting anything other than the Scottish Country stuff'.

The private coming out dances had been neatly slotted into the larger framework of the Scottish social calendar: the Highland Games and, adjuncts to the games, the Highland Summer Balls. The main balls were held in Skye and Oban, Inverness and Perth. At these daunting assemblies the age level was higher and the protocol was stricter than at dances in debutantes' own homes. For the balls in Skye long dresses for the women were compulsory. At all balls in the Highlands – Perth and further north – the men who were entitled to be kilted wore their kilts with sporrans and diamond-pattern knee socks, making a brilliantly vivid scene. However Fife, being a kingdom, had special regulations and if anyone were ignorant or careless enough to come to a ball in Fife wearing a kilt, he would be fined £5.

The Highland Balls were formal programmed dances. We were given little cards with 'Engagement' slots from 1 to 20 waiting to be filled. For the Scottish debs the reels, of course, were second nature: Tessa Prain, for instance, claimed to have started Scottish dancing almost as soon as she could walk. But, for visiting debs from England, Scottish dances in themselves could be a source of terror: we were expected to take part in complicated sequences such as those in Hamilton House where a wrong move could upset the whole pattern of the ballroom. For debs more used to foxtrotting at the Savoy the Scottish balls necessitated learning a new language. Anxious hostesses would sometimes coach the debs in Scottish dancing in case our incompetence disgraced her house party. How to flirt while dancing reels? This was again a new experience: no cheek-to-cheek endearments, no smooching in the shadows. Eye contact was all.

If the debutante Season in England could be tiring, Scotland was exhaustion of quite another order as I am reminded by a note on my

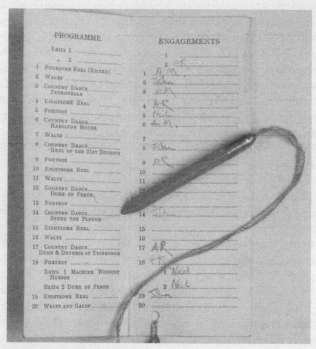

Highland Ball programme

old programme for the Perth Ball. This gives official warning that the Supper Room Service will be closing at 5.15 a.m. Back home perhaps by 6.00 and your host would be reminding you the party for the grouse shoot would be leaving in three hours.

I had lived in Scotland already, conscious of and awestruck by its over-whelming maleness even as a child. Towards the end of the war we had spent a spring and summer at Fort George, living in a house just outside the walls of the massive artillery fortifications built by the English after the 1745 uprising as a defence against the threat from the Highlands and especially the Jacobites. The great grey fortress-town was built on land jutting west into the Moray Firth at Ardersier, eleven miles north of Inverness. Fort George is enormously powerful and grim. The military presence was a still large one in 1945, in what was then the depot of the Seaforth Highlanders. The children, in that wartime house of many children, a house allotted to Fort George's sec-ond in command, would sit on the wall in a row to watch the soldiers marching past towards the station with their bagpipes and drums.

It must, I think, have been appallingly depressing to my mother, widowed less than two years before, to spend that long summer in close proximity to such a powerhouse of war as Fort George with its bastions and firing steps, its ordnance stores and the Grand Magazine constructed to be capable of holding 2,500 barrels of powder. Such an emphasis on gunfire cannot have been a comfort to a young Royal Artillery war widow. But my mother was endemically stoical. The large house, Cromal Lodge, was shared between three families: three mothers, my own mother and her friends Mollie Maynard and Barbara Buchanan; three nannies, our own Isa, Nanny MacLeod from the Highlands and the unfortunately named Nanny Smelling, victim of inevitable stink bombs from small boys. The eight children rampaged around together. In such set-ups in the country it was usual for the children to lead almost independent existences, finding their own amusements, racing through the bluebell woods, thronging past the stable with the carter and his horses, taking the narrow lane that led down to the shingle beach which, once the tide went out, opened out into a dank expanse of muddy sand. On VE Day in early May 1945 we gazed transfixed at a big bonfire on the hillside celebrating Germany's final capitulation. Three months later another, even larger bonfire, was lit on the ramparts of the fort itself to mark the Japanese surrender, and Emperor Hirohito was burned in effigy. An extra excitement for the children was the fireworks, the first fireworks we had ever seen.

One wet summer afternoon the little gang of wartime children had decided we should play at doctors and nurses up in one of the second-floor bedrooms of the Lodge. I, one of the youngest and more passive, was designated patient, stripped and put to bed to await examination by the doctor. The then eight-year-old Andrew Buchanan was designated doctor, attended by small nurses and assistants, his brother, his sisters, a whole entourage of children. The examination was so thorough and so public it provoked my first infant intimations of sex. Little Andrew, the doctor, who succeeded to his father's baronetcy, is now, through one of those magic transformations, Sir Andrew Buchanan, Lord Lieutenant of Nottingham, a figure of considerable official gravitas, the Queen's representative in the county. I have never quite dared tell him of his key role in my burgeoning sexual awareness in a remote Highland lodge at the end of the Second World War.

When I returned to Scotland as an almost grown-up woman it was to stay in a house party at Rowallan. Rowallan Castle is near Kilmarnock in South Ayrshire. I took the night sleeper from King's Cross, getting off at Ayr and finally arriving at the castle around breakfast time. The porridge was still hot on the mahogany sideboard and the house party assembled. The men were deep in talk about politics. This was an austere high-minded Scots-liberal household. Lady Rowallan's brother was Jo Grimond, then leader of the Liberal Party whose prospects were thought to be in the ascendant since Mark Bonham Carter's surprise victory at Torrington. Lord Rowallan was at the time Chief Scout of the British Commonwealth and Empire, often photographed at international scout gatherings. He was a very tall, almost a godlike figure, his appearance bringing a touch of ancient drama to the camp-fire choruses. Lord Rowallan was a man who attracted, indeed demanded, veneration. In July of 1958, he had been installed as Knight of the Most Ancient and Most Noble Order of the Thistle in St Giles's Cathedral. This was shortly before my visit to Rowallan. Impressive as he was in public life, his domestic persona was a little bit unbending. Sitting next to him at dinner I remember as an ordeal. The Chief Scout was not an easy conversationalist.

As so often at these parties it was the house itself that made the most impression. Rowallan Castle was the first important Scottish country

Rowallan Castle in South Ayrshire

mansion by the Scottish Arts and Crafts architect Sir Robert Lorimer. Its first occupant was the then rising young politician Cameron Corbett, later to be enobled as the 1st Lord Rowallan, who had entered Parliament as Liberal member for the Tradeston division of Glasgow. His wife, Alice, was from the Polson family whose fortune had been made from Brown & Polson cornflour. The resplendent new quasi-medieval castle intended as a marriage gift to Alice from her mother was completed, in somewhat reduced form, as her memorial after Alice's early death in 1902. Rowallan Castle is marvellously sited on a hill with views to the coast and Ailsa Craig in the far distance. It was built not as pastiche but in what then seemed a valid recreation of Scottish baronial style. The towers and the gables, the great entrance hall with a high-vaulted stone stairway rising to the left, give an initial impression of ancientness. The coat of arms above the doorway includes a crow and the motto *Deus Pascit Corvus*, God feeds the crows or corbies, a medievalist pun on the family name Corbett. But Rowallan is also an early modern building, like William Morris's Red House in its fluency of planning, in the way in which one room flows through into another. Rowallan is an open-plan castle, a masterpiece of optimism, air and light. When later I wrote a biography of Morris, Rowallan Castle became a kind of reference point, a prime example of the kind of architecture he inspired: architecture that gave old techniques of construction and craftsmanship a new validity; buildings so settled in, so rooted in, their landscapes one could simply not imagine they had ever not been there.

Rowallan became another reference point later, in the early 1960s, when the Hon. Arthur Corbett, the Rowallans' eldest surviving son and heir, abandoned Eleanor, the wife from a well-bred Scottish military family who had by then borne him four children, to pursue April Ashley, the transvestite model and nightclub performer, an equivocally glamorous figure of the time. April Ashley, born a boy and registered as George Jamieson, was brought up in Liverpool and sent to sea as a deck boy, emerging as a star performer in the drag act at Le Carrousel in Paris. Here he was talent-spotted by Salvador Dali who proposed painting him naked as *Hermaphroditos*. By the time that Arthur Corbett was courting April Ashley, she had undergone a sex-change operation in Casablanca involving removal of the testes, surgery on the outer genitalia and construction of a vagina, and changed her name by deed poll. Lord Rowallan, by now promoted from Chief Scout to Governor of Tasmania, is reported to have written to his son from hospital, where he was being treated for cancer of the throat, on the eve of Arthur's marriage to April Ashley entreating him to come to his senses. Arthur's younger brother Bobby, more in the spirit of the enterprise, sent a telegram reading 'Congratulations – can I be a bridesmaid?'

With its backdrop of nightclub drifters, Soho criminals, freak shows and idiotic toffs the April Ashley affair continued irresistibly through the 1960s, staple subject matter of the *News of the World*, linked mysteriously to the larger scandal of Profumo, until the marriage was annulled in November 1969 on grounds that April Ashley was still legally a man. Sociologically the episode shows the increased merging in the 1960s of the traditional classes with what my Uncle Justin would have designated riff-raff. Emotionally, for old men brought up with solemn attitudes to manliness and service to their country, ideals of stability, this was a testing time. What price Chief Scouts, let alone Knights of the Most Ancient and Most Noble Order of the Thistle, in a world not just of wildly fluctuating moral values but a world become so scientifically adept that the manly body itself could be reshaped?

Dodavoe, the shooting lodge at Glen Prosen, Kirriemuir

There was little premeditation in the Season. You took what fate allotted you. By and large you went where you were asked once your mother had approved it: 'Oh, that would be nice, darling.' You packed your leather suitcase, put your shoes into their shoebags, and again you trundled off. Towards the end of September I was staying in a shooting lodge right over on the other side of Scotland from Rowallan, at Kirriemuir near Forfar in Strathmore, Queen Mother country. Dodavoe, the main house, had been rented for the shooting by the mother of a deb's delight called Robert Douglas Miller. He had invited a group of trusty friends, many with similarly complicated names: George Bathurst Norman, Tony Seth-Smith, Ian Stewart-Brown. An equal number of girls were in the party, among them George's sister Victoria Bathurst Norman, Allegra Kent Taylor, Davina Windley. Seven brides for seven brothers, or something of the sort. The young people were housed in a building called the Bothy, a house of rudimentary facilities perhaps originally built for the servants or the ghillies. The girls and the young men had separate dormitories, the demarcation between sexes being rigidly adhered to except when a formal raid was carried out with the purpose of sewing up the men's pyjama trousers or suspending a wet sponge on a string above the pillow, one of many girlish wheezes dreamed up by Victoria and her great friend Davina, alias 'Daveegs'. I must say I regretted this strict

Grouse shooting in the Highlands: the transporter for the guns

sexual segregation, feeling by now a bit susceptible to one of the house party, Paddy Colquhoun, whose deep seductive voice reminded me of Frank Sinatra groaning out 'Begin the Beguine'.

Quite early in the morning the men would go out shooting, mustering each other in a self-important way. There were almost no women among the guns in those days. You were made to feel privileged if asked to be a beater. Otherwise it was merely picnic basket duty, meeting up with the shooters at some prearranged spot *en plein air* in the heather or in some shack or little cottage, always mildewy and cold, to which those fabulous cane picnic hampers would have been transported in a shooting brake. For people with no image of these now surely obsolete items of equipment I should explain they were rectangular baskets in red-brown lacquered wicker with buckled leather closures and carrying handles on each side. They contained knives, forks, spoons, Bakelite plates, Thermos flasks and food containers, all with their allotted places, packed neatly in two tiers. During the sixties it became a kind of fashion in anti-establishment novels, films and plays to use the shooting parties of the British aristocracy as a metaphor for the frenzy of slaughter in the First World War. I have often found that parallel a crude one. But there was indeed a quasi-military precision in the organisation of the lorries for the beaters, the truck for the guns and shot, the truck for the dead birds. And I have to admit that the ritual of bearing in the shooters' picnic baskets did make me feel a little like a maiden on a battlefield proffering the victuals to the brave.

In the evenings we danced, driving miles and miles to do so, the young men in their kilts, since this was indeed the Highlands, the girls in their long dresses. With an absolutely unflagging energy the Douglas Miller house party attended the Hot Air Ball at Brechin; the Angus Ball; and finally the Perth Balls, held during the week of the Perth Races at the end of September, bringing the Scottish Season to its official end. By the time I left for London I'd acquired an unexpected but, as it turned out, redundant talent: I had actually got quite good at reels.

Autumn was in the air. *The Times* was running features on dressing fashionably 'against the wind and rain' and suggesting easy recipes for cooking pheasant. By the end of September the debs were reassembling in a London in which, during their absence on the grouse moors, racial tensions had erupted into clashes with the police. The Queen too was returning to London from Balmoral. Preparations were in train for the State Visit in October of the President of the Federal Republic of Germany, Professor Theodor Heuss, the first German state visit since 1907 when the Kaiser visited King Edward VII at Windsor Castle. Heuss's state visit was felt by many to be premature, at a time when memories of battle and Blitz were raw. Through the autumn up to Christmas the debs' coming-out dances went inexorably on. In that year of record-breaking applications to curtsey there was also an unprecedented number of deb dances scheduled for the so-called 'Little Season'. More than thirty were announced for dates from 1 October to 17 December, most of them in London. For many of the debs, as they now describe it, the return to London for the 'Little Season' was not a happy time, but a period of anticlimax and anxiety. It was now half a year since they had made their curtseys. Just how long could one keep dancing? Some debs' parents were expecting a return on their investment. In such a conventional and circumscribed society, in which most girls' education had been minimal and in which a career was ridiculed as dowdy, what could the future hold?

An early marriage was an easy solution to the problem. The first engagement amongst debs of 1958 was that of Nicolette Harrison, daughter of a Lloyd's underwriter, whose betrothal to the Marquess of Londonderry was announced with what seemed almost indecent speed, only ten days after her presentation. Nicolette's future history developed into a form of tragedy peculiar to its age, as I shall be suggesting in a later chapter. But for the moment her destiny looked settled. She was married in May at Wilton Parish Church, photographed a little later as the radiant young bride at a party held to introduce her to the Londonderry estate staff and the tenants. For Nicolette the marriage market aspects of the Season were now of course superfluous. The marchioness left the debs to their devices, tore up her invitations and was rarely seen again.

It did not even have to be a thoroughgoing marriage. Mere engagement provided a valid form of life after the Season. Once announced in *The Times*, a deb's engagement burgeoned into a full-time occupation in itself, involving the compilation of the wedding list at Harrods and the General Trading Company, decisions on the details of the wedding ceremony and the reception, the choosing of bridesmaids and discussion of their dresses, their headdresses, their shoes. Of our year, one of the first engagements announced on 29 July, was that of the Countess Carolyn Czernin, the girl whose sexual knowingness had so unnerved me at the beginning of the Season. However, her engagement was cancelled just weeks later by a second, much bleaker, announcement in *The Times*, releasing her once again upon the market. Another early engagement, that of Margaret Hamilton to the Hon. Matthew Beaumont, ended satisfactorily – in deb terms – with her wedding in Brompton Oratory in the spring of 1959, attended by several of her still single fellow debutantes.

In fact the vast majority of debs ended that Season not married, not engaged and with little idea of how to occupy their lives. Charity work was the most obvious of the options. 'It is most interesting now to see the debutantes of last year blossoming out into the Committee Chairmen and hostesses at charity ball parties.' Gladys Boyd's approving comments in the *Sketch* on the charitable debs of 1957 suggested that these should be the role models for us. Jennifer in the *Tatler* noted with approval 1958 debs helping with tombolas and raising money for the Distressed Gentlefolk's Aid Association, always a favourite with the upper classes. There but for the grace of God go I. My own single venture into charity work during the Season had not been an encouragement. Having spent a whole morning on Sailors' Day standing near the Law Courts rattling a collection tin, one of thirty girls recruited by a deb's stepmum, the small, bustling Lady Coldstream, I received a little note from the King George's Fund for Sailors: 'You will be interest-

ed to know that your tin contained £1 3s 11d.' This confirmed me in
my view that the true beneficiaries of charitable work were less the
undoubtedly deserving soldiers, sailors, airmen, gentlefolk and so on,
more the unemployed debutantes whose empty hours it filled.

Could a deb get a job? Well yes and no. According to the arcane regulations of employment laid down by many of the parents of the debs,
a girl could work but only if the job was not demanding or indeed
even averagely remunerative. Modelling was approved of since it was
not only extremely lowly paid but was regarded (incorrectly) as somehow rather jolly, an extension of the Berkeley Debutante Dress Show.
Working in a florist with the kudos of say Pulbrook and Gould was
considered as absolutely fine and would stand the deb in good stead in
supervising the flowers in the lovely country mansion to which it was
expected she'd eventually gravitate. Working in an antique furniture
shop was similarly seen to have its uses for the future. Even cutting
sandwiches was regarded as permissable, according to what now
seems a preposterous scale of values, so long as sandwich-making
took place somewhere socially acceptable. Fortnum's Soda Fountain
was at that time almost wholly staffed by ex-debutantes.

I missed the Little Season. I refused all invitations for the autumn
with an alibi so cast iron and convincing I too might have been mar-
rying a 9th marquess or an 11th earl: 'Lady Hayter's daughter Teresa
goes up to Oxford this term as does her friend Miss Fiona MacCarthy,
and both are much looking forward to their studies there.' So the
Sketch informed its readers. We were not the sole defecters. A drift
away from the Season was beginning. By 1958, for women in Britain
in general as well as for the girls of my own privileged – or not so privileged? – subsection of society aspirations were enlarging and greater
opportunities of self-fulfilment were gradually opening out. Many of
my debutante contemporaries were starting to feel critical of the conventional pattern of existence passed down from mother to daughter,
the cycle of coming out, engagement, marriage, childbearing, then
launching one's own daughters, the system repeating itself in perpetuity. It has sometimes seemed to me that the official end of curtseys
helped to concentrate the mind on the kind of futures we actually
wanted. There was a definite breaking of the mould. Often, and sometimes painfully, this entailed rejection of the cultural values and formality of manners in which we had been reared.

I can illustrate this best with the story of the debutante determined to go to university whose mother had insisted she should wear a hat for her interview at Somerville. The girl, Auriol Stevens, had intuited that hats, necessary for debs' luncheons or for presentation day, were unlikely to improve her chances with the dons at Somerville, at the time a highly academic all-female Oxford college. Auriol's mother dropped her at the gates and she deposited the hat surreptitiously at the Porters' Lodge. She got the place at Somerville, and indeed went on to a career of great intellectual glory, ending up as editor of the *Times Higher Education Supplement*. The story of Auriol and the abandoned hat is symbolic of the rejection of old standards of decorum as the traditional English deb died out. It also reminds us that the impetus for change, the urge to reinvent themselves amongst the girls who curtseyed, came not – certainly not – from the debs' mothers but from the girls themselves.

CHAPTER NINE

What Happened to the Season?

In late 1958, the year that curtseys ended, the professionals whose livelihood and status depended on the debutantes began a rearguard action. In the *Tatler* Jennifer, the doyenne of social columnists, took up the defence:

I want to say how heartily sick I am of reading (ever since it was announced from Buckingham Palace that there would be no more Royal presentation parties) such statements as 'Death of the débutante' – 'No more débutantes' – 'The end of the débutantes' seasons'. This is rubbish. There are just as many debutantes coming out in 1959 as in any previous year. The dropping of the presentation parties has made no difference, and the season promises to be as gay as ever.

There was in fact only a very slight reduction in the number of deb dances previewed in the *Tatler*: 99 in 1959, as against 117 in 1958. The deb Season continued more or less in its old format over the next few years. Later attempts were made, and are occasionally still made, to revive it. But its nature had been changed fundamentally by the palace's decision to end the presentations. With the ending of the link between the Queen and the virgin daughters of her well-bred subjects, in a solemn ceremony of initiation not dissimilar to a laying on of hands, the Season lost what element of gravity it had pretended to, and descended into pointlessness. Its spiritual centre had now gone.

The end of presentations meant a larger role for Queen Charlotte's Birthday Ball as the Season's important opening event. Debs still took lessons at Vacani's School of Dancing in the curtsey to be made to the ball president. Curtseying remained a technique considered to be useful, along with arranging flowers and making soufflés. A 1959 deb told me that as well as curtseying she was taught at Vacani's how to pick up the train of the long dress she was wearing and loop it round her forearm, a skill she might possibly be needing in the future. But even Queen Charlotte's was less formal than it used to be, treated with less reverence as the Season itself began to loosen up. Barbara Griggs reported in her *Evening Standard* column in 1959: 'Symptomatic of a less-inhibited, freer (and – should we say – more democratic?) social whirl, a Chelsea note is beginning to be perceptible.' Belinda Bellville, well-known designer of debs' ball gowns in a picturesque quasi-Edwardian style, is quoted as saying, with a touch of bitterness: 'These debs are rather a gay lot this year – black stockings and a rather Chelsea-look and much more fashion conscious – not nearly as worried about waists and full skirts as they used to be.' By the time that joints were being smoked at Queen Charlotte's the traditionalists were lamenting the demise of Lady Hamond-Graeme ('dear Lady Ham-'n-Eggs' as she was known on the deb circuit), a ball president of disciplinarian rigour who had ruled the debs' behaviour with an iron rod.

For Chelsea debs in their black stockings the old set patterns of coming out were now appearing discredited and boring: 'rent-a-crowd dancing to Tommy Kinsman'. No one wanted staid old dances at the Hyde Park any more. Deb dances now needed to include a surprise element. In 1960 Diane Taylor held a South Seas coming out in the quasi-Polynesian decor of the new Beachcomber Restaurant at the Mayfair Hotel, where real macaws sat in imitation palm trees. Sarah Rashleigh Belcher, Virginia Campbell-Johnson and Melanie Hadden were still more enterprising in hiring London Zoo where the roaring of the lions and the yells of the hyenas provided a bizarre accompaniment to the sweet-talking of the debs and the delights. My sister Karin rejected the family duty of a deb dance at the Dorchester in favour of a dance on a boat on the Thames with a steel band playing as it chugged along to Greenwich. The waiters wore the by now fashionable matelot-stripe jerseys. In 1960 Candida Betjeman's coming out took place in a barn on a farm at Duxford, Berkshire. Candida was the daughter of the poet John Betjeman, himself an adorer of the debutante sub-species:

> *Miss J. Hunter Dunn, Miss J. Hunter Dunn,*
> *Furnish'd and burnish'd by Aldershot sun.*

The guests arrived at the party in pony carts, led by Candida's mother, the Hon. Mrs Betjeman, daughter of the late Field-Marshal

Lord Chetwode and herself a considerable horsewoman, driving a skewbald mare to a four-wheeled wagonette. Instead of dinner jackets the men wore open-necked shirts and tweed jackets, the girls loose V-neck jumpers and candy-stripe skirts. This was what might be called an alternative deb dance, more a *fête champêtre*, at the beginning of a whole decade of alternatives in which the more traditional modes of coming out were beginning to look like an embarrassment.

At the opposite end of the spectrum to the barn dance were the balls which purported to be given for a daughter's coming out but were more of an occasion for a grand spectacular. The most lavish of the balls of 1963 was given by Lady Ashcombe, daughter of Viscountess Kemsley, at the Kemsleys' eighteenth-century mansion in Buckinghamshire. Though ostensibly a dance for Tana Alexander, Lady Ashcombe's debutante daughter, it was really a party for the jet set and the no longer youthful international royalty, including Prince Rainier and Princess Grace of Monaco. 'There were over 800 guests, but most of them had been debs and debs' delights *many many* years earlier', recalled the designer Adam Pollock who had been commissioned to transform the 150 foot ballroom at Dropmore into a baroque Roman piazza:

. . . architecturally correct, but everything covered in gold foil dripping with diamonds and brown varnish. A swagged and ragged white silk ceiling was hung with, I think, twenty four jewelled chandeliers. In the corners were grottoes of the elements, each with four ten foot statues holding up the rocky vaults . . . only slightly camp.

All this was enormously more sophisticated than the rose trellises and fountains that constituted decor at the dances I went to in 1958. Lady Ashcombe's ball was quite another sort of party, more stagey, more *mouvementé*. In a way it set the pace for the mind-blowing effects of illusion and psychedelia found at the smartest parties by the middle 1960s. Pollock himself went on to design one of the first of those big psychedelic parties of the sixties. Charles Spencer Churchill gave the party in an empty house in Regent's Park with 'masses of projected quickly changing abstract and Rauschenbergy slides on the blank walls'.

If we accept that by 1958 the English debutante was dying, what exactly had contributed to her demise? Besides the edict of the Queen that put an end to curtseys there were several other factors. The first, and most crucial, was the ongoing erosion of the exclusive and relatively small social grouping known as High Society within which the

Tana Alexander's coming out dance at Dropmore in 1963, with spectacular decor by Adam Pollock (top); and Lady Rosemary Muir at Lady Ashcombe's ball at Dropmore, transformed into a Roman piazza for the night

debutante system was invented and by which it had been nurtured. High Society stood for an acknowledged social leadership based on meaningful political power, titled rank and wealth and land. The American philosopher and Anglophile Ralph Waldo Emerson estimated High Society as containing around 70,000 people when he first visited England in 1833. This exclusivity had lasted up to the First World War and, after a fashion, had continued right through the 1930s. But in his 1962 investigation of the running of the country, *The Anatomy of Britain*, Anthony Sampson raised the question of how far, with a large class of post-war new rich, the old aristocracy was losing ground. Sampson noted that in newspaper gossip columns by the early sixties the worlds of the new millionaires and old aristocrats could be seen to be colliding: breeding had become less newsworthy than money and success. Sampson's socially sensitive antennae detected a new pattern: 'The two worlds of aristocracy and plutocracy overlap in the "Season" – the succession of private dances and balls given between April and July, which serve as the marriage market for richer children.' Debutantes, so far as they continued to exist, included girls that our own mothers with their listings and address books and strict sense of the old networks would have looked on as impostors. If they could afford it anyone could have a Season. The criterion for inclusion was now not birth but wealth.

There was the growing feeling that the upper class itself was getting seedy. In the early 1960s a succession of sex scandals erupted, involving well-known members of the ruling classes and the aristocracy. John Profumo, then Minister for War in Macmillan's cabinet, had been considered one of the most brilliant of his generation of politicians before he was forced to resign from the Cabinet in June 1963 for lying to the House of Commons over his affair with the call girl Christine Keeler. Profumo's brazen denial of any 'impropriety whatsoever' in his 'acquaintanceship with Miss Keeler' created a distrust by extension of Britain's entire ruling elite. As wild rumours accumulated through that summer of nude swimming parties, masked men at whipping sessions, a Cabinet Minister dressed in bondage gear, and other up-to-then unmentionable forms of orgy, the old Tory confidence in preaching morality to the lower classes was forever undermined. The toffs were now revealed as no better than they should be, as many people claimed to have suspected all along. Less than a month after Lord Denning's report into the Profumo affair in all its lurid ramifications of immoral earnings, unlawful abortions and risks to the national security, Macmillan resigned, ostensibly for health reasons, and the way was paved for Labour's 1964 election victory.

The Profumo affair sabotaged what remained of automatic respect towards the upper classes. Even more directly damaging to the reputation of the debutante was the long-running and, to the public, riveting divorce case brought by the Duke of Argyll against his wife. The proceedings were brought to a conclusion in May 1963, that summer of the scandals, when the duke was granted a decree of divorce on grounds of the duchess's adultery. The duchess had, as I have previously mentioned, been Deb of the Year in 1930, a young woman of such fame at the time of her first marriage to the American playboy Charles Sweeny that Cole Porter had hymned her in the song 'You're the Top':

> You're Mussolini,
> You're Mrs. Sweeny,
> You're Camembert.

Perhaps the bracketing with Mussolini was unfortunate. By 1963 she was in appalling trouble, castigated by Lord Wheatley, the judge in the divorce case, as a promiscuous woman whose attitude to marriage was 'wholly immoral'. He dwelt with particular disgust on a set of photographs showing sexual acts in progress between the duchess and an unknown man or men.

Two of the photographs are proved to be photographs of the defender taken during the marriage and they not only establish that the defender was carrying on an adulterous association with those other men or man but revealed that the defender was a highly sexed woman who had ceased to be satisfied with normal relations and had started to indulge in what I can only describe as disgusting sexual activities to gratify a basic sexual appetite.

While the woman in the photographs could be seen to be the duchess the naming of the man was very much more difficult since the pictures showed the body of a nude male but not his head. The identity of the so-called Headless Man was a subject of obsessive speculation, which I well remember since I was working in the *Guardian* office at the time. He has turned out to be not the portly Tory politician Duncan Sandys – for some time the front-runner – but the swashbuckling film star Douglas Fairbanks Junior. The reviling of the duchess in such salacious detail by a judge intent on showing us a monster of depravity could not but affect the old harmless-if-silly image of the debutante as it destroyed respect for duchesses in general. In her memoirs *Forget Not*, the Duchess of Argyll tells a striking story of how, on the day after the court case went against her, she returned home to her house in Upper Grosvenor Street:

I went straight upstairs to my bedroom, where my loyal and devoted maid, Isabel Bennett – then almost eighty – was waiting. She had looked after me for many years, and I saw at once from her face that she had read the judge's words. 'Oh, Your Grace,' she began falteringly, but got no further.

By the early 1960s the scales were falling from loyal and devoted servants' eyes.

We were a jeering generation. The sixties satire boom had its origins in Oxford. It began in a small and esoteric way with *Parson's Pleasure*, a High Tory weekly founded by Adrian Berry, whose father the Hon. Michael Berry, later Lord Hartwell, was proprietor and editor in chief of the *Daily Telegraph*. *Parson's Pleasure* first appeared in autumn 1958, the term in which I arrived at Lady Margaret Hall, a college whose name itself seemed infinitely risible, like that of another idiotic, braying debutante, in that world of obscure and secret jokes. I knew these infant satirists who far from being the bearded left-wing incendiarists now enshrined in legend were amiable young men in British warms and cavalry twill trousers, all of whom had been at public school. *Parson's Pleasure* was inherited from the Old Etonian Berry by the Old Salopians Richard Ingrams and Paul Foot, nephew of Michael and son of Sir Hugh Foot, recently appointed Governor of Cyprus. Another central figure in the little core of contributors and editors who gathered in the Town and Gown, an insalubrious cafe off the High Street, was Andrew Osmond, an immensely handsome and sweet-natured Old Harrovian and ex-Gurkha officer, yearned over by the girls at LMH. *Parson's Pleasure* was absorbed into another short-lived satiric Oxford magazine *Mesopotamia*, familiarly known as 'Messpot'. One early issue had a hessian cover attached to which was the packet of mustard and cress seeds you could grow on it. Out of these rather puerile beginnings emerged *Private Eye*, the satiric magazine which flourished in London in the early 1960s and, with its relentlessly joshing tone and its great resources of insider information, gradually became seriously destructive of establishment self-confidence.

A second cell of satirists was simultaneously emerging in Cambridge in the sixties, centred on the Cambridge Footlights. Peter Cook was Footlights President in 1960, Nick Luard Treasurer, David Frost the Registrar. When Cambridge Footlights took the revue *Beyond the Fringe* to the Edinburgh Festival in the autumn of that year the four performers were Peter Cook, Dudley Moore, Jonathan Miller and Alan Bennett. The revue was a send-up of England and the English, an attack on the outdated attitudes and mores of a fuddy-duddy nation that was perhaps more lethal than even the performers knew. In May 1961 Cook and Luard founded the satirical Soho nightclub, the Establishment, leasing an old stripclub in Green Street with the aim of continuing the political-anarchic spirit of *Beyond the Fringe* after the revue's unexpectedly popular run in the West End. Many of the Oxford–Cambridge satirists were involved as the writers and performers of the Saturday night television satire programme *That Was the Week that Was*. An important element in the success of sixties satire was the closeness of the satirists to their establishment targets: the old buffers, the smooth talkers, the claptrap politicians, the Tory government, the monarchy, the Church of England. Bishops, as I remember, were given an especially rough ride. The minority of satirists who had not been to public schools were from the aspirational grammar schools. The girlfriends and wives of the satirists were from the edges of the deb world if not former debs themselves. Peter Cook was to marry Judy Huxtable, who came out in 1960 with my sister. David Frost married Lady Carina Fitzalan-Howard, the Duke of Norfolk's second daughter, becoming Sir David and a genial upper-class party-giving parody of the people he had ridiculed as a young man.

The satire boom had an almost tragic impact on its victims, needling these derided people into ever more self-destructive outbursts of buffoonishness. It was a culture in which almost no one survived to be taken seriously any more. I addressed this whole dilemma in a *Guardian* column. I called it 'In Fear of the Fringe' and singled out for blame the young and fashionable humourists – Jonathan Miller, Alan Bennett, Michael Frayn – for creating such a climate of general ridicule and scorn:

Who can one own as one's friends when everyone around appears to be a boutique keeper or an artist in a cottage or a modern clergyman or a Foreign Office Wykehamist or Old Etonian banker or a literary agent or something humorous? And who is one to marry? The satirists between them have made the choice of partner more or less impossible. With everybody funny, the sacred vows of marriage seem – to say the least – a little inappropriate.

A typically 1960s *cri de coeur*.

On *That Was the Week that Was* Fenella Fielding impersonated Jennifer. In what had become a national frenzy of debunking, the Season could no longer be taken absolutely straight even by the magazines that recorded and promoted it. In 1959 the *Tatler* ran a feature by Andrew Sinclair, billed as the irreverent young author of 'a bestseller that mocks the Season'. Sinclair's cult novel *The Breaking of Bumbo* was about to be staged by Wolf Mankowitz as a West End musical. His disdainful article about what he claimed to be the now redundant Season compared it to 'the skeleton of a dinosaur in the desert'. *Queen*, *Tatler*'s chief rival as a magazine which traditionally drew its circulation from the landed and moneyed classes, made similar attempts to have it all ways, teasing its readership without alienating it. The proprietor of *Queen* in the sixties was Jocelyn Stevens, a young energetic hot tempered and some ways brilliantly iconoclastic man, nephew of Edward Hulton, famous publisher of *Picture Post*. He bought *Queen* as a 25th birthday present for himself and appointed a Cambridge friend, Mark Boxer, as art editor. Boxer was a formidably observant cartoonist, inventor of the Stringalongs, the archetypically trendy sixties couple who lived in NW1. Another of Stevens's early hirings had been Jennifer, tempted away from the *Tatler* in 1959. But this was in effect a token hiring. In what Stevens assessed as a new climate, social comment was a matter of asperity and irony and jokes, not simply lists of names and velvet smooth responses that flattered the hostesses and buttered up the debs. Jennifer complains in her memoirs that her diary was given very little space. The doings of the debutantes were now considered of only marginal interest to *Queen* readers and – horror of horrors – the cruel lens of Henri Cartier-Bresson was brought in to photograph Queen Charlotte's Ball.

In 1963 a book was published that altered fundamentally the public perception of the Season. It was a short novel, not an especially well written or profound one, but there was something about the tenor and the timing that made it influential. Debs' escorts in particular, derided as foolish, unattractive chinless wonders, could not be the same again. *Coronet Among the Weeds* was the work of the twenty-year-old Charlotte Bingham or, to give her her full name, the Hon. Charlotte Mary Thérèse Bingham, daughter of the 7th Baron Clanmorris. She had gone to a very unacademic convent school, The Priory, Haywards Heath, and had been 'finished' in Paris, living with an impoverished aristocratic family and going to lectures at the Sorbonne. She had then returned to London for the Season. *Coronet Among the Weeds*, undisguised autobiography, shows coming out to be unremitting awfulness.

There had been attempts before to satirise the Season. A sharp-eyed deb of my own year, Dominie Riley-Smith, had written a novel, *Curtains for Curtseys*, about a fat, vague mother bringing out her own smart daughter and a bumbling cousin from the country. *Curtains* had been accepted by a publisher, Secker & Warburg, who in the end had failed to bring it out. Charlotte Bingham's *Coronet Among the Weeds* was the first public send-up of the Season from the point of view of a disgruntled debutante. The tea parties:

Tea parties went on for practically ever. Everyone went on and on giving them. If they liked you they didn't only ask you to one, they asked you to half a dozen. And if there was some corny bit in the newspapers about you they'd all swoon.

The cocktail parties:

Cocktail parties are worse than tea parties. They're worse than dances too, come to think of it. In fact they're the worst thing you could possibly do. Except shorthand. It's all the weeds you have to talk to. They're much worse than the girls. Millions of times worse. If you find the girls chilling you wait and see what you'll find the men. You really get fond of the girls after you've met the men. I thought I knew how weedy a weed could get. But I didn't. I didn't know even half how weedy a weed could get.

With her endearing frankness and her *faux naif* approach Charlotte Bingham gave a true insider's view of a girl's Season, analysing the worst of a deb's social dilemmas:

You can't tell some po old hostess you don't want to go with someone because he's a sex maniac, and being raped by a weed would be no joke. I'm not exaggerating: some of those weeds there was nothing they wouldn't stop at. Mostly because they're so stupid. No intelligence at all.

For the early 1960s this was a new tone: anti-romantic, painfully realistic, rudely discontented with the debs' delights on offer, like an early, posher version of Bridget Jones.

The Season had been based on ideas of the inheritance of elegance, the debutante looking like as well as emulating the behaviour of her mother. By the early sixties this was no longer so. Once Mary Quant had introduced the miniskirt the concept of dressing in a style that reflected your position in society was fatally undermined. Following the youth cult of the period debs turned into dolly birds, parading down King's Road in little gymslips, keyhole dresses, skinny rib sweaters, paper knickers (or no knickers), op art earrings and enormous floppy hats. The debutante pink lips had given way to splurged white lipstick. Thick black eyeliner made the girls look rather waifish under their Vidal Sassoon geometric haircuts. There was the craze for hot pants and I still have a picture of myself standing in a white cave like boutique wearing the pair of white Courrèges boots I'd bought in Paris and a long shiny white mac.

The girls of this generation were abandoning the labels still popular in the 1950s: Jean Allen and Frank Usher now looked frumpy. They took up the young designers who had begun producing clothes for an emphatically young market: Mary Quant, Kiki Byrne, Jean Muir, Marian Foale and Sally Tuffin, Gerald McCann, Emmanuelle Khahn, inventors of the lean and classless 'London Look'. All aspects of the Season were affected by the youth cult. The once staid Berkeley Debutante Dress Show reinvented itself. No more Monsieur Cardin. The girls now modelled clothes from Young Jaegar and from Annacat, the ultra fashionable South Kensington boutique set up by two ex-debs Maggie Keswick and Janet Lyle. A deb of my own year, Annette Bradshaw, another of the girls involved in running Annacat, remembers the excitement and the chaos of the scene in a shop that epitomised the swinging sixties: *everyone* shopped at Annacat, from Christine Keeler to Mrs David Bruce, wife of the American Ambassador to London. The sixties was a period of social fluidity in which fashion models had more kudos than the daughters of the upper classes and ex-debs (not always too convincingly) attempted to look and behave like fashion models. I remember being stopped by a film crew in Woollands 21 shop, the 'young designer' section in a once completely middle-aged Knightsbridge department store, and asked if I dreamed of looking like Jean Shrimpton, the sixties' most iconic face. I denied this indignantly, refusing to be interviewed. But I was not being truthful. Anyone of my generation longed to be Jean Shrimpton, whether or not they had curtseyed to the Queen.

Another factor in the death of the debutante was Biba, which had started in a small way as a mail order catalogue, then enlarging into retail. The Polish designer Barbara Hulanicki and her entrepreneur

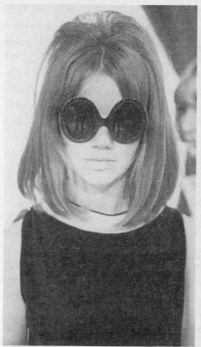

Annette Fletcher modelling Young Jaeger beachwear at the Berkeley Debutante Dress Show in 1966 (left); and Sarah Harman modelling Annacat palazzo pyjamas at the Berkeley Dress Show in 1967

husband Stephen Fitz-Simon opened the first Biba shop in a converted Victorian chemist's shop in Abingdon Road in 1964. Two years later, such was Biba's success, they took a larger shop in Kensington Church Street before expanding yet again into the beautiful Biba designed by Julie Hodgess on the site in Kensington High Street which was formerly a Cyril Lord carpet showroom. With its decor of giant potted ferns, dark wood panelling and stained glass (retrieved from neighbouring St Paul's School, about to be demolished) that Biba store lives on in many people's minds as one of the dream experiences of the sixties, a fantasy of opulence and sexiness. In a recent interview in the *Observer* the singer Jane Birkin made the comment that 'People know exactly where they were, or who they were in bed with, when they first heard "Je T'aime (Moi Non Plus)"', the 1969 hit song she recorded with her lover Serge Gainsbourg and which was banned as indecent by the BBC. I know I was in Biba's, ascending the grand staircase, and that astonishingly arousing song had had an extra magic in that Jane Birkin, a war-hero's wayward daughter, was a former pupil at my own old school, Miss Ironside's. Stylistically Biba was unlike Bazaar, in some ways its antithesis. Where Bazaar promoted a pert teenage look of stripes and spots and daisies Biba was marketing a notion of sinfulness. This was fashion for young vamps: body-clinging satin dresses, feather boas, shoes with high-stack heels, suede boots with long long zips. The colours were those of the fashionable brothel: black, purple, dusky pink. The point about Biba style was that it was pastiche High Society, replicating the etiolated glamour of debs of the year in c.1930. Biba clothes were not expensive. Teenagers from the suburbs raided Biba every Saturday, returning home with carrier bags bulging with their spoils. Once the style of the elite was taken over by the people once regarded as an underclass the mystique of the debutante was undermined.

The traditional deb escort was hit hard by the fashion revolution. Henry Blofeld, in his memoirs, recalls the purchase of his city gentleman's wardrobe in 1959: the impeccably tailored three-piece dark-grey suit, the bowler hat from Lock's, St James's, the rolled umbrella. These clothes would have made him look a cartoon character a few years further on. The catalyst for change was John Stephen, a design entrepreneur who introduced into men's fashion a new mood of flamboyance, an element of camp, using often lurid colours, shiny textures, patterned fabrics, pleated pockets. These were clothes my Tattersall-shirted Uncle Justin would have certainly denounced as pansy stuff. But they suited the mood of the time, the urge for performance, the shock tactics of the pop scene. John Stephen's first shop, His Clothes, opened in Beak Street in Soho. He soon moved into Carnaby Street with Lord John, Mod Male, Male West One, virtually taking over the street with his chain of consciously subversive menswear shops. Gradually the debs' delights adapted, even if they never totally abandoned the uniform announcing them as officers and gentlemen. The fashionable Mayfair tailors, Blades, opened in 1963 by Rupert Lycett Green, grandson of a baronet and Candida Betjeman's husband-to-be, sold the Carnaby Street look in a much better cut and more expensive version. In 1960s London the aristocracy were followers rather than setters of the trend.

'I can't bear chinless people talking about sex. I think chinless people should be eunuchs.' Charlotte Bingham's onslaught on the chinless wonders in *Coronet Among the Weeds* is a reminder of a time in which the smoothness and effeteness of traditional debs' delights, murmuring their innuendos and reeking of Old Spice, was being challenged by the unkempt glamour of the working-class professionals: designers, actors, photographers with East End accents. If ex-debs were dreaming of looking like Jean Shrimpton, some at least of the escorts must have felt a twinge of envy at the swaggering and blatantly unshaven David Bailey, as I remember him in Vogue House Studios, shouting at the models: 'Stick your tits out.' The romantic ideal of working-class authenticity caused the London Season to lose much of its appeal.

The old predictable social patterns were dissolving. Fewer people were assembling for drinks at 6.30 when there were all-day parties. The merging of the deb world with a more rackety, ostensibly less-snobbish subsection of society had started in the fifties with the so-called 'Chelsea Set', a throwback to the louche and flamboyant arty Chelsea personified by Augustus John. The attractions of that scene are well explained in Andrew Sinclair's *The Breaking of Bumbo* in which the young Guards officer, desperately bored with the conventional deb parties, looks for an alternative in the espresso bars and pubs of Chelsea amongst the arty drunks and models, old painters, heavy blondes. The Chelsea Set was a small world of fashionable drifters which revolved around the ever-crowded Markham Arms, the pub beside Bazaar, the Pheasantry, the Chelsea Potter, the Picasso Café. No debs' mums' address books. Entrée to the Chelsea Set was more a matter of style than family credentials. No embossed invitation cards. You sniffed out the best party and brought along a bottle of undistinguished *vino*. As yet not many drugs.

By the sixties the once coherent structures of the deb world had been further dissipated by the growth of hippydom. There was the picturesque and in the end ill-fated exodus in gypsy caravans by the hippy children of the upper classes, hoping to find the good life in the West Country or in Wales. One of these disaffected deb escorts was Sir Mark Palmer, whose father, the 4th Baronet, had been killed in action in 1941, the year when Mark was born, and whose mother was a lady in waiting to the Queen. I remember being partnered by Mark Palmer at one of those London dances. Was it at the Anglo-Belgian Club or the Hyde Park Hotel? This was before he was transformed into 'the King hippie', as Penelope Betjeman described him, deeply disapproving of the way he and his friends cut out the knees of their jeans and the elbows of their jerseys to make themselves look as unkempt as they could. Mark Palmer was at Oxford, got sent down for drugs and

. . . started this gypsy thing of getting caravans and horses and getting lots of girls and boys together who wanted to lead that sort of dropout life. They went all over England. They went down to Cornwall and he was beaten up in Padstow because he rather stole the thunder from the Padstow 'Obby dance, with his pretty debs and caravans.

The Hon. Mrs Betjeman, somewhat misguidedly, went on to stay at Palmer's later commune in Montgomeryshire:

They had an old gypsy doing fencing on their smallholding. I can't describe the squalor, I CANNOT describe the squalor. The next morning I realised there was a large hole in the wall of my bedroom which was covered up by a piece of old carpet on the outside. And their great theory at the time was that you must never never spend one moment doing any housework, it was an absolute waste of time. The *gypsy* took me aside and complained of the dirt and the mess!

The story is told in Bevis Hillier's definitive biography of John Betjeman. This particular debs' mother was relieved that her daughter Candida had not settled for Mark Palmer, as had at one time been a possibility. But in such conditions of social anarchy all ideas of hand-picking a husband for your daughter, let alone vetting escorts for their likely good behaviour in a taxi, were becoming utterly irrelevant.

In 1958 Britain was on the edge of feminism. Women's achievements were beginning to be singled out and recognised. In that summer of our dances a Women of the Year luncheon was held at the Savoy, attended by over seven hundred women including the artist Dame Laura Knight, the ballerina Beryl Grey, Marjorie Marriott, Matron of the Middlesex Hospital, the Salvation Army leader Colonel Mary Booth, the Holloway bus conductress Mrs Waymark, a signal that Women of the Year were not just middle class. There was also Joyce Grenfell, the comedian and writer, who (as Joyce Phipps) had curtseyed to Queen Mary in 1928 and therefore could be seen to bear another kind of message: that of upper-class women's potential in the world. In autumn 1958, the first year in which the State Opening of Parliament was televised, four women were among the fourteen new peers created under the Life Peerages Bill, the first women ever to take their places in the House of Lords. These were Baroness Swanborough, founder of the WVS, Baroness Elliott of Harwood, Baroness Ravensdale of Kedleston and Baroness Wootton of Abinger.

There was increasingly vociferous debate over the next few years on what it meant to be a woman, on how women could break through the traditional social mores that circumscribed their lives. In 1963 the first widely influential study of contemporary women's discontents, *The Feminine Mystique*, was published. The author, Betty Friedan, drew on a series of interviews with American graduate wives to explode the myth of the happy housewife, maintaining that millions of women in the United States were surviving on tranquillisers, leading lives that felt empty and unfulfilled. I covered Friedan's first visit to Britain for the *Guardian*. Her controversial study was followed in 1970 by Germaine Greer's *The Female Eunuch* which within my own circle was to have an even stronger impact. *The Female Eunuch*, a trenchantly argued, often wildly funny book, dealt less with the problems of American suburban housewives, more with the social and sexual dilemmas we knew from our own often bitter experience. I cannot claim that every deb I knew had read *The Female Eunuch*, though I treasure the story told me by a friend of how she travelled through France sharing a night-sleeper with her husband, she reading Germaine Greer, he snoring up above. By the end of the journey, she had dismissed her husband from her heart, arriving in the end at a handsome divorce settlement. But even if most daughters of the upper class baulked at signing up as bona fide feminists – and feminism certainly had its wilder shores – no woman of my generation could be unaffected by the prospect of expanding possibilities that became so potent a feeling in the air.

The final act of destruction to the debutante Season was the end of virginity. The whole cycle had its basis in ideals of the virgin: the queen's benison, the courtship, the engagement and the wedding, leading up to the ritual deflowering on the marriage bed. By the early 1960s there were many fewer virgins. To put it candidly there were now simply not enough virgins to go round. Partly this was the result of the now easily available contraceptive pill which allowed a single girl to make her own decisions about intercourse without the fear of pregnancy that I have described as paralysing sexual activity in 1958. The ending of virginity also came from an attitude of mind much altered from the secrecy and mystery surrounding sex throughout our teenage years when my own clandestine source of information had been my mother's copy of Marie Stopes's *Radiant Motherhood*. The widely publicised trial of D.H. Lawrence's novel *Lady Chatterley's Lover* for obscenity in 1959 released into the public domain words and actions that had up to then been hushed and furtive: as fucks, cunts, and anal intercourse became a part of everyday vocabulary there seemed less to fear in the sexual acts themselves.

The poet Philip Larkin set the year in which sexual intercourse began as 1963. I would put it two years earlier. In 1961 the Oxford Union held its Chastity Debate in which the Earl of Longford, Esther Pedlar of St. Hilda's, and A.S. Neill, headmaster of the (to some) alarmingly permissive Summerhill School, considered the question 'That the Christian ideal of chastity is outmoded.' And in 1961 my group of female Oxford friends at Lady Margaret Hall met together and agreed that in the previous vacation we had all gone down like ninepins. When it actually happened, after all the fuss surrounding it, the loss of our virginity seemed such a little thing. My mother made a token objection when, engaged but not yet married, I proposed to go on holiday in Wales with my fiancé. But she knew the game was up and she quite quickly acquiesced.

Poster for the Oxford Union Chastity Debate in 1961

Things changed in and around my mother's house in Chelsea as that mobile symbol of 1960s irresponsibility – the Bubble car – began careering round our bend in the King's Road. In my teenage years King's Road was quite an ordinary shopping street with butchers, grocers, fishmongers, a Timothy White's, Sidney Smith the drapers and Beeton's the baker where you could buy potato cakes still warm from the griddle and scrumptious Chelsea buns. At the bottom of Limerston Street, Ted-in-the-Shed, an old-time London trader, sold us our fruit and veg with lots of winking innuendo in the *Carry On* film mode. But gradually these normal shops, and even Ted, were ousted by boutique after boutique, the wildest of which came to colonise World's End. We could hardly believe our eyes when Granny Takes a Trip opened just around the corner from our Limerston Street house in 1965. Granny was an antique clothes shop, psychedelic in its concept and startling in its decor, which changed from day to day. The tour de force was the Dodge car belonging to the owner, John Pearse, which he had sawn in half and welded to the shop front instead of the glass window, an act of subversiveness which was reported back to us by Isa, our old nanny, in some alarm. Like I Was Lord Kitchener's Valet, a similarly mickey-taking retro fashion shop in Portobello Road, Granny Takes a Trip specialised in the reconstituted military jackets, Boer War helmets, the equipment of old British militarism that entranced the pop world of the sixties. This was the same love-and-loathe-the-Empire feeling that inspired the Beatles' *Sgt Pepper's Lonely Hearts Club Band*. If Isa had been shocked by Granny Takes a Trip she would have been still more so (had she lived to see it) by SEX, the punk shop opened in the seventies by Vivienne Westwood and Malcolm McLaren, manager of the Sex Pistols, on that same curve of the King's Road. The gay-bar cowboys in their Stetsons, nude from the waist down; the torn up Union Jack with the Sex Pistols logo superimposed; the Queen with a safety pin stuck through her lip. The shock images of SEX were our old world deconstructed. As King's Road itself transformed, the links with the old innocent life of the deb dances grew ever more remote.

My sister Karin had paid only minimal attention to her coming out in 1960. She was training as an actress and a dancer and had already had her first professional engagements as a Sherman Fisher girl in the pantomime *Aladdin* at Streatham Hill and as a dancer in Gillian Lynne's cabarets on New Year's Eve at the Cumberland Hotel. She also had a boyfriend, not a debs' delight, but a boy on the fringes of

Karin MacCarthy photographed in her coming-out year in 1960, looking more Chelsea Set than debutante

the Chelsea Set. Peter Stansbury was very young, with an appealing fallen angel look. He dressed in the King's Road uniform of nicely faded tight blue jeans, Cuban heels and pretty coloured shirts. Peter had artistic aspirations and played the classical guitar. He lived with his mother in a rather gloomy Earl's Court mansion block. He and Karin spent many hours together in the Troubadour café on Fulham Road. When they felt they could afford an evening out they went not to the Berkeley but the Café des Artistes with its check gingham table-cloths and sputtering red candles. Otherwise it was the Bistro d'Agran where they tried to forget about the filthy kitchens which no modern health inspector would possibly have passed. In what was meant to be her Season Karin did go to deb dances, often insinuating Peter, but she could not face the house parties. Her style of life that summer was less the conventional ingénue debutante, more the self directed and sexually sophisticated Chelsea Bird, as defined in Virginia Ironside's evocative 1964 novel of that title. My sister really had no need for coming out. Ironically enough her first breakthrough as an actress was taking over the part Anna Massey had been playing in *The Right Honourable Gentleman*, the dramatisation of the Charles Dilke scandal. It seemed as if our family was destined to be haunted by the reluctant debutante.

As the sixties wore on the Limerston Street household came more and more to resemble a theatrical lodging house. It has to be said that things got out of hand. One of the PGs, tended fondly by my mother, was the actor Robert Lloyd whose long run in the Peter Brook production of *Marat/Sade* was followed by a stint in the Theatre of Cruelty. My mother's theory was that all this had, not surprisingly, turned Robert slightly mad. Another PG was Petronella Barker, daughter of the comedians Eric Barker and Pearl Hackney. Peta, who had been at the Central School with Karin, was herself a wonderful comic actress, memorable as Phoebe in the National Theatre *As You Like It* and in the Feydeau farce *A Flea in Her Ear*. Anthony Hopkins was also in the National Theatre Company, then based at the Old Vic, and they had formed a relationship which was often stormy, exacerbated by his drinking. One night at Limerston Street, where Peta's room was in the basement, there was a violent scene. My mother and Karin, woken up by frenzied screaming, both rushed out of the front door and saw Tony running down the street. Peta had meanwhile emerged from the basement, in a state of near-hysteria, maintaining that Tony was trying to kill her. The story was that he had sat on her head, attempting to smother her. Certainly the cane bedhead, of a twirly design then popular in Chelsea, which I remember buying with my mother at Peter Jones, was showing signs of damage. The episode was reported to the police and my mother set off indignantly to the Old Vic to take the matter up with the National Theatre management. As a landlady she cared about the welfare of her lodgers. No action was taken. Tony Hopkins and Peta married in September 1967. But the marriage was short-lived.

I often think about the transformation of my mother from fairly conventional lieutenant colonel's widow to the ruler of this risqué, unpredictable lodging house in Chelsea. The theatrical connections are easily explicable. The world of theatre was the one she had longed for for herself. It was also, I think, that she was making up for her obedient, repressed McAlpine upbringing. She loved young people, even trippy Phena, who secreted in her Limerston Street cupboard a considerable stash of LSD. Was my mother never afraid of being busted? I suppose she took a chance on it. Her life had opened out in ways that at last made her contented. She had never been exactly keen on debs.

Social pundits agreed that 1958 had been the last good year for debutantes. By the mid 1960s, by which time the socialists were back in power, the elegant, exclusive deb Season as we knew it was in terminal decline. Drugs took over from drinking at deb parties. Dress standards declined sharply. Where in 1958 traditionalists lamented the growing tendency for men to wear dinner jackets at deb dances instead of white tie and tails, dinner jackets were themselves becoming rarer by the middle 1960s. People turned up at deb dances in whatever they happened to have on. There was an enormous rise in promiscuity. Nigel Dempster, self-appointed expert on debutante virginity, who had estimated in 1958 that only 5 per cent of girls doing the Season had ever slept with anyone, reversed his estimate for 1965, finding only 5 per cent of debutantes were still virgins. The number of coming-out parties, in their hundreds in their heyday in the 1950s, twenty years later had reduced to a mere trickle. In 1974 only nineteen cocktail parties and twenty-four dances were pre-announced in *Queen* by Jennifer. By 1975 she had stopped listing private dances altogether. In that same year doubts were raised about the continued viability of Queen Charlotte's Ball now that ticket sales were so much slowing down. The last Queen Charlotte's was in 1976. In 1977 the writer Margaret Pringle asked the Marchioness of Tavistock who, as Henrietta Tiarks, had been Deb of the Year in 1957, whether she would want her daughter to be a deb today. Henrietta replied:

The answer is that it would not work anymore, it would be meaningless. You cannot go to disco parties, wear make-up, smoke and go out with boyfriends before the age of seventeen and *then* be a deb. . . . The deb era has gone.

There were some valiant attempts to resuscitate the Season. Peter Townend, Jennifer's successor as the *Tatler*'s social editor, saw it as his mission to prolong the social system that had dominated England for so long. Townend, an obsessively meticulous man, had started his professional life as archivist for his local Wolverhampton council before editing *Burke's Peerage*. He was in a position to keep records of ex-debutante mothers who now themselves had daughters of an age to make their debuts and would write to them or telephone to offer his assistance. Up to a point his persistence was effective. Some of the debs of 1958 have described how Peter Townend brought them together in organising dances for their own daughters in the late 1970s and early 1980s. He also kept a list and held an annual party at Raffles for his approved debs' escorts. But even Peter Townend's near religious fervour in preserving what he saw as the system's ancient purity was not enough to stem the tide of social change. Even Townend had to recognise that England's once highly stratified society had changed into a relative free for all in which the credentials for inclusion were no longer those of lineage but celebrity and glamour. Nicholas Coleridge analysed these changes in the address he gave at Townend's memorial service:

His social pages, which once championed the Winter Ball, the White Knight's Ball and the Rose Ball, were soon contaminated, as he saw it, by funkier, more egalitarian parties, at which the Honourable Fenella Sporran cavorted with rock stars, and many of the young men at the raves found no place on Peter's respectable list. The social stars were no longer the Lord Lieutenant of Derbyshire, but supermodels and self-publicists and entrepreneurs.

Attempts made, from 1989, to revive Queen Charlotte's Ball fizzled out a few years later. The bored and bolshy teenage girls, who turned up for their curtsey rehearsals in Doc Martens, refused to take seriously the once-solemn processional rituals. The final straw came when Queen Charlotte's was featured in *Hello!* with Angela Rippon seated at the central table. By the year 2000, as debutantes mutated into 'celebutantes', the Season was a shadow of its former self.

CHAPTER TEN

What Happened to the Debs?

Ex-debutantes of 1958 photographed by Terry O'Neill for a 'Last of the Debs' feature in the *Sunday Telegraph* in 1993. From left, standing: Holly Eley (formerly Urquhart), Penny Graham, Lady Kindersley (formerly Tita Norman). Seated, Zia Kruger (Foxwell), Annette Bradshaw, Susanna Swallow (Crawley), Melanie Black (Lowson), Elfrida Fallowfield (Eden)

In June 1990 a reunion of the debs who had curtseyed in 1958 was held at the Vanderbilt Racquet Club in Kensington. Of the 231 girls on Jennifer's original list of debutantes published in the *Tatler* 46 came to the luncheon. Some could not be traced. Some refused the invitation, one ex-deb explaining piteously she had got too fat. Four of us were dead. Of these 46 ex-debs, now on the verge of fifty, 44 were married, a high proportion (well over half) to men I remembered, sometimes only too clearly, from the deb-dance circuit. Jennifer, who was of course invited to the party and whose attitude to the debutantes was still in her old age proprietorial and exacting, looked around her with some satisfaction, noting the most impressive transformations:

Maxine Hodson now Lady Jenkins, whom I recently visited in the Netherlands where Sir Michael Jenkins is our Ambassador; Miss Sally Hunter now Mrs. Henry Clive; Miss Melanie Lowson, now Mrs. Charles Black who celebrated her fiftieth birthday with a party at the Berkeley the previous evening; the Hon. Teresa Pearson now the Hon. Mrs. Stopford Sackville; her cousin Miss Miranda Smiley now the Countess of Iveagh; Miss Dominie Riley-Smith now Mrs. George Courtauld; Miss Elfrida Eden now Mrs. Richard Fallowfield; Miss Zia Foxwell now Mrs. David Kruger and an authoress; Miss Alexandra Bridgewater now Lady Cotterell, the mother of four and a successful artist; Mlle. Eliane de Miramon now the Hon. Mrs. Anthony Grigg; the Hon. Annabel Hawke now the Hon. Mrs Brook; Miss Tita Norman now Lady Kindersley; Miss Georgina Scott now Lady O'Neill; Miss Tessa Prain now Mrs. Vere Fane; Miss Christine Stucley now Lady Cobbold; and Miss Antonia Palmer now Lady Christopher Thynne.

Jennifer extended a smile of sympathy for one of the two as yet unmarried debs, 'a successful career lady', who had been 'one of the prettiest debutantes and still is very attractive!' But by and large, in terms of the conventions of the Season, the gels of 1958 had turned out well.

The notable absentee from the reunion, but the name inevitably on everybody's lips, was that of Sally Croker-Poole who, since the Season, had first become Lady James Crichton-Stuart and was now translated into Her Highness Princess Salima, wife of Karim, His Highness Aga Khan IV, spiritual leader of 20 million Ismaili Muslims and a man whose riches entered the realms of fantasy. One of the questions that rippled round the gathering of her one-time rivals in the ballroom was why Sally, a young woman of evidently formidable ambition, had settled in the first place for Lord James Crichton-Stuart, who though

The Aga Khan and his bride, 1958 debutante Sally Croker-Poole, at the reception for Ismaili leaders at the Prince's farm at Lassy near Paris held the day before their marriage ceremony on 28 October 1969

from an impeccably aristocratic Scots Catholic family, was just the younger son. It was his twin brother, the elder by a few crucial minutes, who had recently succeeded their father, becoming the 6th Marquess of Bute. Had Sally herself indeed had cold feet about the marriage, saying she was only doing it to please her mother? Had she actually been crying at her wedding in the Brompton Oratory, as one of her bridesmaids was later heard to claim? The Crichton-Stuart marriage was over two years later and was eventually annulled by the Roman Catholic church. And what of Sally's second marriage to the Aga Khan in Paris in October 1969? She had by now become a Muslim. Did she see her new future as Begum Aga Khan a more optimistic one? They were married first in a private civil ceremony; then seven days later there was an Ismaili ritual marriage at the Aga Khan's chateau on the Ile de la Cité, with Sally smiling bravely, swathed in a white sari. The signing of the marriage contract was accompanied by reading from the word of the prophet Mohammed, from whom the Aga Khan claimed direct descent.

Besides the Aga Khan's Uncle Sadruddin, his brother Amyan and leaders of Ismailic communities in twenty-three countries, Lieutenant

Colonel Croker-Poole, formerly of the Bengal Lancers, and Sally's stolid brother Anthony were in attendance at the Islamic marriage: a bizarre link with Sally's Limerston Street days and a reminder of just how far she had now travelled. Were we really debs together in those stuccoed Chelsea houses opposite to one another, slamming our two doors in concert, descending the steps in our dressmaker clothes, off to the palace, off to Ascot, off to cocktails at the Cavalry Club? Or had I merely dreamed the semi-feud between my mother and Mrs Croker-Poole? Within another decade Sally had become a legendary figure, a goddess of the jet set, ignoring her old friends if she encountered them in Bond Street, a woman removed to a completely distant sphere.

By 1990 her marriage to the Aga Khan was over. The playboy element in his family was strong. Since the early 1980s Sally had been living with their three children in a rented house in a luxurious estate overlooking Lake Geneva. A cash settlement of around £20 million had been bestowed on her in order to keep the Aga Khan's private life out of the divorce courts. Their divorce was to be finally made public in 1994. Sally showed a feistiness in common with other 1990s millionaire divorcées in refusing to go quietly. In 1995 she defeated the Aga Khan's attempts through the courts to stop her selling at auction at Christie's in Geneva the wondrous collection of jewels he had given her on grounds that these were not hers to sell, having family or religious connotations. All 261 jewels sold, bringing in a total £17.8 million. The Begum Blue diamond went way above the estimate, selling for over £5 million. This was, Mrs Croker-Poole would have reminded us, Sally's reward for being very beautiful indeed.

By the time of the 1958 debutante reunion, I had been away from this world for many years. The lunch party at the Vanderbilt gave me that sharp sad stab of déjà vu that one is conscious of at almost all reunions, school or university or work. The feeling is universal, equally applicable to an assembly of middle-aged women who thirty-two years earlier had curtseyed to the Queen. You look at once familiar faces and you wonder what has happened in the intervening period. I suppose it was the 1990 debs' reunion that first gave me the idea for the writing of this book.

It was then that it first began to dawn on me that the experiences of many of these girls I had once known was not so very different from that of other women of all classes in this country in rethinking and expanding the roles that their mothers had accepted as the norm. The ex-deb who organised the party at the Vanderbilt – Susanna Crawley – was a case in point. Her schooling had been sketchy since her father, a lawyer, did not approve of education for women. She was married early, in 1961, to Charles Swallow in whose arms we all remember her as clasped throughout the Season. Charles taught history at Harrow and became headmaster of a comprehensive school. Susanna, having had two children, took on the running of Nell Gwynn House, a large block of flats in Chelsea. She discovered her considerable skills in management. Charles resigned from his teaching job and together they embarked on an ambitious scheme to redevelop a series of redundant sheds in Shepherd's Bush, originally built as exhibition sheds for the 1907 White City Exhibition, into a luxurious tennis club and social club with eight tennis courts, a gym, a snooker room, a beauty salon and a library. For some years the Vanderbilt Racquet Club was a fashionable success, 'a non-stop cocktail party' as Susanna now describes it, with Princess Diana among the regulars. At the time of the reunion – which Susanna had herself conceived and organised in all its complex detail of searching out the girls who had once been debutantes – Susanna was by no means the drifting socialite that debs were reputed to turn into, but an energetic and highly motivated 1990s London entrepreneur.

'The generation of our mothers accepted they were wives and mothers and that was that', wrote Annabel Greene (now Annabel Gooch) in a letter to me recently. 'They *were* expected to do charity work of course, but not to *earn money*! Oh dear no!' In the changing of attitudes from mothers' to their daughters' generation this question of financial reward for work was crucial as traditional boundaries between the amateur and the professional were eroded. Upper-class young women of the post-war generation were the first to accept and exploit the commercial possibilities of their historic areas of expertise – gardening, interior decoration, entertaining, organising a large household. Annabel herself, who had married into a well-known Essex family with a sense of its own dignity, had to tread carefully but managed to establish herself as a professional gardener. She became knowledgeable about temperate plants, and had the foresight to build a conservatory at her house in Essex in the years before the boom in exotic plants. Soon she was giving professional advice to other people establishing indoor gardens. She became a consultant to a wholesale importer and won a medal at the Chelsea Flower Show for her orangery in one of the show gardens. 'All of these activities happened because I was not happy just to be a wife and mother,' she explains.

The horizons of what was both socially acceptable and practically possible expanded for those who had been debs in 1958. Tessa Prain became a professional interior decorator, assistant successively to two of the most famous English twentieth-century country house designers John Fowler and David Hicks. In the early 1960s, the years when Tessa worked for him, David Hicks, who was connected by marriage to the royal family, was already greatly in demand in country-house circles for his affable blending of the classical and modern. Hicks was a populariser, an early incarnation of the modern television makeover designers, who maintained that the country-house style was achievable by anyone. All you needed was flair and ingenuity. Another of our contemporaries, Philippa Drummond, was part of the professional 'foodie' revolution that, again, was just beginning in the 1960s. Her recipe columns appeared in the *Financial Times* and *Country Living* and Philippa became an authority on cookery. Elfrida Eden took over the Vacani School of Dancing, where she had once been the star pupil, in the early 1980s, combining the running of the much-expanded school with her own independent career as a choreographer. The girl who had been trained in that most esoteric skill of curtseying was now making her own living passing on the technique.

As old prejudice against opening historic houses to a paying public receded, the ex-debs of my generation were frequently drawn into plans for making great houses financially viable, generating enough income to support necessary future restoration work on buildings which were by their very nature vulnerable. Elisabeth Hyde Parker, whose coming-out dance, readers will remember, had been held at her own family home, Melford Hall, just two years before its transfer to the National Trust, married Thomas Stonor in 1966. He became the 7th Baron Camoys ten years later, inheriting Stonor, near Henley-on-Thames, Oxfordshire, the beautiful and atmospheric red-brick house important in the history of the recusants in England. The priest hole once occupied by St Edmund Campion, the Jesuit and martyr, is still there. In a sense, as a young wife, Elisabeth had gone from one problematic great house to another. Stonor in the middle 1970s was looking rather hopeless, depleted of much of its historic furniture, in need of extensive restoration. The revival of Stonor has been much of her life's work. Beth's special achievement has been the old kitchen garden, which she totally replanted and replanned during the 1980s. Its rose and shrub borders are interspersed with apple trees. Clipped yew trees and long home-grown box hedges give the garden the studied informality of a painting in a medieval illuminated manuscript. Great swathes of daffodils and narcissi spread out to the north of the walled garden in the spring.

Similarly Christine Stucley took on some unexpected responsibilities when she married David Cobbold, with whom she had been very visibly in love through most of the Season of 1958. Christine has described their meeting in her memoir *Board Meetings in the Bath*. It was at a dance: 'Attracted by my low-cut green dress and long hair, he had wandered over and asked, "Are you a mermaid?" "Yes," I replied, "and I live in the sea off Hartland Point in north Devon."'

This was a very 1958 exchange. David Cobbold was the eldest son of Lord and Lady Cobbold and heir to Knebworth in Hertfordshire, the crazily magnificent edifice that had been in his mother's family, the Lyttons, for five hundred years. The house, originally a relatively simple Elizabethan manor house, had been fabulously Gothicised by the Victorian writer and poseur Edward Bulwer-Lytton who had superimposed on the façade copper domes and minarets and gargoyles, and commissioned exuberant interior decorations from John Crace, a follower of Pugin. It was a demanding house to run. His parents were worn out with the problems of maintaining Knebworth and were thinking of giving it away to Hertfordshire County Council to make a university headquarters, a popular idea among owners of redundant stately homes at that time of massive university expansion. But even giving Knebworth away had proved impossible: people were frightened off by the state of the building, 'riddled as it was with dry rot and every sort of beetle'. However, as Chryssie Cobbold writes,

David and I were young and energetic; the sixties had seen a huge expansion in car ownership and tourism, and the idea of 'the stately homes' had been pioneered at Woburn, Longleat and Beaulieu. Suddenly it occurred to us that we could perhaps keep Knebworth as a home.

In 1970 David's parents moved into the bungalow they had for years been longing for and the young Cobbolds, with their family, moved into the all-too-daunting house.

Like Elisabeth Camoys at Stonor, in her work for the resuscitation of Knebworth Christine Cobbold was to some extent developing exist-

Lord and Lady Cobbold, the former Christine Stucley, and their children
Richard, Rosina and Peter in costume for an Elizabethan joust at Knebworth

ing skills. In the hope of stabilising their income, her parents Sir
Dennis and the Hon. Lady Stucley had been running their enormous
house in Devon, the twelfth-century Hartland Abbey, as a hotel. Their
five children had been involved in this labour intensive and, by all
accounts, somewhat precarious enterprise as Hartland Abbey sometimes lurched into an aristocratic Fawlty Towers. Chryssie had learned
the lessons in her childhood of that old-fashioned upper class
resilience. The Stucleys as a tribe had been good at buckling down. But
hers and David's energies on behalf of Knebworth proved how far
Chryssie was also a woman of the modern world. Their development
of the Knebworth site in Hertfordshire showed great imaginative flair:
building their own exit road off the A1 to make the house and park
more accessible to visitors; moving two 400-year-old tithe barns from
elsewhere on the estate to make a restaurant architecturally in keeping
with the house; inventing an adventure playground as an attraction
for children and constructing a narrow-gauge railway line to carry
passengers right around the park. They generated a whole series of
attractions – jousting tournaments and Elizabethan banquets, car rallies and the large-scale rock festivals, verging on the riotous, at which
bands of the calibre of Pink Floyd, the Rolling Stones and Led

Zeppelin performed. Chryssie was involved in every detail of planning, to the extent of dressing up her whole family for the photographers in Elizabethan clothes. In 1984, once the proceeds of the Cobbolds' sales of land in Knebworth village had been invested, producing a reliable annual income for the house and the estate, a trust was set up and the future secured for coming generations of the Lytton family. We should not forget that this success had been achieved with entrepreneurial flair that would have been denounced as embarrassingly vulgar by many of our parents' more commercially inhibited generation.

It was part of the accepted duties of the country-house chatelaine, the lady of the manor, to take an active part in country life. There was a distinct trend among the married women I had known as debutantes towards taking public office not as their husbands' consorts but in their own right. The Hon. Mary Bridgeman, for example, was married in 1962 to Jeremy Bayliss, an upright and very charming escort of our year who had a distinguished and high-profile career, becoming President of the Royal Institution of Chartered Surveyors and Chief Executive of the Foundation, Royal Botanic Gardens, Kew. They live a contented married life in Berkshire. It was Mary not her husband who became High Sheriff of that county, her appointment starting in 2005.

Alexandra Bridgewater, who featured as a deb with her friend and cousin Georgie Milner in Tom Hustler's double portrait, had also married young. She had met John Cotterell during the London Season at the dinner dance given by the Duke of Norfolk for his daughter Mary. They were married in 1959. John came from an old Herefordshire family, succeeding his father as 6th Baronet in 1978. With his sporting and historical interests, he has been a popular and influential figure in the county. From the late 1980s he led the campaign to keep the medieval Mappa Mundi at Hereford Cathedral and has been Vice Lord Lieutenant of Herefordshire since 1998. It would have been easy for Alexandra to accept the role of high-up county wife and mother to four children. But she developed another, indeed several other careers in parallel. She enrolled as a full-time mature student at Hereford Art College, developing her painting to a level which enabled her to have three professional London exhibitions. She pursued her fund-raising projects, especially car-boot sales, with an entrepreneurial energy that lifted them far beyond the level of the conventional country ladies' charitable works. One car-boot sale held at the Cotterells' house,

Garnons, raised £26,000 for the Samaritans. Alexandra was given the MBE for charitable services to the community and became known locally as 'Lady Carboot'. When she became High Sheriff of Herefordshire and Worcestershire in 1992 she was the first woman to hold this office in her county. Al died of cancer in 2006. Her last communications with me came from hospital, notes written post-chemo in a very shaky hand. Seven hundred people crowded into Hereford Cathedral for her funeral, mourning a woman of great radiance and capability.

Annabella Loudon, one of the few debs of our year en route for Oxford, makes an appearance in James Lees-Milne's diaries for 1991. She was by this time married to Jonathan Scott, banker, art historian and Chairman of the government Export of Works of Art Committee: 'We had the Jonathan Scotts to luncheon. She clever and formidable, a J.P. etc. He rather like Tom Bridges, slight, aquiline features, the same grim mouth . . . I like him.'

James Lees-Milne had not quite got Annabella's measure. Certainly she was a JP. She had been a JP for twenty or so years. Presiding as a magistrate was one of the traditional voluntary unpaid occupations for those who had the time and inclination for it. It was seen as a perfectly acceptable, indeed an admirable, calling for a well-off married woman. But Annabella, who had gravitated into the legal world after university, was a more than ordinary magistrate in that she had always been more interested in formulating legal policy than in implementing it in day-to-day court work. She chaired numerous Bench Committees and panels. She was a member of the Youth Justice Board for England and Wales, a quango established by Jack Straw, from its inception in 1998, and a member of the Coulsfield Inquiry into Alternatives to Prison which reported in 2004 after spending eighteen months investigating alternatives to custody. Annabella is an admirable example of a one-time deb who survived the Season to become a power in the land.

Annabella's later career might have been predicted: even as a deb she showed a streak of seriousness which prevented her from ever appearing quite attuned to that intensive party-going scene. Of Diane Kirk, now Lady Nutting OBE and a formidable figure in British public life, the opposite is true. Diane was only sixteen when she did the Season: this was a year younger than the norm. With her sparkling vivacity and air of wide eyed innocence Diane had always struck me as one of the most frivolous of debutantes, seen at all the dances, always ready with a quip for the reporters who adored her. The *Evening Standard* gossip columnist caught her at a party at the Duke of Bedford's house in Cheyne Walk in Chelsea:

Miss DIANE KIRK, her complexion marble smooth, her dimensions right for Paris fashion designer Pierre Cardin, who chose her as one of his top 12 models, was outlined against a gilt-framed painting by Gainsborough.

Guests studied Miss Kirk, ignored Gainsborough. 'You should see her in leopard skin trousers' said an emphatic escort, who was later observed on his knees asking Miss Kirk out to dinner.

Yes, in 1958 that was our Diane.

What happened to transform the girl who then appeared as the epitome of debbiness into an authoritative member of some of the most influential national committees, particularly those concerned with architecture, heritage and the environment? Diane herself attributes her involvement in public service to her marriage, in 1959, to Earl Beatty, a distinguished wartime naval commander, himself the son of the famous First World War Admiral, the 1st Earl Beatty. At the time of Diane's wedding to the already three-times-married David Beatty he was, at fifty-four, old enough to be her father, even at a pinch her grandfather, as many of our mothers noted with alarm. It was however a great love match, a sensationally swashbuckling Regency romance that Georgette Heyer might have written, and many of the debs both envied and applauded Diane in attracting such a glamorous, experienced older man.

David Beatty had had his own political career. He was Unionist MP for Peckham from 1931 to 1936 and later a Councillor for Peckham on the LCC. He encouraged Diane to enter politics and in 1968 she was elected to Westminster City Council, serving for ten years and becoming a member of the Town Planning Committee. Right back in her childhood buildings and the landscape had mattered greatly to her, and she revelled in the big pitched battles of that period over conservation versus urban renewal and commercial development. Diane, in speaking up for conservation, often found herself allied with the LCC's Labour members rather than her own constituency of the Tories. In tackling issues that affected the face of Britain so profoundly she had found her cause.

David Beatty died in 1972. Diane's second husband, Sir John Nutting, QC, a lawyer and since 1998 a Deputy High Court Judge, similarly supported Diane's wide-ranging public work, viewing it a

Lady Beatty, the former Diane Kirk, photographed by Cecil Beaton at
Chicheley Hall soon after her marriage to Earl Beatty in 1959

stimulating basis for a marriage that his wife should have her separate
sphere of influence. From 1980 to 1995 Diane was the first woman on
the board of Anglia TV. Simultaneously she was serving on the
Council of the National Trust, she was a member of the Royal Fine
Art Commission and, from 1991 to 1997, was a trustee of the
National Heritage Memorial Fund and Heritage Lottery Fund,
empowered with the spending of enormous sums of money at what
often seemed an impossibly fast pace. Diane had little formal education. She went, as most debs did, to a non-academic school and only
caught up with her A-levels in her early thirties. But she has enormous
curiosity and an instinct for arriving quickly at the crux of any given
issue. She knows precisely what can be achieved by a committee and
she loves her involvement in the processes of power. Currently she is
Chairman of the Georgian Group, a member of the Cathedrals Fabric
Commission and Chairman of the Prince of Wales's Drawing School.
The girl who told the newspapers in 1958 she was looking for a job
'ideally as a film star' has surprised us by becoming a magnificent
grande dame.

So far we have been looking at ex-debs operating within the conventions of previous generations, finding new possibilities within existing frameworks of ways of life considered socially acceptable. But there were also notable departures as some of my contemporaries baulked at the restrictions of the life they saw ahead:

Much as I enjoyed the Season I am glad that I decided on my particular path – the alternative seemed to be arranging another bowl of flowers and organising another dinner party ad infinitum, which though fun for a while palls after a bit.

This is the retrospective view of Margaret Chilton, who, as Margaret McKay, was one of the best-liked and most gregarious of debs. She changed course completely in the 1980s, once her four children were growing up. She took a degree in English at Reading University, a discipline which gave her her first psychological insights into character: insights notably absent from the social world we knew. She then trained as a counsellor and now has her own practice as a psychotherapist. These moves were opposed bitterly by her parents, who had brought her out so splendidly, especially her mother who had her sights set on an earl. But as Margaret soon learned from her professional experience, release from the burden of one's parents' expectations is basic to the recovery of self.

This was an era when many new careers were opening to women. Judy Grinling, the last of the debs to make her curtsey, became one of the new breed of graphic designers, a profession that burgeoned in the image-conscious sixties. Having trained in graphics at the Munich Akademie für das Graphische Gewerbe and the Central School of Arts and Crafts in London, Judy worked as an assistant to one of the rising stars of graphics: Derek Birdsall at BDMW Associates. Once she married the journalist and wine writer Hugh Johnson she freelanced in design and used a treadle press at home for letterpress printing. There were gradually more opportunities for women on newspapers and magazines and on television. Penny Graham gravitated from modelling to fashion journalism, becoming fashion editor on the *Evening News*. Auriol Stevens was the *Observer*'s education correspondent and a reporter for the TV programme *A Week in Politics* before she became editor of the *Times Higher Education Supplement*. Holly Eley (the former Holly Urquhart) was assistant editor of the *New Review* before moving, in 1979, to the *Times Literary Supplement* where she is now art history editor.

Caroline Cuthbert (right) and Camilla Paravicini with Frank Sinatra in his house in Beverly Hills in 1962. The photograph was taken on Caroline's Box Brownie by Robin Douglas-Home

Two other of my contemporaries rose high in the new world of arts administration. Annette Bradshaw joined the ICA in the early 1970s as the Director Norman Rosenthal's assistant, then moved with Rosenthal to the Royal Academy where she eventually became Deputy Secretary. Caroline Cuthbert's career had started as an art dealer. Before the Season she studied art history in Florence, Rome and Paris. Her background and contacts stood out as more cosmopolitan than those of the home-grown English debutantes. It was Caroline who wore a sensational deep-red satin dress by Lanvin at her own deb dance. She went to the States after her Season, travelling from coast to coast by Greyhound bus, stopping off in LA where she met Warren Beatty, Natalie Wood, Frank Sinatra, 'the film stars we'd dreamt about'. She worked at Christie's in New York and then returned to London, joining Anthony d'Offay's Dering Street gallery in 1973 and becoming a director three years later. It was the highly driven and charismatic d'Offay who sharpened her appreciation of twentieth-century British modern painters – Wyndham Lewis, the Bloomsbury artists, David Jones. She learned a great deal of the psychology of artists since d'Offay also dealt in living artists, for example Richard Long and Gilbert & George. In 1984 she was invited to apply for a new post at the Tate: Curator in the Archives Department with special responsibility for acquisitions, negotiating with living artists and their heirs, persuading them to sell or leave their records to the nation. Caroline was instrumental in acquiring the Tate's substantial Bloomsbury collections, the Edward Burra letters, the records of the painters' muse Isabel Rawsthorne. She loved the job's aspects of a treasure hunt, each new discovery leading to another, and it proved an important post in relation to the shaping of the history of British modern art.

Caroline's career has been doubly interesting in that, even as a debutante, she had been determined never to get married, negating at the outset what the Season had in theory been all about. Besides what she had suffered through her own parents' separation, she was terrified of what she saw as the innate restrictiveness of the married state, the tedium of having to refer your decisions and actions to another person. She described this to me as a dread of being 'subsumed'. She held out until she was in her early forties when she married the writer Jonathan Raban who had similarly been resisting marriage. They were together for the next five years.

Jennifer Murray, the former Jennifer Mather, record-breaking helicopter pilot

I do not think that I am forcing things in claiming ours as an exceptional year in which quite a proportion of the upper-class young girls sloughed off their old image of routine frivolity and began a process of reinvention. The departure of the debs into unexpected spheres is epitomised by Jennifer Murray, formerly Jennifer Mather, who in 1997 was the first woman to pilot a helicopter around the world. At the age of fifty-seven she entered the *Guinness Book of Records*, having flown 22,173 miles in 99 days and raised $100,000 for the Save the Children fund. She now claims that she had never quite conformed. She had been the 'country bumpkin' in the Season, not even knowing how to paint her toenails like the other more sophisticated girls. She was deeply influenced by her hugely energetic industrialist father, Sir William Mather, Chairman of Mather & Platt, the Manchester engineering firm, who was always setting her new challenges. After the Season Jennifer had gone to art school, studying textile design. She started her own textile company in Thailand in the 1960s, the decade in which Thai silks became high fashion. She then formed another textile company in Hong Kong. From the early 1990s, as we have seen, her ambitions refocussed on aviation. In 2000, dispensing with co-pilots, Jennifer achieved another record of being the first woman to fly solo around the world in a helicopter. The journey took her eastward from England through Saudi Arabia, Bangladesh, Vietnam and onwards around the circle of the globe. She is now making her second attempt to fly from Pole to Pole. As with the apotheosis of Sally Croker-Poole, one's initial response is of total disbelief. Is 'Jeffa', the heroine helicopter pilot who posts those upbeat bulletins on the internet, really the same Jennifer whose dance at Whirley Hall in Macclesfield, shared with her sister Gillian, I remember going to in 1958? Jennifer's press statements are wonderfully positive. Her intrepid circumnavigation of the world in a small piston-engine helicopter without autopilot must surely act as encouragement to others: 'Hopefully this shows people they can do anything if they really want to – no matter what their age or gender.' She has certainly succeeded in challenging the image of the vapid and unadventurous ex-deb.

In one of the most fascinating chapters of his book *The Decline and Fall of the British Aristocracy*, David Cannadine points out that 'throughout its long history as the governing class of the nation, the British landed establishment had always spawned its fair share of mavericks and rebels, dissidents and revolutionaries'. He cites the seventeenth-century country squire Oliver Cromwell; Charles James Fox, eighteenth-century aristocratic chief spokesman of the Whiggery; the twentieth-century Labour aristocrats and 'the Fascist notables' as part of 'a long line of titled and genteel renegades'. He could have included as part of this phenomenon a particular strain of female rebelliousness within the upper classes: the conscience of the debutante.

One example of an attitude frequently regarded as a form of class betrayal can be found in the memoirs of Margaret Haig Thomas, later Viscountess Rhondda, who became a militant suffragette member of the Women's Social and Political Union, was arrested and sent to Usk Prison where she went on hunger strike. As founder and editor of *Time and Tide* she was a staunch campaigner for political freedom and individual liberty. In the early 1900s, her years of coming out, she endured three London Seasons which she describes bitterly in her reminiscences *This Was My World* as a form of tyranny:

A system which hypnotized a perfectly intelligent, though perhaps rather a naïve young woman already anxious to investigate most accepted notions impersonally and dispassionately, into acceding without question to indulgence in this odd form of occupation, which in fact she was hating so much.

In the growth of her feminist politics those three debutante Seasons had been her baptism of fire.

In a later generation, in 1935, Jessica Mitford had glowered through a Season whose meaningless rituals and foolish luxuries seemed to her increasingly obscene in a world in which fascism was growing. She had fallen in love with Esmond Romilly, Winston Churchill's cousin, a precocious class rebel who had run away from Wellington College where he had been publishing a left-wing magazine entitled *Out of Bounds*. Encouraged by Romilly, Lord Redesdale's fifth daughter became a Communist. She read the *Daily Worker*, immersed herself in Marxist books and pamphlets. 'Now I was really a Ballroom Communist with a vengeance', she wrote of her coming out, describing its frustrations and ennui: 'I had made no real friends, had learned nothing, was no further advanced in the planning of my life. I cursed myself for not having the brains or the ability to find my own way out of the deadly boredom that was enveloping me like a thick fog.' Eventually she and Romilly left for Spain together,

supporting the Republicans in the Spanish Civil War. With her tren-
chant politics and her caustic turn of phrase in describing the sheer
idiocy of the upper classes, Jessica Mitford was the prime pre-war
example of the anti-debutante.

For anyone with the disposition to be critical the contrasts within
the Season were dramatic, like a medieval painting simplifying the
distinctions between luxury and poverty. The gawping crowds
around the palace watching the debs coming to be presented:
'Crowds used to watch because they enjoyed looking at pretty people and pretty clothes . . . we were pretty butterflies', one debutante
recorded at the height of the Depression. The armies of retainers:
waiters waiting, cloakroom ladies hanging coats and running the
warm water for the debutante ablutions, dance bands playing, photographers capturing and posing the most impressive guests. At my
own dance at the Dorchester, the ancient fortune teller paid to tell
young girls what they were wanting to hear most. For the most far-
thinking of the girls who found such scenes of conspicuous consumption sickening it was not a simple matter of resenting the
unfairness of the rich having the parties while the underclass sustained them. The most dissident of debutantes arrived at a position
of believing that the upper classes should not exist at all. Such debutantes, content at nothing short of a dismantling of the system, have
inevitably been looked upon as traitors by many of their peers. This
was Jessica Mitford's political position. Nearer our own time there
has been Vanessa Redgrave, whose Season in 1956 pre-dated her
involvement with the Workers' Revolutionary Party, and my own
friend Teresa Hayter whose considerable journey from an embassy
childhood to International Marxism is described in her autobiography *Hayter of the Bourgeoisie*, published in 1971.

Thinking back over Teresa's Season I cannot find the signs of her
incipient revolutionary politics. There are pictures in the scrapbooks of
Teresa at deb tea parties looking a bit bored and out of things, but
docile. We see her in the long receiving line for her own deb dance,
shared with two others, Olga Hohler and Delia Dupree, standing
between her parents Lady Hayter and the enormously distinguished Sir
William in his stiff white shirt, glittering with decorations. He had just
retired from the Foreign Office, having been Ambassador in Moscow,
and was now the Warden of New College in Oxford. Teresa's dance was
held at Mercers' Hall, one of the ancient city livery halls only recently

rebuilt after its destruction in the Blitz. According to Jennifer's report of the occasion, 'The three girls, in dresses of pastel shades, created a memorable picture as they stood with their mothers receiving the guests.' It is interesting in view of Sir William's recent Moscow incumbency, and indeed Teresa's later history, that one of the guests listed at the Hayter ball is Sir Anthony Blunt, at the time Surveyor of the Queen's Pictures, who was subsequently revealed as a long-term Marxist and a Soviet spy.

Teresa does not mention her Season in *Hayter of the Bourgeoisie*, an otherwise detailed personal account of her radicalisation to the point of joining the International Marxists, a revolutionary Trotskyist group. She examines with rigorous honesty a childhood exposed to 'the blandishments of bourgeois apologetics' in a charming and well-meaning intellectual household, describing her parents as 'fine representatives of what is best in bourgeois ideology: liberal values, a belief in progress and reform, aesthetic and literary appreciation'. She confesses to the laziness and callowness of her three years at Lady Margaret Hall in an Oxford of snobbery and indolence, virtually unchanged since the days of Evelyn Waugh:

The prominent students, those of fame and notoriety, were overwhelmingly public school, by acquired mannerism if not fact. They sprawled on the lawn of Peckwater Quad, went to 'balls' and parties, frequented exclusive clubs like the Gridiron Club and, even more select, the Bullingdon Club.

She castigates herself for her 'unthinking' acceptance of the 'bourgeois system of values' and indeed for going to far too many parties: Teresa had been seen attending sixty-four parties in fifty-six days during her first Oxford term. Why does Teresa give no account of her ritual curtsey to the Queen in this otherwise candid confessional? Why no mortified description of Queen Charlotte's, the Berkeley Debutante Dress Show, her own dance at Mercers' Hall amidst the Canalettos and beneath the crystal chandeliers? For, I think, the self-same reason she does not include any reference to her appearance, dressed in pinky-purple silk and carrying a bouquet, in the retinue of bridesmaids that followed me down the aisle on my first marriage, in the chapel at New College where her father was the Warden. Sir William made the speech afterwards at the reception in the college hall. For people unfamiliar with such arcane scenes there is no way of describing them. Some things are just too thoroughly, mysteriously bourgeois to be included in an exposé of the bourgeoisie.

Teresa Hayter (far right) with Karin MacCarthy and Sarah Friedberger, bridesmaids at Fiona MacCarthy's wedding to Ian White-Thomson in New College Chapel, Oxford in 1961

Teresa left Oxford, as I did, in 1961. She has always been an inveterate traveller. Born in Shanghai, at nursery school in Washington, at primary school in London and then Paris: her peripatetic diplomatic childhood had given her the taste for being on the move. In the early 1960s she was in New York. She lived for a time with a taxi driver whose father was a vermin extinguisher by trade and a member of the Communist Party. She describes in her memoirs the exhilaration of driving every morning in the taxi from the Bronx into Manhattan 'under and over an astonishing series of bridges'. She then spent a year in Asia, which was really the start of her political awareness. Five long journeys that she made at this stage in the east – Hong Kong, Japan, China, Cambodia, and through India – brought her closely in touch with the social problems and the underlying politics of the so-called underdeveloped countries. Each one, as she explains 'put me a stage further on the road to becoming a revolutionary'.

In 1968 Teresa was back in Oxford, taking a B.Phil, a postgraduate degree in economics. This was the year of the student rebellion that brought Paris to a standstill, of protests and sit-ins in many universities and colleges in Britain. She found an Oxford completely changed from the politically complacent place she had remembered. Activism was in the air. All students were affected. She wrote: 'I am convinced that by then it was impossible for any student to ignore Marxist ideas.' 1968 was the year of what I can only describe as her conversion: '. . . this second Oxford period finally turned me into a revolutionary'.

Teresa's transformation from debutante to Marxist has baffled, in some cases infuriated, many former friends. The response, especially amongst ex-debs who knew her, has been to ridicule a volte-face so extreme they cannot quite accept that it is serious or even genuine. This is not the way I feel. Teresa's total change in outlook of course reminds me strongly of the quasi-religious conversion of William Morris, whose biography I wrote. Morris, in the 1880s, turned his back on his own comfortable middle class to join the revolutionary Socialist Democratic Federation. In the case of Teresa I am conscious of a similar almost total cut-off between her old life and her new. We are still friends. But I, although leftist in my politics, am nowhere near a Marxist. And I have to accept that a part of Teresa has now been lost to me. She has written many books, closely argued and provocative, on aid, world poverty, environmental exploitation, global piracy. She was closely involved in protests against the partial closure of the Rover Group's car plant at Cowley in 1988 which caused a substantial rise in local unemployment. From 1993 she was active in the campaign to close the immigration detention centre at Campsfield. Her most recent book *Open Borders* puts the case against immigration controls. Could this possibly have been the girl who held a record for Oxford party-going, let alone my bridesmaid? I have come to admire her decades of tenacity and to respect her fierce integrity.

The last two stories are of girls with whom I have a double link. As well as having curtseyed in 1958, Nicolette Harrison and Rose Dugdale were my more or less contemporaries at Miss Ironside's School. A full account of that marvellously idiosyncratic educational establishment, in some ways behind the times but in many ways ahead of them, has been given by Miss Ironside's great-niece, Virginia Ironside, in her memoir *Janey and Me: Growing Up with My Mother*. Suffice it to say here that the school had been founded in the years between the wars by the highly principled daughter of an Aberdeen doctor who had taken a

Froebel teachers' training course and was progressive in her views of education. Rene was emphatically the headmistress, tall and upright with her hair swept up into a bun, backed up by her rounder, more domestic sister Nellie who was in charge of the housekeeping. The school building was a large stuccoed house in Elvaston Place, South Kensington, into which the 150 pupils were crammed with only three lavatories and a basement dining room to which we descended to eat our frugal lunches sitting on long oak benches at oak tables – a little like the children in a workhouse, although the pupils of Miss Ironside came in fact from highly cultured homes.

Although she looked and often was intimidating, Rene was in some ways a free spirit. She had a great respect for individuality: her ruling principle was 'We must protect the child'. It was a school in which there was no uniform and children were encouraged to address staff by their Christian names or affectionate nicknames such as 'Snorks' for the maths teacher Miss Norcross, 'Focky' for the infant class teacher Mrs Fox. It was assumed that we would concentrate in lessons and enjoy what we were learning. There was lots of tuition in italic handwriting using broad-nibbed calligraphic pens, one of Rene's specialities, and classes in Dalcroze Eurhythmics, for which we wore floaty pseudo-Grecian tunics. The music mistress, Mrs Kelvin, had been a concert pianist in her native Austria. There was very little science in Miss Ironside's curriculum and, as my sister has reminded me, no religious instruction. She remains to this day uncertain what the Resurrection actually was.

Word must have got around the London theatrical-artistic coteries that Miss Ironside's was a good school to send your children to. Rene's nephews Robin and Christopher Ironside were both well known in the art world, Robin as a neo-Romantic painter and gallery curator who was Deputy Director at the Tate under John Rothenstein, Christopher as a brilliantly versatile designer recently recruited to teach life drawing at the newly revitalised Royal College of Art. The children at Miss Ironside's were also fortunate in being taught by Christopher whose services, his daughter Virginia assumes, had been extracted in lieu of payment of fees for her own attendance at the school. The arty children flocked in. The three daughters of Sir Hugh and Lady Casson; Juliet, the daughter of John Mills and Mary Hayley Bell; Susan and Tessa Price, daughters of Dennis Price who starred as the charismatic poet in the film *The Bad Lord Byron* soon after I arrived at Miss Ironside's school. There was Tracy Pelissier, stepdaughter of Carol

Reed, famous producer of the films *The Fallen Idol* and *The Third Man*, and Harriet Devine, daughter of George Devine, recently appointed Director of the English Stage Company at the Royal Court. Jane Birkin was to arrive a little later on. This was the context – talented, theatrical, original, a little wayward – in which Nicolette Harrison and Rose Dugdale received their early years of education.

Nicolette was in the form beneath me at Miss Ironside's. Even then I registered her as a particularly beautiful child, blonde haired with the delicate Pre-Raphaelite good looks that were to come back into fashion in the sixties. She could have been an angel painted by Burne-Jones. Her best friend at the school was Tracy Pelissier. Tracy's mother was the well-known socialite and actress Penelope Dudley Ward, known to her intimates as Pempy; her grandmother Freda Dudley Ward had been the Duke of Windsor's close companion before Mrs Simpson arrived on the scene. Tracy came from a racy and sophisticated world. Where Nicolette was so blonde, Tracy was a dark little girl, very striking, rather sallow. At Miss Ironside's School the two of them were quite inseparable, feared by the other children, forming a conspiracy of knowingness. If a classmate told them she was going to the cinema Nicolette would sneer at her: 'How frightfully common.' Every morning Virginia Ironside dreaded being picked up by Sir Carol's limousine, on what sounds like a superior version of a school run, since she knew that Nicolette and Tracy were waiting in the back seat to torment her while the driver made his leisurely way through the streets of South Kensington. A cruel little pair.

Nico was sixteen when she met the Marquess of Londonderry, introduced by his sister Lady Annabel Birley. The publicity that followed the announcement of their engagement in 1958, so soon after Nico had curtseyed to the Queen, brought reminders of the young Lord Londonderry's earlier notoriety. In 1957 Londonderry had supported Lord Altrincham's onslaught on the monarchy, attacking in a letter published in the *New Statesman* the 'toothpaste smiles' and 'deplorable taste in clothes' of the royal family. It should not be forgotten that Lord Londonderry's elder sister Lady Jane Vane-Tempest-Stewart had been one of the maids of honour who attended the Queen at her coronation. The Londonderrys as a family have had a special penchant for social contradictions. As reported by the *Daily Express*, the defiantly unconventional young marquess, who had run a jazz band – the Eton Five – while still at school, had refused to give his fiancée an engagement ring. Nicolette had been accommodating: she didn't like rings anyway. Such a symbolic disregard for the conventions suited the mildly rebellious spirit of the times. The beautiful, original young pair were seized on by the press as examples of a new unstuffy aristocracy, reported to have celebrated their engagement dining quietly à deux at a Chinese restaurant in Brompton Road.

That dream was over within another decade. The Londonderrys had two daughters, Lady Sophia and Lady Cosima. In September 1969 Nicolette had a son, Tristan Alexander, who was assumed to be heir to the Londonderry title, growing up as little Viscount Castlereagh. Alastair Londonderry claimed that the baby was not his. Blood tests confirmed his contention and showed that the actual father was the singer and jazz musician Georgie Fame. In the sixties Georgie Fame, born Clive Powell, was at the height of his popularity, performing with his band the Blue Flames at the Flamingo and scoring three number-one hit singles in the decade. Ironically, in this family tale of many ironies, it was Lord Londonderry's sister Lady Annabel who first drew the marchioness's attention to the rock star. She recalls in her memoirs *Annabel: An Unconventional Life* how she was sitting at home sometime in 1964 watching *Top of the Pops* on television and was so struck by the good looks of the young singer whose record had reached the number-one slot she immediately rang Nico to tell her to switch on the programme. 'She was just in time to catch the end of Georgie Fame singing "Yeh, Yeh" and she was star struck.'

Nico's story does not finish well. In 1970 the Londonderry marriage ended in divorce on grounds of her adultery with 'the pop singer' Georgie Fame, discretion being exercised in respect of adultery committed by Lord Londonderry. Tristan had been stripped of his title and eventually became a recording engineer and guitarist with his rightful father's band, the Blue Flames. In 1972 she and Georgie Fame were married at Marylebone registry office, she still looking like an angel. They were mobbed when they emerged by the singer's screaming fans. They attempted to live quietly and they had another son together. But by the 1990s Nico was suffering from clinical depression. She died after what was officially termed 'a fall from Clifton Suspension Bridge'.

Though Nico and Tracy, that impenetrable duo, linger a little dubiously in the memories of the past pupils of Miss Ironside, no one ever speaks ill of Rose Dugdale. She is generally remembered as warm-hearted and

Nicolette Powell, the former Marchioness of Lodonderry, after her marriage at Marylebone Register Office to the singer Georgie Fame in 1972

original. One old friend recalls Rose's scathing wit: 'she was very very funny'. Another speaks of Rose as 'the highlight' of her school years. Virginia Ironside voiced the feelings of the majority: 'Everyone adored this generous, clever and dashing millionaire's daughter, who was life and laughter.' Rose Dugdale's former English teacher, Jillian Staynes, saw that she had a potential streak of anarchy: for instance, when rebuked for cheating Rose was unrepentant saying, 'Well, I don't see why not.' But such unusual early independence of thought is not sufficient to explain the whole of Rose's later history. The lasting mystery to everyone who knew her is how this clever boisterous child, whose attitude to life was so sturdily irreverent, ever became serious about the IRA.

My own connection with the Dugdales was a close one since for a time I was best friends with Rose's older sister Caroline who is seated in the place of honour on my right in the picture of my tenth birthday tea party at the Dorchester. The Dugdales took me out on memorable treats: I watched Margot Fonteyn dance in *Cinderella* from the family box at Covent Garden. Reciprocal nursery teas were a feature of our childhood and I was quite often dropped off by my nanny at the Dugdales' house in St Leonard's Terrace, alongside Chelsea Hospital. We would meet again on Sundays at morning service in the Chelsea

Children's fancy dress party given by Rose Dugdale, in front row, second from left. Karin MacCarthy sits fourth from left, wearing one of the bridesmaids' dresses from our mother's wedding

Pensioners' chapel, the two Dugdale sisters and their little brother James dressed in what was a family uniform of navy-blue wool coats and navy berets. For musical afternoon performances at Rene's, the girls wore identical white *broderie anglaise* dresses, their long hair beribboned and beautifully brushed. They looked like sisters in a Renoir painting. They played duets together, a critical Mrs Dugdale looking on. On one Christmas-time visit to their house I remember being amazed at being told the children had to reach the age of ten before being allowed to decorate the Christmas tree. It seemed to me the Dugdale house was one of daunting rules and regulations laid down by Rose and Caroline's mother, Carol Dugdale, a large imperious woman whose family had made its fortune out of soap in Liverpool and whose previous husband was John Mosley, Oswald Mosley's brother. My mother was as terrified of Mrs Dugdale as I was, so totally unbending did she seem.

The family was a rich one. Rose's father, Eric Dugdale, was a Lloyd's underwriter and the owner of a six-hundred-acre estate near Axminster in Devon. Rose's friends who were invited to stay at Yarty Farm have recollections of a farmhouse smartened up to the extent of being 'ludicrously overdone', with immaculate grounds, a gravel drive, shiny limousines, a dressage ring in which the children practised on their ponies and a highly structured educational routine in force in Devon as it had been in London. Dugdale children were brought up to improve the shining hour. Rose was sent abroad to 'finish' before she did the Season. She curtseyed, as we did, in 1958 although her dance, at the River Club, was not held until 1959. She was by then showing signs of reluctance at involving herself in such a full-scale coming out as her sister Caroline had undergone. She resisted going to deb tea parties and only agreed at the last moment, under what one imagines was huge pressure from her mother, to have a dance at all. According to the later legend of Rose Dugdale the fact that she had her deb dance on a Sunday, an almost unheard of day for dances in the Season, was an early sign of revolutionary tendencies. In fact there was a simpler explanation: all the weekday slots for dances had by this time been booked up.

Rose Dugdale in male disguise, having successfully
infiltrated the Oxford Union in the early 1960s

Rose arrived at St Anne's College in Oxford in the autumn of 1959 to read philosophy, politics and economics. I was by then myself at Oxford but saw little of her. She was gaining a certain notoriety by the way she was said to be swaggering around wearing men's shirts and trousers and by the reported squalor of her room, a pile-up of filthy coffee cups, cigarette ends, discarded garments, mountains of old books and newspapers. A reversal of her mother's ultra-orderly environment. The rumours were that Rose was getting very odd. There were press reports and pictures of Rose Dugdale and a friend from her college having gatecrashed the Oxford Union, wearing men's clothes and wigs. This was a protest against the all-male union's refusal to let in women members. They sat amongst the men in the debating hall for two hours without being recognised. The subsequent publicity was gratifying proof of the power of such protests. Oxford saw the beginning of what the newspapers were later to revel in describing as ex-debutante Rose Dugdale's 'lunge to the left'.

In the early 1970s Rose's increasingly reckless political activities and the bitter rift with her family became public. Like Teresa Hayter, Rose Dugdale had been radicalised by the student protests of 1968, and again like Teresa she had visited and been inspired by the revolutionary Cuba of that time. She held a master's degree in philosophy from Mount Holyoke women's college in Massachusetts, having submitted a thesis on Wittgenstein. But by 1972 Rose had abandoned her academic and government advisory career as an economist, sold her Chelsea house and was living in a flat in Tottenham, north London, with her lover Walter Heaton, an ex-Guardsman and shop steward who was married with two daughters and who had been in prison for a number of minor criminal offences, ranging from burglary to fraudulent consumption of electricity and obstruction of the police. Rose had cashed in her share of the family syndicate at Lloyd's, estimated at around £150,000, distributing the proceeds – over £50,000 in 1972 and 1973 alone – amongst the north London poor and to Wally's ex-wife with rather random generosity. She and Wally ran the Tottenham Claimants' Union from a corner shop in Broad Lane. Through their work for civil rights they had developed a shared interest in the civil rights movement in Northern Ireland and visited Ulster together several times.

In June 1973 Rose was arrested and stood trial in October at Exeter Crown Court charged with taking part in a burglary at Yarty Farm, the Dugdale home in Devon where Rose had been brought up.

Rose Dugdale on her release in 1980 from Limerick prison after serving six years of a nine year sentence for her part in the Russborough art robbery and for helicopter hijacking near the border with Northern Ireland

Paintings and family silver valued at £82,000 had been stolen. Police knowledge of her's and Wally's IRA connections and suspicions that they had been involved in smuggling arms were factors in making the arrest. Rose, who pleaded not guilty, claiming to have been coerced by her associates, used the trial to repudiate publicly her family and background. The majority of the stolen goods had been recovered and were assembled as exhibits in the courtroom, symbols of an upbringing Rose by now regarded as iniquitous. During the trial she interrogated her own father, a witness for the prosecution. She told Eric Dugdale: 'I love you, but hate everything you stand for.' At the end of the trial she turned upon the jury: 'In finding me guilty you have turned me from an intellectual recalcitrant into a freedom fighter. I know no finer title.'

Finally Rose was given a two-year suspended sentence while Wally was given six years in jail. She denounced this as yet another blatant example of capitalist injustice: the rich girl being let off lightly in relation to the poor man convicted on the lesser charge.

In June 1974 Rose Dugdale was on trial again, this time at the Special Criminal Court in Dublin. She was charged with receiving nineteen Old Master paintings stolen in a raid on 26 April from

Russborough, the Palladian mansion in the Wicklow mountains belonging to Sir Alfred Beit. The Beits were amongst the wealthiest of all the 'Randlords', dynasties made vastly rich through mining gold and diamonds in South Africa. Sir Alfred's father had used his money to amass one of the world's great private art collections, half of which had descended to his son. Rose – in apparently convincing disguise as a Frenchwoman – with three IRA accomplices broke into Russborough late at night, pistol whipping Sir Arthur and his wife, tying them up and gagging them. The haul included a Vermeer, two Rubens, paintings by Velázquez and Gainsborough and a famous Goya, *Portrait of Doña Antonia de Zarate*. The Beits looked on in helpless anguish as these and other masterpieces were wrenched out of their frames with a screwdriver. Their total value was said to be around £8 million. The objective behind the robbery was to trade the paintings for the release of Dolours and Marion Price, sisters who had been jailed for life on explosives charges and were on hunger strike in Brixton Prison. However, three of the paintings were discovered two weeks later in a wardrobe in a cottage in west Cork which Rose – keeping up her French alias – had rented, and the rest were found rolled up in the boot of a Morris she had borrowed from her landlord. Fingerprints left at the cottage were identified by the army as belonging to the Provisional IRA leader David O'Connell. This time Rose Dugdale pleaded 'proudly and incorruptibly guilty' at her trial.

Once again she used the courtroom as a political platform, denouncing Britain as 'a filthy enemy'. In her submission to the court she maintained that the Irish people had the sole right to the wealth of Ireland; that the Dublin government was guilty of 'treacherous collaboration' with England; and that victory would eventually be granted to what she referred to as 'the army of the people'. She did her best to prevent what she considered irrelevant details of her earlier existence being mentioned in court: she was reported to have 'laughed contemptuously' as a prosecution witness stumbled through a list of her European finishing schools, mispronouncing all the names. Rose's Dublin court appearance and indeed the raid itself on people well known to her parents, Lady Beit being connected to the Churchills and the Mitfords, marked another ruthless step in the rejection of her past. When Rose was sentenced to nine years' imprisonment she turned to her supporters in the crowded public gallery, giving a defiant clenched fist salute. In 1974, a son, Ruari, was born in her cell in Limerick

Prison and in 1978 by special dispensation Rose was married to the father, Eddie Gallagher, an IRA terrorist himself serving a twenty-year sentence in Portlaoise High Security Jail for the kidnapping of Dr Tiede Herrema, the Dutch businessman. The wedding was held in the heavily guarded oratory of the prison at Limerick, the first time a marriage between convicted prisoners had been permitted in the history of the Irish Republic.

One can see Rose in part as a figure of her period, the family denying 1970s. She connects with the active terrorism of the German Red Army Faction, otherwise known as the Baader–Meinhof Gang, whose attacks on property and murders of prominent individuals from 1974 onwards posed a grave threat to German democracy. Like its leaders Andreas Baader and Ulrike Meinhof the members of the group were predominantly middle-class, well-educated people in their thirties, born in the uncertain years of the Second World War, as Rose herself had been. There is also an obvious parallel with the case of the American newspaper heiress Patty Hearst who in 1974 was kidnapped by a radical gang calling itself the Symbionese Liberation Army (SLA). Her father Randolph Hearst had begun by meeting the demands of her captors, organising multi-million-dollar food distribution programmes for the poor, only to see his daughter turn against him. Taped messages from Patty Hearst became increasingly hostile to her family and class until in the end she told them: 'I have chosen to stay and fight.' Video footage of her participation in an SLA bank robbery, the heiress turned into gun-wielding terrorist, remains as an eerie memento of that time.

In some respects Rose was just another politically radical, profoundly disaffected child of the seventies. But what makes her case particular and to me so poignant is the way that it is rooted in the then declining English upper class. This was a drama played out amongst the country landowners, the Lloyd's underwriters, the acquirers of great collections of art, all people of a kind Rose lumped together as obsolete. Her reactions had their own simplicity and logic: 'For years', she said, 'my family have been taking money from the poor. I am just trying to restore the balance by giving some of it back.' Her coming-out ball she remembered as a horror: 'One of those pornographic affairs which cost what 60 old-age pensioners receive in six months.' To call Rose a reluctant debutante would be inadequate, toweringly so. As an example of committed and in its way heroic resistance to the Season the story of Rose Dugdale can never be surpassed.

And my own case history? What had *I* been doing between 1958 and the Racquet Club reunion in 1990? My story is certainly a tamer one than Rose's. But the Season set up a species of resistance with me too. In October 1961, the autumn after I left Oxford, I married Ian White-Thomson, who had been at Oxford with me. We made a nostalgic return for a large wedding, which was held in the chapel of Ian's old college, New College, as I have described. I cannot blame Ian for the gradual disintegration of the marriage. He was then tall and good-looking, highly intelligent, generous and sensitive, and I expect that he still is. It was not Ian himself, it was the life that went with him. The life of the young married Mrs Ian White-Thomson, wife of the rising young business executive in a firm called Borax, came less and less to suit me. I hated the monotony, the repetitiousness, the London dinner parties with two or three carefully chosen, smartly dressed, charming, articulate and infinitely boring married couples, mirror images of us. Most of all I loathed the weekends with Ian's sociable military family in Essex. The shoots, the tennis parties, the before-lunch Sunday drinks parties. The routine became anathema. The moment of truth came in the middle of a rather ramshackle and drunken hunt ball held in Chelmsford Town Hall. I looked around and realised that this was like the Season only worse.

One effect of the Season was to make me very serious. I was in any case a natural swot, irritating my contemporaries at Miss Ironside's by getting 99 per cent for maths. I used to listen avidly to *Top of the Form*, yearning to join one of the teams of little geniuses showing off their knowledge to quiz-master Lionel Gamlin. The most popular girls in the Season were the silly ones, but silliness had never come easily to me. What had been a long summer of disguising my intellectual interests in order to survive brought about a perhaps predictable reaction. I wanted a career as a writer and intended to be more professional than the professionals. No one was going to brand me as an ex-deb amateur.

In 1963 I joined the *Guardian*. It was a turning point. To say I joined the paper with something very like the relief and gratitude with which my friend Teresa Hayter joined the International Marxists may sound ridiculous. But that is the way it was. Arriving from a very different way of life in which the deadlines were those of the next social occasion, I loved the sense of urgency, the rethinks and the crises on which the lifeblood of a daily newspaper depends and the feeling of

Fiona MacCarthy, feature writer on the Guardian

Should women have teeth?

Fiona MacCarthy in advertisement promoting *Guardian* women journalists
in 1965

attachment to a paper dedicated to upholding moral values (yes, the
Guardian in those days was a little sanctimonious) within which I had
my own albeit minor role. I loved the easy camaraderie of a culture in
which the chief reporter could come over to my desk holding out a
battered copy of Simone de Beavoir's *The Second Sex* and tell me: 'You
ought to read this book.' In effect I was the *Guardian*'s Swinging
Sixties correspondent, recruited as the voice of metropolitan youth at
a time when the paper had only very recently ceased to be the

Manchester Guardian and was much expanding its London base. I interviewed John Lennon, David Hockney, Ossie Clark (who I described, correctly, as the rudest man in London) and all the other obvious 1960s interviewees, and I wrote an early feminist column for the women's page. I was thrilled when Jonathan Aitken, in his book *The Young Meteors* (1967), a study of young people's precocious impact on the public in the sixties, referred to Fiona MacCarthy's 'alarming views'. Energised by my excitement at working for the *Guardian* I was so productive that, faced with what had become an *embarras de richesses*, the editor suggested my pieces should appear under two different by-lines, giving the paper two journalists for one. I had become what would now be seen as a workaholic. I have come to blame the Season for these and many subsequent symptoms of excess. Would I, for instance, have felt the need to spend eight years – eight *years* – on the researching and writing of the life of Byron, reading every single letter that he ever wrote, leaving not a stone unturned in the Byronic haunts in Italy, Greece and even Aberdeen if I had not been disowning my own past life as a debutante? Maybe; but I think most likely not.

I escaped to find my own working-class hero, David Mellor, a designer and silversmith. He was already fairly famous, a young man with an E-type, when I went to interview him for the *Guardian* in 1964. A little later I moved north to live with him in Sheffield, a city where no deb has ever danced. It was an exciting time to be young and living in what was soon to become known as the People's Republic of South Yorkshire. Sheffield was still a working city of cutlery and steelworks. I liked feeling a part of this environment of *making*. We had two children and sent them to Sheffield comprehensive schools, believing in the ethics of the social mix. The miners' strike of 1974 impinged upon the city. Collection points for food and money for the striking miners' families were set up in the street and outside the Town Hall. There was a mood of grim determination mingled, oddly, with a sense of carnival, the warmth and sheer exuberance of people united in a common cause.

In my own writing as a biographer I gravitated towards the utopians, people seeking better alternatives to the world they had examined and found wanting. All the books I have written have been about outsiders. C.R. Ashbee, the Arts and Crafts architect who led an exodus of craftsmen from the slums of the East End in search of an idyllic existence in the Cotswolds. Eric Gill, Roman Catholic patriarch and sculptor, whose back-to-the-land communities purported to be cells of good living 'in the chaos of the world'. William Morris with his radical and generous ideals of art for the people in the face of widespread social inequalities and Victorian imperialist greed. Lord Byron: a lord yes, but a poet and iconoclast who attacked the venality of English high society with devastating wit.

These were busy, fulfilled years. A lot of work, a lot of travel. Our friends now tended to be artists, designers, architects, theatre people, other writers. Any links with the old deb world were broken. The memories of the queues outside the palace, debs' mums' lunches, Allegra Kent Taylor's cocktail dance, the descent of the virgins down the staircase at Queen Charlotte's, the Fourth of June at Eton, the bread-and-butter letters, Lady Ham-'n-Eggs, Royal Ascot, the rained-off Henley Royal Regatta, the party at Luttrellstown, high jinks in the Bothy, the whole panorama of the Season, had receded into one of those jumbled, intermittently beautiful and slightly shaming dreams.

Diana, Princess of Wales

Lady Diana Spencer came upon the scene as a ghost of Seasons past when the royal engagement was announced in February 1981. Prince Charles, who when he became King would also be Supreme Governor of the Church of England and Defender of the Faith, was bound by an anachronistic set of royal rules to marry a Protestant girl of preferably noble stock who was also a virgin. By 1981 such a girl was hard to find. The Prince's attendants scoured the country with a growing desperation that reminds one of the search for the elusive girl in *Cinderella*. All too often the slipper did not fit. Diana succeeded where others had failed because she was so young, so naive and so old-fashioned. Earl Spencer's daughter was a then unusual throwback to the sweet and blushing debutantes of three decades before.

She was born into an ancient English family of landowners and aristocrats, third daughter in a family in which the lines of succession had for centuries descended through the sons. On the usual assumption in such families that daughters did not need much education Diana was sent to an unambitious boarding school for girls, West Heath at Sevenoaks in Kent, where she failed all of the five O levels she took. After leaving West Heath she went to a finishing school in Switzerland. If the curtsey ceremony had continued as before, she would certainly have been in line to curtsey to the Queen – as indeed would the future Camilla Parker Bowles in her own debutante year of 1965. As it was Diana Spencer did not have a formal Season. But the flats in Chelsea and South Kensington shared with one or two other Sloaney girls; the socially acceptable but meagrely paid jobs babysitting for friends, cleaning, working as a waitress; the cookery course; the temporary teaching post at the Vacani School of Dancing; the job

Lady Diana Spencer leaving the Royal Academy of Arts in June 1981, after an evening party she attended with her fiancé, Prince Charles

as an assistant at the all-too-appropriately named Young England kindergarten; the Old Etonian and Guards officer suitors; the girlish confidences and old-time practical jokes: it was as if even the sixties had not happened. Lady Diana's peculiarly sheltered life as a single girl in London was precisely that of the debs of my own generation in the fifties, as was Diana's remarkably determined sexual purity. She clung to her virginity as we had done, and with perhaps the same mixed motives of fear, ignorance and preserving one's intactness for Mr or (ideally) Lord Right. Lady Diana Spencer was after all the step-granddaughter of the romantic novelist Barbara Cartland whose books she had read avidly through her teenage years, presumably absorbing a philosophy of love which is a curious blend of calculation and effusiveness. One of Diana's flatmates quoted her as saying: 'I knew I had to keep myself tidy for what lay ahead.'

The tragedies that lay ahead cannot quite have been predicted from the television interview given at Balmoral at the time of their engagement by a rather sheepish kilted and sporraned heir to the throne and the still childish beauty who gazed at him adoringly, the fiancé from a time-warp. Is it just with hindsight that one senses the unease? Diana was accepting the life of the consort, the admirer, the eternal looker-on in a world in which male privilege and prowess in battle and in sport was the long-accepted norm. She was entering the world accurately described by Beatrix Campbell in her book about Diana as 'the sexist culture of masculine performance and female spectatorship'. It was also a world of crude and cruel double standards in which kings and future kings were permitted infidelities – Edward VII and his high- and low-born 'beauties', Prince Charles and his long-running liaison with Camilla – with a tacit approval not extended to their wives. In the circles I grew up in it was more or less accepted that men from time to time would have their little fling and you were better to ignore it because when it came down to it, financially and socially dependent on your husband as you were, what was the alternative?

Diana herself had been reared in an environment in which, by and large, these conventions persisted. She was not, at least to begin with, a brave spirit. When, goaded to retaliation, Princess Diana found herself what appeared the perfect lover, the man she later claimed to have adored, it was James Hewitt, a career soldier, a Captain in the Life Guards, a very good rider and an expert polo player, a brave and handsome man who was a bit of a philanderer, a military hero who lacked the sense of irony to see that his professions of loyalty to Queen and country were in some ways contradicted by the fact he was committing adultery with the Queen's son's wife. One might claim that James Hewitt was a well-deserved diversion for Diana, but he certainly had his limitations. Reading his memoirs *Moving On* his antediluvian attitudes strike me as painfully familiar. This was just the sort of man I used to meet at house parties, watch at polo matches, fend off in dark nightclubs. Fundamentally James Hewitt was a debs' delight of yesteryear.

When the marriage between the Prince and the Princess had evidently reached a crisis, the conventional wisdom amongst those who knew or pretended to know the royal couple was that the troubles would die down or be glossed over. The important thing was to preserve the status quo. A typical insider's view was that of Woodrow Wyatt writing to John Bowes Lyon in 1992:

I think they will jog along and at the end they will survive all these difficulties and have a *modus vivendi* because she is a well brought up girl with proper standards and obviously he is, too. They are not going to do anything which is going to put the crown in danger or become a most fearful scandal.

A nicely brought up girl was bound to quieten down and compromise. The fascinating thing is that she did not.

Diana's gradual emboldening was one of the remarkable turning points in recent memory. The people who had vetted her, approved her ancient lineage and innocently docile personality, had assured themselves of her technical virginity, made certain she was physically equipped to bear the future King of England's children, indoctrinated her in meek acceptance of her duty in relation to the monarchy and God, were aghast when Diana turned upon them in all her pent-up anger and indignation, first by her collaboration with Andrew Morton in the book *Diana: Her True Story*, published in 1992, and then in the famous *Panorama* interview with Martin Bashir in 1995. Among the 22 million people watching her dramatic accusations and disclosures was James Lees-Milne who recorded in his diary:

An astonishing performance. Never having heard her speak before, I imagined she would be like a silly little debutante. On the contrary, she was adult and articulate. A low, croaky voice slipping into Northolt 'eows'. Very beautiful, cocking her head to the left, lovely mouth, enormous clear eyes . . . She didn't criticise the Prince or Family directly, yet left watchers with no doubt that she hated the lot. Venom visible in every gesture and look. Said they held her to be an embarrassment and danger. I dare say.

The shock value of the interview lay in its candour, its quite beautiful vulgarity: a princess transformed into an emotionally manipulative media star. The wonder of it was the way she overturned all the decorum and passivity her upbringing and class had battened into her. Perhaps Diana's *Panorama* interview marked the final death of the English debutante.

Select Bibliography

Nigel Arch and Joanna Marschner, *Splendour at Court, Dressing for Royal Occasions Since 1700*, 1987

Margaret Argyll, *Forget Not*, 1976

Patrick Balfour, *Society Racket*, 1933

Cecil Beaton, *Self Portrait with Friends: Selected Diaries 1926–74*, 1979

Mark Bence-Jones, *A Guide to Irish Country Houses*, 1988

David Benedictus, *The Fourth of June*, 1962

Charlotte Bingham, *Coronet Among the Weeds*, 1963

Caroline Blackwood, *Great Granny Webster*, 1977

Henry Blofeld, *A Thirst for Life*, 2000

Ronald Blythe, *The Age of Illusion: Some Glimpses of Britain Between the Wars 1919–1940*, 1963

Elizabeth Bowen, *Bowen's Court*, 1942

Sarah Bradford, *Elizabeth: A Biography of Her Majesty the Queen*, 1996

Kate Caffrey, *'37–'39 Last Look Round*, 1978

Beatrix Campbell, *Diana, Princess of Wales: How Sexual Politics Shook the Monarchy*, 1998

David Cannadine, *The Decline and Fall of the British Aristocracy*, 1990
Class in Britain, 1998

Leonora Carrington, *The House of Fear: Notes from Down Below*, 1989

Anne Chisholm, *Nancy Cunard*, 1979

Chryssie Lytton Cobbold, *Board Meetings in the Bath*, 1999

Diana Cooper, *The Rainbow Comes and Goes*, 1958
The Light of Common Day, 1959

John Cornforth, *London Interiors*, 2000

Anne de Courcy, *1939 The Last Season*, 1989
Debs at War 1939-45, 2005

Marian Crawford, *The Little Princesses*, 1950

Quentin Crewe, *The Frontiers of Privilege*, 1961

Sarah Curtis (ed.), *The Journals of Woodrow Wyatt*, 3 vols, 1998–2000

Leonore Davidoff, *The Best Circles. Society, Etiquette and the Season*, 1973

Mark Décharné, *King's Road*, 2005

Terence Dooley, *The Decline of the Big House in Ireland. A Study of Irish Landed Families 1860–1960*, 2001

Daphne Fielding, *Emerald and Nancy: Lady Cunard and Her Daughter*, 1968

Theodora FitzGibbon, *With Love*, 1982

Zia Foxwell, *Borrowed Time*, 1989

Jonathan Gathorne-Hardy, *The Rise and Fall of the British Nanny*, 1972

Lady Annabel Goldsmith, *Annabel: An Unconventional Life*, 2004

Robert Graves, *The Long Weekend: A Social History of Great Britain 1918–1939*, 1940

Norman Hartnell, *Silver and Gold*, 1956

Teresa Hayter, *Hayter of the Bourgeoisie*, 1971

Robert Hewison, *Under Siege: Literary Life in London 1939–45*, 1977
Too Much: Art and Society in the Sixties, 1960–75, 1986

William Douglas Home, *The Reluctant Debutante*, 1955
Mr Home Pronounced Hume: An Autobiography, 1979
Old Men Remember, 1991

Virginia Ironside, *Chelsea Bird*, 1964
Janey and Me, 2003

Robert Rhodes James (ed.), *Chips: The Diaries of Sir Henry Channon*, 1967

Molly Keane, *Good Behaviour*, 2001

Betty Kenward, *Jennifer's Memoirs: Eighty-five Years of Fun and Functions*, 1992

Ian Kershaw, *Making Friends with Hitler: Lord Londonderry and Britain's Road to War*, 2004

Angela Lambert, *1939: The Last Season of Peace*, 1989

James Lees-Milne, *Ancestral Voices: Diaries 1941–3*, 1975
Prophesying Peace: Diaries 1944–5, 1977
Caves of Ice: Diaries 1946–7, 1983

Rosamond Lehmann, *Invitation to the Waltz*, 1932

Shaun Levy, *Ready, Steady, Go! Swinging London and the Invention of Cool*, 2002

Jeremy Lewis, *Playing for Time*, 1987

Lesley Lewis, *The Private Life of a Country House (1912–1939)*, 1980

Lady Sybil Lubbock, *The Child in the Crystal*, 1939

Randal MacDonnell, *The Lost Houses of Ireland*, 2002

Sarah Maitland (ed.), *Very Heaven: Looking Back at the 1960s*, 1988

Tom Maschler (ed.), *Declaration*, 1957

Charles McKean, *The Scottish Chateau*, 2001

Jessica Mitford, *Hons and Rebels*, 1960

Nancy Mitford, *The Pursuit of Love*, 1945

Nancy Mitford and others, *Noblesse Oblige: An Enquiry into the Identifiable Characteristics of the English Aristocracy*, 1956

Hugh Montgomery-Massingberd and Christopher Simon Sykes, *Great*

Houses of Ireland, 1999

Andrew Morton, *Diana: In Pursuit of Love*, 2004

John Osborne, *Look Back in Anger*, 1956

Mary Pakenham, *Brought Up and Brought Out*, 1938

Roy Perrott, *The Aristocrats*, 1968

Ben Pimlott, *The Queen: A Biography of Elizabeth II*, 1996

Petronella Portobello, *How to be a Deb's Mum*, 1957

Anthony Powell, *A Dance to the Music of Time*, 12 vols, 1951–1975

Violet Powell, *Five Out of Six*, 1960

Margaret Pringle, *Dance Little Ladies: The Days of the Debutante*, 1977

Philippa Pullar, *Gilded Butterflies: The Rise and Fall of the London Season*, 1978

Mary Quant, *Quant by Quant*, 1966

Simon Raven, *The Old School: A Study in the Oddities of the English Public School System*, 1986

The Viscountess Rhondda, *This Was My World*, 1933

Sheila Rowbotham, *Promise of a Dream: Remembering the Sixties*, 2000

Ianthe Ruthven, *The Irish Home*, 1998

The Scottish House, 2000

Anthony Sampson, *Anatomy of Britain*, 1962

Dominic Sandbrook, *Never Had it So Good*, 2005

Nancy Schoenberger, *Dangerous Muse: A Life of Caroline Blackwood*, 2001

Caroline Seebohm, *The Country House: A Wartime History 1939–45*, 1989

Christopher Simon Sykes, *The Big House: The Story of a Country House and its Family*, 2004

Andrew Sinclair, *The Breaking of Bumbo*, 1959

My Friend Judas, 1959

Michael Sissons and Philip French (eds.), *Age of Austerity 1945–1951*, 1963

Lavinia Smiley, *A Nice Clean Plate: Recollections 1919–1931*, 1981

Godfrey Smith, *The English Season*, 1987

Louis T. Stanley, *The London Season*, 1955

Roy Strong, Marcus Binney and John Harris, *The Destruction of the Country House, 1875–1975*, 1974

A.V. Swaebe, *Photographer Royal*, 1967

Laura Talbot, *The Gentlewoman*, 1952

Emma Tennant, *Girlitude: A Portrait of the 50s and 60s*, 1999

Rebecca Tyrrel, *Camilla*, 2004

Evelyn Waugh, *Brideshead Revisited*, 1945

The Sword of Honour, 3 vols, 1952–1961

Loelia, Duchess of Westminster, *Grace and Favour*, 1961

A.N. Wilson, *After the Victorians, 1901–1953*, 2005

Simon Winchester, *Their Noble Lords: The Hereditary Peerage Today*, 1981

Giles Worsley, *England's Lost Houses*, 2002

Peregrine Worsthorne, *In Defence of Aristocracy*, 2004

Sources

PREFACE
'It was such' – Annabella Scott, conversation with the author, 23 February 2005

CHAPTER ONE
'flimsy finery' – *The Times*, 21 March 1953
'the full perfection' – E.H. Ruddock, *The Common Diseases of Woman*, 1888
'the specific, upper-class' – Jessica Mitford, *Hons and Rebels*, 1960
'Now darlings, throw out' – Philippa Pullar, *Gilded Butterflies*, 1978
'you had to make' – Lady Clodagh Anson, *Victorian Days*, 1957
'there was something' – Lady Sybil Lubbock, *The Child in the Crystal*, 1939
'After the presentations' – Betty Vacani, quoted Margaret Pringle, *Dance Little Ladies*, 1977
'The splendour of the 1930s' – Margaret Argyll, *Forget Not*, 1976
'Now, there were' – Philippa Pullar, *Gilded Butterflies*, 1978
'The crowning mischief' – *Queen* magazine, 1861, quoted Pat Jalland, *Women, Marriage and Politics*, 1986
'In my humble opinion' – Betty Kenward, *Jennifer's Memoirs*, 1992
'We had to put a stop' – Thomas Blaikie, *You Look Awfully Like the Queen*, 2002
'I knew of two peeresses' – Betty Kenward, *Jennifer's Memoirs*, 1992
'will be more' – Malcolm Muggeridge, *New Statesman*, 22 October 1955
' "Crawfie", Sir Henry Marten' – Lord Altrincham (John Grigg), *National and English Review*, August 1957
'she carried on' – Sarah Bradford, *Elizabeth: A Biography of Her Majesty the Queen*, 1996
'the present age' – *The Times*, 15 November 1957
'One girl had drunk' – *Daily Express*, 15 November 1957
'INNOCENT DAZZLE' – *New York Herald Tribune*, 21 March 1958
'Epitaph for a Deb' competition – *Daily Express*, 22 March 1958

'Deb decorum' – *Daily Express*, 13 March 1958
'a dainty honey blonde' – *Daily Express*, 21 March 1958
'a symbol of loyalty' – *Sketch*, 1 January 1958
'a little wobbly' – *Daily Express*, 21 March 1958
'I don't think' – *Daily Express*, 21 March 1958
'Goodbye to the Debs' – *Evening Standard*, 12 and 13 March 1958
'What's the new play?' – William Douglas Home, *Mr Home Pronounced Hume*, 1979
'very alarming' – Diana Cooper, *The Rainbow Comes and Goes*, 1958
'a split second' – Emma Tennant, *Girlitude*, 1999
' "SQUASHY" BELCHER' – *Evening Standard*, 19 March 1958

CHAPTER TWO
'Riding's my hobby' – *Evening Standard*, 19 March 1958
'resembling the evacuation' – Jessica Mitford, *Hons and Rebels*, 1960
'as fixed' – Jessica Mitford, *Hons and Rebels*, 1960
'London season' – *The Times*, 24 March 1958
'Penelope Riches' – *Sketch*, 12 March 1958
'Miss Lola Wigan' – *Evening Standard*, 8 April 1958
'We seemed to fill' – Margaret Argyll, *Forget Not*, 1975
'Miss Miranda Smiley' – *Sketch*, 12 February 1958
'a strawberry blonde' – *Evening Standard*, 8 April 1958
'that large, handsome' – *Evening Standard*, 23 June 1953
'There is little' – *Sketch*, 12 February 1958
'We used buckets' – Thalia Stone, conversation with author, 15 March 2005
'the invisible bonds' – Peregrine Worsthorne, *In Defence of Aristocracy*, 2004
'cycle is non-U' – Nancy Mitford, 'The English Aristocracy', essay in *Noblesse Oblige*, 1956
'no girl would willingly' – *Sketch*, 12 February 1958
'Caroline has 300' – *Evening Standard*, 8 April 1958
'I had enough' – *Evening Standard*, 10 May 1958
'I know girls' – Judith Listowel, 'The cost of coming out', *Tatler*, 9 April 1958

CHAPTER THREE
'laughing over' – *Sketch*, 9 April 1958
'As I listened' – Antonia Fraser, 'It's the Cinderella flavour I remember', *Tatler*, 9 April 1958
'Irene Ravensdale' – Evelyn Waugh, diary 15–16 March 1956, ed. Michael Davie, *The Diaries of Evelyn Waugh*, 1976
'often studiously' – *Sketch*, 21 May 1958
'I also met' – *Tatler*, May–June 1958
'the new order' – *The Times*, 1 July 1940
'the outside world' – Lindsay Anderson, 'Get Out and Push!', essay in

Declaration, 1957

'Are we going to?' – John Osborne, 'They Call it Cricket', essay in
   Declaration 1957

'Enter James Bond' – *Daily Express*, 19 March 1958

'most delightful' – *Sketch*, 9 April 1958

'little scarlet gods' – Andrew Sinclair, *The Breaking of Bumbo*, 1959

'a good dancer' – 'Debutantes Escorts', *Sketch*, 4 June 1958

'went into paroxysms' – Candida Lycett Green, funeral address for Molly
   Baring, *Well Remembered Friends*, ed. Angela Huth, 2004

'She was my enemy' – Auriol Stevens, conversation with the author, 27
   February 2005

'Please be kind' – Elfrida Fallowfield, conversation with the author, 24
   February 2005

'at the top' – Zia Foxwell, *Borrowed Time*, 1989

'growing up girls' – Noel Streatfield, *The Years of Grace*, 1950

'young marrieds' – *Tatler*, 2 April 1958

'his grey suit' – *Daily Express*, 22 March 1958

'to exchange' – *Sketch*, 19 November 1958

'a sparkling girl' – *Evening Standard*, 16 April 1958

'Big thing recently' – Georgina Milner, notebook entry, April 1958

'the appalling deportment' – *Tatler*, 2 April 1958

CHAPTER FOUR

'looking enchanting' – *Tatler*, 14 May 1958

'They are now' – *Sketch*, 21 May 1958

'striped awnings' – Cynthia Asquith, *Remember and Be Glad*, 1952

'not in our street' – Virginia Woolf, 'A Dance in Queen's Gate', 1903, ed.
   Mitchell A. Leaska, *A Passionate Apprentice: The Early Journals*, 1990

'Though I am' – Violet Powell, *Five Out of Six*, 1960

'Walking at 2 or 3' – Evelyn Waugh, diary entry for 28 June 1956, ed.
   Michael Davie, *The Diaries of Evelyn Waugh*, 1976

'all magnificent, gilded' – Diana Cooper, *The Rainbow Comes and Goes*,
   1958

'All the parties' – Joyce Phipps, quoted Margaret Pringle, *Dance Little
   Ladies*, 1977

'probably at Brook House' – Margaret Argyll, *Forget Not*, 1975

'Holland House too' – Chips Channon, diary entry for 14 October 1940, ed.
   Robert Rhodes James, *Chips: The Diaries of Sir Henry Channon*, 1967

'It is sad' – Chips Channon, diary entry for 2 November 1940, ed. Robert
   Rhodes James, *Chips: The Diaries of Sir Henry Channon*, 1967

'Aristocracy no longer' – Nancy Mitford, *Noblesse Oblige*, 1956

'It doesn't happen' – *Evening Standard*, 22 May 1958

'the most dazzling' – *Evening Standard*, 28 May 1958

'He beamed' – *Evening Standard*, 23 May 1958

'two very common' – Sonia York, 1958 scrapbooks, lent to the author

'Though You're Only Seventeen' – Noël Coward, *Dance Little Lady*, Chappell Music Ltd.

'Byronic youth' – Cyril Connolly, *Enemies of Promise*, 1938

'secretly engaged' – *Daily Express*, 22 March 1958

'Age Succeeds Class' – *The Times*, 16 May 1958

CHAPTER FIVE

'Hulking young Old Etonians' – *Daily Express*, 5 June 1958

'you were going into' – Henry Blofeld, *A Thirst for Life*, 2000

'The Tory Ministers' – *Daily Express*, 5 June 1958

'We openly' – Professor Francis Sherlock, essay in *The Old School*, ed. Simon Raven, 1986

'on trust' – Henry Blofeld, *A Thirst for Life*, 2000

'it seemed to me' – Simon Raven, *The Old School*, 1986

'whorehouse pink' – General Eisenhower, quoted Patrick Gale, *The Dorchester: A History*, privately published, 1990

'What a mixed crew' – Cecil Beaton, quoted Patrick Gale, *The Dorchester: A History*, privately published, 1990

'the air of a witches' lair' – *Christopher McAlpine: A Life*, privately published, 2005

'shining ones who dwell' – John Betjeman, 'Christmas', *A Few Late Chrysanthemums*, 1954

'a dark lilac satin' – *Tatler*, 25 June 1958

'Discipline has declined' – Quentin Crewe, *The Frontiers of Privilege*, 1961

CHAPTER SIX

'The Thames's most social' – *Tatler*, 16 July 1958

'Like so many' – *Tatler*, 9 July 1958

'I have seen much' – Chips Channon, diary entry for 7 July 1958, ed. Robert Rhodes James, *Chips: The Diaries of Sir Henry Channon*, 1967

'The stately homes of England' – Noël Coward, *The Stately Homes of England*, Chappell Music Ltd.

'One thing is quite certain' – James Lees-Milne, 'The Country House in our Heritage', essay in *The Destruction of the Country House*, 1974

'You were our godparent' – John Joliffe, *Clive Pearson: A Life*, 1992

'There were 200' – *Melford Hall*, The National Trust, 2004

'I join 800' – *Tatler*, 2 July 1958

'I have been to' – Betty Kenward, *Jennifer's Memoirs*, 1992

'stiff sets of tennis' – Violet Powell, *The Departure Lounge*, 1952

'except that' – 'Somerhill History', The Schools at Somerhill, 2005

'Mrs. Wenger has asked' – Petrina Hall to Mrs George McKay, 1958

'This is just to tell' – Nan Danby to Margaret McKay, 4 June 1958

'The other people' – Petrina Hall to Mrs George McKay, 1958

'The trouble with' – *Evening Standard*, 6 June 1958

'deb escorts drive' – *Evening Standard*, 18 June 1958

'After Sarah Norman's ball' – *Tatler*, 2 July 1958
'you are at the head' – Millicent Fawcett, *What I Remember*, 1925
'Growing up' – Jessica Mitford, *Hons and Rebels*, 1960
'In his office' – Ludovic Kennedy address at memorial service for Sonia
  Heathcoat-Amory, 21 January 2000, *Well Remembered Friends*, ed.
  Angela Huth, 2004

CHAPTER SEVEN
'a wild Rabelaisian week' – Margaret Pringle, *Dance Little Ladies*, 1977
'the finest and best-preserved' – Mark Bence-Jones, *A Guide to Irish
  Country Houses*, 1988
'singularly satisfying' – Hugh Montgomery-Massingberd and Christopher
  Simon Sykes, *Great Houses of Ireland*, 1999
'V. nervous' – Penny Graham diary, 2 August 1958
'sleep till lunch' – Penny Graham diary, 3–10 August 1958
'a mixture of years' – Penny Graham to the author, 2005
'a beautiful mover' – *Tatler*, 21 August 1957
'possessing an estate' – *Tatler*, 8 January 1958
'a pretty 22 year old' – *Daily Express*, 9 August 1958
'tempestuous outburst' – *Tatler*, 20 August 1958
'All Irish houses' – James Lees-Milne, diary entry for 12 November 1996,
  ed. Michael Bloch, *The Milk of Paradise*, 2005
'the most cheery' – Lord Castletown, *Ego: Random Records of Sport,
  Service and Travel in Many Lands*, 1923
'the estate of Borris' – James Norris Brewer, *The Beauties of Ireland*,
  1825–6
'skirts were short' – Rosemary FitzGerald, conversation with the author,
  August 2005

CHAPTER EIGHT
'the Scottish season' – Margaret Pringle, *Dance Little Ladies*, 1977
'Tessa, dark and pretty' – *Tatler*, 10 September 1958
'semi-Socialist views' – Holly Eley to the author, 24 November 2005
'the bands' – Holly Eley to the author, 17 March 2006
'Congratulations' – Duncan Fallowell and April Ashley, *April Ashley's
  Odyssey*, 1982
'It is most interesting' – *Sketch*, 26 March 1958
'Lady Hayter's daughter' – *Sketch*, 24 September 1958

CHAPTER NINE
'I want to say' – *Tatler*, 17 December 1958
'Symptomatic of' – Margaret Pringle, *Dance Little Ladies*, 1977
'There were over 800' – Adam Pollock to the author, 29 January 2006
'The two worlds' – Anthony Sampson, *Anatomy of Britain*, 1962
'wholly immoral' – *The Times*, report of court proceedings, 9 May 1963
'I went straight' – Margaret, Duchess of Argyll, *Forget Not*, 1976

'Who can one own' – Fiona MacCarthy, 'In Fear of the Fringe', *Guardian*, 19 August 1968

'the skeleton' – Andrew Sinclair, 'Anthropologically speaking', *Tatler*, 15 April 1959

'Tea parties' – Charlotte Bingham, *Coronet Among the Weeds*, 1963

'People knew' – *Observer Magazine*, 12 March 2006

'the King hippie' – The Hon. Penelope Betjeman, quoted Bevis Hillier, *Betjeman: The Bonus of Laughter*, 2004

'The answer is' – Margaret Pringle, *Dance Little Ladies*, 1977

'His social pages' – Nicholas Coleridge, address at memorial service for Peter Townsend, 6 November 2001, ed. Angela Huth, *Well-Remembered Friends*, 2004

CHAPTER TEN

'Maxine Hodson' – *Harpers & Queen*, October 1960

'a non-stop cocktail party' – Susanna Swallow, conversation with the author, 21 April 2006

'The generation' – Annabel Gooch to the author, 25 November 2005

'Attracted by' – Chryssie Lytton Cobbold, *Board Meetings in the Bath: The Knebworth House Story*, 1999

'We had the Jonathan Scotts' – James Lees-Milne, diary entry for 20 July 1991, ed. Michael Bloch, *Ceaseless Turmoil*, 2004

'Miss DIANE KIRK' – *Evening Standard*, 8 April 1958

'ideally as a film star' – *Evening Standard*, 6 July 1958

'Much as I enjoyed' – Margaret Chilton to the author, 7 November 2005

'the film stars' – Caroline Cuthbert to the author, 28 April 2006

'the Fascist notables' – David Cannadine, *The Decline and Fall of the British Aristocracy*, 1992

'A system which hypnotized' – The Viscountess Rhondda, *This Was My World*, 1933

'Now I was really' – Jessica Mitford, *Hons and Rebels*, 1960

'Crowds used to' – Margaret, Duchess of Argyll, *Forget Not*, 1976

'The three girls' – *Tatler*, 15 October 1958

'the blandishments' – Teresa Hayter, *Hayter of the Bourgeoisie*, 1971

'toothpaste smiles' – Nicolette Powell obit., *The Times*, 15 August 1993

'She was just' – Lady Annabel Goldsmith, *Annabel: An Unconventional Life*, 2004

'Well, I don't see' – Jillian Staynes, conversation with the author, 15 November 2005

'ludicrously overdone' – Julia Mount, conversation with the author, 15 November 2005

'lunge to the left' – *Sunday Times*, 30 June 1974

'I love you' – *The Times*, 23 October 1973

'proudly and incorruptibly' – *The Times*, 26 June 1974

'I have chosen' – Patricia Campbell Hearst with Alvin Moscow, *Patty*

Hearst: Her Own Story, 1982
'For years' – *The Times*, 26 June 1974

EPILOGUE
'I knew I had to' – Andrew Morton, *Diana: Her True Story*, 1992
'the sexist culture' – Beatrix Campbell, *Diana, Princess of Wales*, 1988
'I think' – Woodrow Wyatt to John Bowes Lyon, 1 February 1992,
　　Woodrow Wyatt Journals, vol. 2
'An astonishing performance' – James Lees-Milne, diary entry for 21
　　November 1995, ed. Michael Bloch, *The Milk of Paradise*

Picture Acknowledgements

hostess, Lady Lowson, at the cocktail party for her daughter Melanie. (© Desmond O'Neill Features)

76 Group photograph taken after the marriage of Lady Mary Maitland and the Hon. Robert Biddulph in April 1958. (*Illustrated London News* Picture Library)

80 Ingestre in Staffordshire, Lady Ursula Stewart's family home, photographed in 1958. (*Illustrated London News* Picture Library)

82 The Berkeley Debutante Dress Show. The Hon. Penelope Allsopp, Georgina Milner and Gillian Gough model Cardin's clothes. (© Barry Swaebe Collection)

83 Debs not chosen to be models were given the consolation prize of selling posies to the audience at the Berkeley Debutante Dress Show. (© Barry Swaebe Collection)

88 The maids of honour descending the grand staircase in the Grosvenor House ballroom. (© Barry Swaebe Collection)

89 The Dowager Duchess of Northumberland cutting the cake at Queen Charlotte's Ball. (© Barry Swaebe Collection)

91 Tommy Kinsman serenading a debutante. (© Barry Swaebe Collection)

97 Sally O'Rorke at her dance at Hampton Court. (© Barry Swaebe Collection)

105 Georgina Milner dancing. (© Desmond O'Neill Features)

106 Fiona MacCarthy with a now-forgotten escort at Dominie Riley-Smith's ball. (© Desmond O'Neill Features)

113 The Countess of Dalkeith (now Jane, Duchess of Buccleuch). Portrait in oils by John Merton. (Reproduced by kind permission of His Grace the Duke of Buccleuch & Queensberry, KT.)

115 Victoria Bathurst Norman at the Fourth of June. (© Barry Swaebe Collection)

129 The Dorchester Hotel elaborately decorated by Oliver Messel for the Coronation of Queen Elizabeth II in 1953. (Reproduced by permission of the Dorchester Hotel Archive)

133 Isabella Hughes with Fiona and Karin MacCarthy. (Reproduced by kind permission of Jean Barbour.)

134 The MacCarthy–Burness dance at the Dorchester. Petie and Kenneth Burness with Jennifer, Yolande MacCarthy with Fiona, just before the guests arrive. (© Barry Swaebe Collection)

136 The McCarthy–Burness dance going with a swing. (© Barry Swaebe Collection)

142 Bucolic scene at Belinda Bucknill and Sara Barnett's dance in Windsor Forest. (© Barry Swaebe Collection)

144 Bramham Park, West Yorkshire, where Marcia Lane Fox's coming out ball was held. (© *Country Life* Picture Library)

145 Miranda Smiley on the night of her dance at Parham Park. (© Barry Swaebe Collection)

150 Clandon Park where the Countess of Iveagh held a dance for the Hon.

Eliza Guinness and Lady Teresa Onslow in her former family home. (© *Country Life* Picture Library)

157 Barn dance given for Mary Groves and Eliza Buckingham at Speen Farm, Buckinghamshire. (© Barry Swaebe Collection)

157 The two debutantes Eliza Buckingham (left) and Mary Groves (right) with their parents at the barn dance. (© Barry Swaebe Collection)

166 Sally Croker-Poole being given a word of advice by her mother before her dance at Quaglino's, shared with Julie Stratford. (© Barry Swaebe Collection)

169 The girls in the Beaulieu house party. From left: Sally Nelson, Zia Foxwell, Fiona MacCarthy, Penny Graham, Coral Knowles, unknown, Gabriel Waddington, unknown, Jane Holden. (Reproduced by kind permission of Penny Graham)

170 Nesbit Waddington with Lady Ainsworth at the Irish Grand National in 1958. (*Illustrated London News* Picture Library / photo by C.C. Fennell)

171 Penny Graham's five-year diary, including her account of Dublin Horse Show Week in 1958. (Reproduced by kind permission of Penny Graham)

174 The Hon. Diana Connolly-Carew and her brother the Hon. Patrick Connolly-Carew. (*Illustrated London News* Picture Library)

176 The Kildare Hunt Club meet at Castletown, Lord and Lady Carew's house at Celbridge, County Kildare. (*Illustrated London News* Picture Library)

177 Luttrellstown House, County Dublin. (© *Country Life* Picture Library)

179 William Montgomery, Master of the Eton beagles in summer 1958. (© Desmond O'Neill Features)

189 The 110th Royal Caledonian Ball held at Grosvenor House in May 1958. Leading the dancers down for the set reels: the young Duke of Atholl, one of the top deb escorts of 1958, with Lady Malvina Murray; Captain John and Lady Gillian Anderson; Major David Butter and Serena Murray. (*Illustrated London News* Picture Library)

189 1958 deb Lady Carolyn Townshend with Alasdair MacInnes of the Cameron Highlanders. (*Illustrated London News* Picture Library)

192 Tessa Prain and Ann Carington Smith before their dance at Mugdrum in Fife. (© Barry Swaebe Collection)

192 Dancers at Tessa Prain and Ann Carington Smith's ball. (© Barry Swaebe Collection)

193 Holly Urquhart with her parents before her dance at Craigston Castle. (© Barry Swaebe Collection)

198 Rowallan Castle in South Ayrshire. (© *Country Life* Picture Library)

200 Dodavoe, the shooting lodge at Glen Prosen, Kirriemuir. (Reproduced by kind permission of Frans ten Bos)

201 Grouse shooting in the Highlands: the transporter for the guns. (© Barry Swaebe Collection)

209 Tana Alexander's coming out dance at Dropmore in 1963, with spectacular

decor by Adam Pollock. (© Barry Swaebe Collection)

209 Lady Rosemary Muir at Lady Ashcombe's ball at Dropmore, transformed into a Roman piazza for the night. (© Barry Swaebe Collection)

217 Annette Fletcher modelling Young Jaeger beachwear at the Berkeley Debutante Dress Show in 1966. (© Barry Swaebe Collection)

217 Sarah Harman modelling Annacat palazzo pyjamas at the Berkeley Dress Show in 1967. (© Barry Swaebe Collection)

228 Ex-debutantes of 1958 photographed by Terry O'Neill for a 'Last of the Debs' feature in the *Sunday Telegraph* in 1993. From left, standing: Holly Eley (formerly Urquhart), Penny Graham, Lady Kindersley (formerly Tita Norman). Seated, Zia Kruger (Foxwell), Annette Bradshaw, Susanna Swallow (Crawley), Melanie Black (Lowson), Elfrida Fallowfield (Eden). (© Terry O' Neill)

230 The Aga Khan and his bride, 1958 debutante Sally Croker-Poole, at the reception for Ismaili leaders at the Prince's farm at Lassy near Paris held the day before their marriage ceremony on 28 October 1969. (© PA/Empics)

235 Lord and Lady Cobbold, the former Christine Stucley, and their children Richard, Rosina and Peter in costume for an Elizabethan joust at Knebworth. (Reproduced by kind permission of Lady Cobbold)

239 Lady Beatty, the former Diane Kirk, photographed by Cecil Beaton at Chicheley Hall soon after her marriage to Earl Beatty in 1959. (Reproduced by kind permission of Lady Nutting)

241 Caroline Cuthbert (right) and Camilla Paravicini with Frank Sinatra in his house in Beverly Hills in 1962. The photograph was taken on Caroline's Box Brownie by Robin Douglas-Home. (Reproduced by kind permission of Caroline Cuthbert)

242 Jennifer Murray, the former Jennifer Mather, record-breaking helicopter pilot. (Reproduced by kind permission of Jennifer Murray.)

252 Nicolette Powell, the former Marchioness of Londonderry, after her marriage at Marylebone Register Office to the singer Georgie Fame in 1972. (© Getty Images)

253 Children's fancy dress party given by Rose Dugdale, in front row, second from left. Karin MacCarthy sits fourth from left, wearing one of the bridesmaids' dresses from our mother's wedding. (Reproduced by kind permission of Virginia Ironside)

256 Rose Dugdale on her release in 1980 from Limerick prison after serving six years of a nine year sentence for her part in the Russborough art robbery and for helicopter hijacking near the border with Northern Ireland (© PA/Empics)

264 Lady Diana Spencer leaving the Royal Academy of Arts in June 1981, after an evening party she attended with her fiancé, Prince Charles. (© PA/Empics)

Endpapers from 1958 debutante scrapbooks reproduced by kind permission of Mary Douglas-Bate and Lady Rosemary Fitzgerald

Acknowledgements

~

I am grateful to the following 1958 debs for sharing their memories and impressions of the Season and, in many cases, for lending me their personal collections of photographs, invitations, dance programmes and letters. Their help with my research has been invaluable. However, I must emphasise that their view of the Season does not necessarily coincide with mine:

Mary Bayliss, Melanie Black, Annette Bradshaw, Maggie Chilton, Sonia Coode-Adams, the late Alexandra Cotterell, Dominie Courtauld, Caroline Cuthbert, Mary Douglas-Bate, Tessa Downshire, Sally Dudley-Smith, Holly Eley, Elfrida Fallowfield, Rosemary FitzGerald, Annabel Gooch, Penny Graham, Georgie Grattan-Bellew, Judy Johnson, Joanna Mersey, Jennifer Murray, Diane Nutting, Davina Portarlington, Annabella Scott, Auriol Stevens, Susanna Swallow.

I have enjoyed an opposite perspective on the Season from the following one-time debs' delights: Jeremy Bayliss, Paddy Colquhoun, Robert Douglas Miller, Giles Havergal, Adam Pollock, Neil Stratford.

For background on Miss Ironside's School I must thank Virginia Ironside, Georgina Howell, Caroline Ground, Julia Mount, Meg Poole and our exceptional English mistress, Jillian Staynes. It cannot be a coincidence that Miss Ironside's produced so many writers.

I must also acknowledge useful reminiscences of the war years in Ardersier from Andrew Buchanan, Georgina Clayton, Carol Lindsay and Venetia Roskinner and more information on Patricia Medina than I had thought possible from Philip French. Anne Hobson shared her vast knowledge of Queen Charlotte's Birthday Ball and Barry Swaebe guided me through his extraordinary photographic archive, covering 50 years of debutante seasons, with unflagging helpfulness.

It was a special pleasure to be in touch again with Jean Barbour and Margaret Blackstock, the two nieces of my nanny, Isabella Hughes.

Above all I am grateful to my sister Karin for remembering people and things I had myself forgotten and to my friend Karl Miller who encouraged me to think a book about the debs could be a good idea.

My thanks too to my incomparable agent Michael Sissons and, at Faber, first and foremost to my editor Julian Loose, to Ron Costley who has designed so many of my books, to Lesley Felce, Henry Volans, Katherine Armstrong and Donna Payne for their care and enthusiasm for this project. Also to Martin Bryant who copy-edited the book and to Diana le Core who compiled such an excellent index. My dear daughter-in-law Helen Mellor, as well as our picture researcher Amanda Russell, gave much appreciated advice and help with photographs of those now distant days.

Index